ADAMSON

Story of a Life

STORY OF A LIFE

*

Childhood and Schooldays

KONSTANTIN
PAUSTOVSKY

translated by
Manya Harari and
Michael Duncan

READERS UNION
Harvill Press
LONDON 1966

This RU edition was produced in 1966 for sale to its
members only by Readers Union Ltd at Aldine House,
10-13 Bedford Street, London W.C.2 and at Letch-
worth Garden City, Herts. Full details of membership
may be obtained from our London address. The book
is set in 11 pt Garamond leaded and has been reprinted
by Collins Clear-Type Press, Glasgow. It was first
published by The Harvill Press.

Contents

Contents

I
Death of my Father

I was in my last year at school in Kiev when the telegram came saying that my father was dying at the Gorodishche farm near Belaya Tserkov.

Next day I went to Belaya Tserkov and stopped at the house of my father's friend Feokistov, the head of the local post-office. He was a short-sighted old man with thick glasses and a long beard who wore an old jacket and the brass insignia of the postal service —crossed horns and lightnings—sewn to its lapels.

It was the end of March. Rain came down in a steady drizzle. Naked poplars loomed through the mist.

Feokistov told me that the night before the broken ice had swept down the fast-flowing Ros. The farm where my father was dying was on an island in the middle of this river, some twenty versts from Belaya Tserkov. A stone causeway ran across the river to the farm.

Now the flood-water was flowing over the causeway, so naturally no one would wish to drive me to the island—not even the most reckless driver in town.

Feokistov sat for a long time pondering as to which of the drivers in Belaya Tserkov was indeed the most reckless. In the half-dark drawing room his schoolgirl daughter Zina was diligently practising the piano. The music shook the leaves of a potted fig-tree. I stared at a pale, squeezed piece of lemon in a saucer and kept silent.

'Well, why not—let's call Bregman, the old rascal,' Feokistov decided at last. 'He'd take on the devil himself.'

Soon, into Feokistov's study cluttered up with volumes of *Niva*[1] in their gold-tooled bindings, stepped Bregman the driver, 'the most

7

desperate character' in Belaya Tserkov. He was a thick-set little
Jew with a sparse beard and blue eyes like a cat's. His weathered
cheeks were as red as apples. He listened mockingly to Feokistov,
twisting a small whip in his hands.

'Oh, what a misfortune,' he said at last in a falsetto voice. 'Oh,
what bad luck, Pan Feokistov! My carriage is light and my horses
are weak. They're only gypsy horses, they'll never pull us across.
We'll all drown, the carriage, the horses, the young man and the
old driver. As to going, of course we can go. Why not? As you
yourself know, a driver's life is only worth three silver roubles—
though I wouldn't swear it isn't five or, let's say, ten.'

'Thank you, Bregman,' said Feokistov. 'I knew you'd take it on.
You're the bravest man in Belaya Tserkov. For this I'll subscribe to
Niva for you till the end of the year.'

'If I'm as brave as that,' laughed Bregman, 'you'd better make it
Russian Pensioner. At least there I can read about the *kantonisti* and the
Knights of St. George.'[2]

Bregman went off.

The telegram I had received in Kiev had contained a curious
sentence: 'Bring a priest from Belaya Tserkov, Orthodox or Catholic,
it doesn't matter which so long as he agrees'.

Knowing my father, I was disturbed by this. My father was an
atheist. His jokes about the clergy, whether Orthodox or Catholic,
brought him into endless clashes with my grandmother, a Pole and
a religious fanatic like nearly all Polish women.

I guessed that it was my father's sister Feodosia Maximovna—
Aunt Dosia as everyone called her—who had insisted on getting a
priest. She believed in absolution, though not in any other rites of
the Church. In place of a Bible she kept Shevchenko's *Kobzar*[3]
hidden in her iron-bound trunk; it was as yellow and as wax-
spattered as a Bible. Now and then Aunt Dosia got it out at night
and read 'Katerina' by candle-light, wiping her eyes ceaselessly with
her dark shawl.

She grieved over Katerina's fate which was so like her own. In
the damp woods behind her cottage was the green grave of her son,
'the little laddie' who had died many years ago when Aunt Dosia
was still quite young. The 'laddie' was, as people said in those days,
her 'illegal' son.

Death of my Father

The man whom Aunt Dosia loved had betrayed her. He had deserted her, but she was faithful to him unto death and was still awaiting his return; for some reason she was convinced that he would come back ill, penniless and damaged by life; she would bawl him out as he deserved but in the end would give him shelter and warmth.

None of the Orthodox clergy would go to Gorodishche, all excused themselves on grounds of illness or of being busy. Only a young Catholic priest consented to go. He warned me that we would first have to call at the church to fetch the Blessed Sacrament to give communion to the dying man, and that it was forbidden to speak to the priest who carried the Host.

The priest wore a long-skirted black coat and a strange round hat which was also black.

Inside the church it was gloomy and cold. Red paper roses drooped at the foot of the crucifix. Without candles, without the sound of the communion bell, without the rolling of the organ, the church looked like the wings of a theatre by daylight.

At first we two travelled in silence while Bregman smacked his lips and hurried on his skinny bays, shouting at them as all drivers do: 'G'on' and 'Oop'. The rain drummed on the low-lying gardens. The priest held the pyx wrapped in a piece of black serge. My school overcoat became soaked and its grey turned to black.

Out of the smoking rain, Countess Branitskaya's famous Alexandrian gardens rose, it seemed, to the very sky. These were vast gardens, equal in size, Feokistov had told me, to those of Versailles. The snow was melting in them, wrapping the trees in trails of cold steam. Bregman turned to us and said there were wild deer in the gardens.

'Mickiewicz[4] was very fond of these gardens,' I said to the priest forgetting that he must keep silent all the way.

I had felt like saying something pleasant to him in gratitude for his willingness to undertake this hard and dangerous journey. The priest smiled in answer.

Pools of rain-water stood in the sodden fields. Reflected in them, you could see the jackdaws flying overhead. I pulled up the collar of my coat and thought about my father and how little I knew him. He was a statistician who had worked almost all his life on various railways—the Moscow-Brest, the Petersburg-Warsaw, the Kharkov-Sebastopol and the South-Western.

We often moved from town to town—from Moscow to Pskov, then to Vilno, then to Kiev. Nowhere did my father get on with his superiors. He was a very touchy, hot-tempered but kind man.

A year ago my father had left Kiev and taken the post of statistician at a Bryansk factory in the Orlov province. After staying in it only a short while he left it suddenly and without apparent reason, and went off to his father's old farm, Gorodishche. His brother Ilko, a village teacher, and Aunt Dosia were living there.

My father's inexplicable action upset all his relations, but above all my mother. At that time she was living with my elder brother in Moscow.

A month after he came to Gorodishche my father fell ill; now he was dying.

The road led downhill through a ravine. From its end came the persistent noise of rushing water. Bregman fidgeted on his box.

'The causeway,' he said in an anxious voice. 'Now's the time to say your prayers.'

The causeway appeared suddenly round a bend of the road. The priest half rose and grabbed Bregman by his faded red belt. Confined between granite rocks, the water rushed swiftly, for here the river Ros breaks in fury through the Avratinsky hills. In a wide clear wave which fell like thunder and filled the air with a cold mist, the water overflowed the causeway.

Across the river, beyond the causeway, enormous poplars seemed to leap into the sky, and I could see a small white house. I recognised the farm on the island where I had lived in my early childhood—its thickets and wattle fences, the tall pumps by the wells and the rocks along the shore; they cut the river into several strong streams. Long ago my father and I had fished for whiskered gudgeon from those rocks.

Bregman stopped the horses near the causeway, climbed down, straightened the harness with his whip, looked his carriage over doubtfully and shook his head. Then for the first time the priest broke his rule of silence.

'Jesus—Mary,' he said in a low voice. 'How can we get across?'

'Eh,' Bregman answered, 'how should I know? You sit still. The horses are shaking all over as it is.'

Death of my Father

The horses, tossing their heads and snorting, stepped into the rushing water. It roared and pushed the carriage towards the unprotected edge of the causeway. The carriage slid sideways, its iron-rimmed wheels grinding against the stones. The horses trembled, hung back and almost lay on the water to avoid being swept off their feet. Bregman whirled his whip above his head.

In the middle of the causeway, where the current was strongest and made a kind of ringing noise, the horses stopped. Foaming rapids swirled around their spindly legs. Bregman cried out in a wailing voice and began to flog them mercilessly. They backed and pushed the carriage to the very edge.

At that moment I saw Uncle Ilko. He was galloping on a grey horse from the farm to the causeway. He was shouting something and swinging a coil of thin rope above his head.

Riding on to the causeway, he flung the rope to Bregman. Bregman quickly tied it up beneath his seat; then the three horses—the two bays and the grey—finally dragged the carriage out on to the island.

The priest made a broad Catholic sign of the cross. Bregman winked at Uncle Ilko, saying a driver such as Bregman would long be remembered. I asked how my father was.

'He's still alive,' Ilko replied; he kissed me, scratching me with his beard. 'He's waiting for you. But where's your mother?'

'I sent her a telegram to Moscow. I suppose she'll arrive tomorrow.'

Uncle Ilko looked at the river.

'It's still rising,' he said. 'That's bad, my dear Kostik. Still, perhaps it will fall. Let's go.'

Aunt Dosia met us on the steps, her eyes dry, her tears already shed.

The stuffy rooms smelled of mint. In the old man with yellow cheeks bristling with grey stubble I did not at once recognise my father. He was only fifty. I remembered him as slightly stooping but well-built, elegant, dark-haired, with an unusual, sad smile and grey attentive eyes.

Now he sat in an armchair, breathing with difficulty and keeping his eyes fixed on my face while a tear rolled slowly down his dry cheek. The tear hung on his beard and Aunt Dosia wiped it away with a clean handkerchief.

My father could not speak. He was dying of cancer of the throat. All night I sat beside him. Everyone else slept. The rain stopped. Outside the window the stars burned gloomily. The river roared louder and louder. Its waters were rising fast. Bregman and the priest could not get back and were marooned on the island.

In the middle of the night my father stirred and opened his eyes. I leaned over him. He tried to put his arms round my neck but he could not do it; he said in a whistling whisper:

'I am afraid . . . your lack of character . . . will destroy you.'

'No,' I answered quietly. 'That won't happen.'

'You'll see your mother,' Father whispered. 'I've treated her badly . . . Ask her to forgive me . . .'

I did not understand his words at the time, and not until much later, after many years, did their bitter meaning become clear to me. It was not until then too that I understood that my father had not really been a statistician at all, but a poet.

He died at dawn but I did not realise it at once. It seemed to me that he had fallen quietly asleep.

There was an old man named Nechipor living with us on the island. He was called in to read the Psalms over my father.

Nechipor often interrupted his reading to go out into the porch to smoke *makhorka*.[5] There, in a whisper, he would tell me simple stories which had stirred his imagination: about a bottle of wine he had drunk the summer before in Belaya Tserkov, about how he had once seen Colonel Skobelev himself near Plevna—'as close as that hedge I was to him'—and about an extraordinary American threshing machine which worked off a lightning conductor. Nechipor was, as they said on the island, 'a frivolous man'—a windbag and a liar.

He read the Psalms all that day and all through the following night, picking the guttering wax off the candles with his dirty fingernails; sometimes he would fall asleep on his feet, give a snore, then waking up, go on muttering inaudible prayers.

That night on the far bank of the river someone waved a lantern and kept on shouting. I went to the river bank with Uncle Ilko. The river was racing. The waters tore across the causeway in a cold cascade. It was late and dark and there was not a single star above our heads. The wind blew in our faces, carrying the wild freshness of the spring floods and the thawing earth. And all the while someone on the other bank went on waving a lantern and calling, but because of the noise of the river we could not make out a single word.

'It must be Mama,' I said to Uncle Ilko.

But he did not answer. Then he broke the silence, saying:

'Let's go in. It's cold. You'll catch a chill.'

I did not want to go back. Uncle Ilko stood silent a while longer, then he went in while I stood where I was, watching the distant lantern. The wind blew stronger and stronger, making the poplars sway and bringing from somewhere the sweetish smell of straw.

We buried my father in the morning. Nechipor and Uncle Ilko dug the grave in a thicket on the edge of the ravine. From there you could see the woods far beyond the Ros, and the white March sky.

We carried the coffin out of the house on wide, embroidered slings. The priest walked in front. He looked straight before him with his quiet grey eyes, saying Latin prayers in a low voice.

When we carried the coffin out on to the steps, I saw an old carriage on the far side of the river, with unharnessed horses tethered to it, and a small woman in black—Mama. She was standing motionless on the bank. She watched my father being carried out. Then she sank to her knees and let herself fall with her face to the ground.

A tall, gaunt driver went up to her, leaned down and said something, but she continued to lie motionless.

Then she jumped up and ran towards the causeway. The driver grabbed her. She sank helplessly to the ground and covered her face with her hands.

We carried my father along the road to the woods. At a turning I looked back. My mother still sat as before with her face hidden in her hands.

No one spoke, but Bregman kept rapping his whip against his boot.

Standing at the grave, the priest raised his grey eyes to the cold sky and said clearly and slowly in Latin:

'Requiem aeternam dona eis, Domine, et lux perpetua luceat eis.' —'Eternal rest give to them, O Lord, and may perpetual light shine upon them.'

The priest stopped and stood listening. The river roared and above our heads tomtits twittered to each other in the branches of old elms. The priest sighed and went on speaking about man's

13

eternal longing for happiness and about the valley of tears. These words were amazingly well fitted to my father's life. They made my heart ache. Since then I have often felt the same anguish on coming upon evidence of man's thirst for happiness and of the imperfection of human relations.

The river went on roaring, the birds twittered cautiously; scraping against the damp earth, the coffin dislodged some clods as it settled slowly down into the grave.

I was seventeen.

2
My Grandfather

I stayed on in Gorodishche for several days after my father's funeral.

It was only on the third day that the river fell and my mother was able to get across the causeway.

Her face had a dark, pinched look. She was no longer crying but she sat for hours by my father's grave.

There were no fresh flowers, so the grave was decorated with paper peonies. They were made by the girls in a neighbouring village, who were fond of wearing them braided with coloured silk ribbons in their hair.

Aunt Dosia did her best to comfort and to distract me. She dragged a trunk crammed with old family belongings out of the lumber room. Its lid opened with a loud crack.

Inside I found a yellowed hetman's[6] charter-deed written in Latin, a copper seal with a coat of arms, a St. George's medal for the Turkish War, a book of interpretations of dreams, several smoked-out pipes and some very delicate black lace.

The charter and the seal had been handed down in our family from our remote ancestor, Hetman Sagaidachny. My father used to laugh at his 'hetman descent' and was fond of explaining that our ancestors had ploughed the soil as the most plodding of farmers, for all that they considered themselves scions of the Zaporozhye Cossacks.

When the Zaporozhye[7] Cossacks were disbanded by Catherine II some of them were settled on the banks of the Ros around Belaya Tserkov. They were unwilling to settle down and their turbulent past continued for some time to simmer in their veins. Even I—born at the end of the nineteenth century—heard from the old people tales about the hetmen, the battles with the Poles, the raids against the Turks, and the 'bloodletting of Uman'.[8]

Our minds filled with such stories, my brothers and I used to play at Zaporozhye battles. We played at the back of the farm in a gulley thickly overgrown with weeds. On hot days their red flowers and prickly leaves gave off a sickly smell. The clouds stood still in the sky over the gully—true Ukrainian clouds, lazy and magnificent. And so strong are the impressions we form in childhood that ever since, battles against Poles and Turks have been linked in my imagination with a wilderness of weeds and their heady, dusty smell in the sun. The very flowers were like clotted drops of Cossack blood.

With the years the Zaporozhye turbulence had died down. All that was left of it by the time of my childhood was the persistent poaching, the endless lawsuits against Countess Branitskaya over ownership of land—and the Cossack songs. The songs were sung to us by my grandfather, Maxim Grigoryevich.

Small, grey-haired and with kindly, faded eyes, he used to live all summer long beside his beehives on the far side of the meadow, in hiding from the irate disposition of my Turkish grandmother.

In the distant past my grandfather had been an ox-cart driver and had travelled as far as Perekop and Armyansk for salt and dried fish. It was from him I learned that somewhere beyond 'Empress Catherine's Country' and Kherson lay the heavenly land of the Crimea.

Before he became an ox-cart driver, Grandfather had served in the army and fought in the Turkish War; he was taken prisoner and brought back with him from captivity a beautiful Turkish wife who came from Kazanlyk in Thrace. She was called Fatima but when she married my grandfather she adopted the Christian faith and with it a new name—Honorata.

We were as scared of her as my grandfather was and we always tried to keep out of her sight.

Sitting among the yellow pumpkin blossoms in front of his hut, my grandfather used to tell us stories and sing for us in his quavering tenor the songs of the ox-cart drivers and the Cossacks.

I liked the ox-cart drivers' songs for their nostalgic monotony. They were songs you could sing for hours on end to the creaking of the cart-wheels as you lay on your cart, looking at the sky. The

Cossack songs evoked an obscure sadness in me. They sounded, now like marching and battle songs with the beat of horses' hooves in them, and now like the wailing of captives held in Turkish chains.

As for Grandfather's stories, the one we liked best was the tale of the blind musician Ostap.

I don't know if you have ever seen a Ukrainian lyre. You would hardly find one nowadays outside a museum. But in my childhood you would often come across blind lyre-players and not only at markets and fairs in small towns but even in the streets of Kiev itself.

The lyre-player walked with his hand on the shoulder of his guide, a small bare-footed boy in a hempen shirt. Slung on his back was a canvas sack with bread, onions and salt in a rag in it, and the lyre hung across his chest. It reminded you of a violin but it had a handle attached to it, and a wooden rod with a small wheel.

The musician turned the handle, the wheel revolved, rubbing against the strings, and the strings vibrated in different keys as if a whole swarm of tame bees were buzzing around him.

The lyre-players hardly ever sang, they recited their ballads and 'psalms' in a sing-song chant. When they finished they stood silently listening while the humming died away, then they begged for alms, staring in front of them with their sightless eyes.

Their begging was different from that of ordinary beggars. I remember a blind lyre-player in the town of Cherkassy who used to say: 'Give me a kopeck—for me because I am blind, and for my boy because a blind man when he dies would be lost without his guide and would never find his way to Heaven.'

I cannot remember a market without its musician, sitting on the ground with his back against a dusty poplar, and compassionate women around him, sighing as they dropped their greenish copper coins into his wooden bowl.

For me the image of the blind musicians is linked forever with the memory of the markets held early in the morning when the dew is still on the grass, when cool shadows lie across the roads and bluish smoke drifts over the fields already lit by the sun.

It recalls for me the misted stoneware jugs of ice-cold milk, wet marigolds in pails of water, pots of buckwheat honey, hot cheese-cakes with raisins, sieves full of cherries, the smell of roach, pealing church bells, wrangling marketwomen, parasols shading the faces of provincial young ladies of fashion, and the sudden rumbling of a copper pot carried on the shoulders of a wild-eyed Rumanian— every old man in the market felt obliged to rap on the pot with his stick to see if Rumanian copper was any good.

I knew the story of Ostap, the musician, almost by heart.

'It happened in the village of Zamoshye near the town of Vasilkovo,' my grandfather would begin. 'Ostap was the blacksmith. His forge stood at the end of the village, under the dark brooding willows overhanging the river. There was nothing Ostap wasn't good at making—he made horseshoes and nails, and axles for the ox-carts.

'One summer evening he was in his forge when a thunderstorm swept over the village, scattering the leaves into the puddles and blowing an old willow to the ground. Then Ostap heard the trampling of hooves as two riders galloped up, and a young woman's voice calling for the blacksmith.

'Ostap came out and stood amazed at what he saw. In front of his door was a prancing black steed and on it a woman of heavenly beauty in a velvet habit, with a crop in her hand and a veil over her face. Her eyes were laughing behind her veil, and her teeth sparkling, and the velvet of her habit was blue and spangled with raindrops. With her was a young cavalry officer—a regiment of Uhlans was at that time quartered in Vasilkovo.

' "Blacksmith, my dear," she said. "Shoe my horse for me, he's lost a shoe. The road is terribly slippery after the storm."

'She dismounted and sat down on a block of wood while Ostap began to shoe the horse. As he worked he kept glancing at the woman, and suddenly her expression became troubled and she raised her veil and met his eyes.

' "I don't seem to have seen you before," said Ostap. "Maybe you're not from our parts?"

' "I'm from Petersburg," she replied. "You're deft with your work."

' "That's nothing," Ostap said softly. "What's a horseshoe? For you I could forge out of this very same steel a jewel fit for an empress."

' "What kind of a jewel?"

' "Whatever you like. Shall I make you a rose with its leaves and thorns?"

' "Good," said the woman, speaking as softly as Ostap. "Thank you, blacksmith. I'll come for it in a week."

'Ostap helped her into the saddle. Her gloved hand rested in his and he could not restrain himself from kissing it with fervour. But hardly had she pulled her hand away when the officer struck Ostap across the face with his whip, shouting "You lout! Remember who you are!"

'The horses reared and galloped off. Ostap had seized his hammer, meaning to throw it at the officer but he had to put it down. He could see nothing for the blood pouring down his face. The blow had damaged one of his eyes.

'But he pulled himself together and worked for six days, and he made the rose he had promised the woman. And everyone who looked at it said that never had there been such craftsmanship—even in the land of Italy.

'On the seventh night a rider pulled up outside and dismounted and tied up the horse. Fearing to show himself, Ostap sat and waited, his hands over his face.

'He heard light footsteps and a light breath, and he felt a pair of gentle arms embracing him, and a single tear fell on his face.

' "I know, my dear, I know," said the woman. "My heart has been aching and aching. Forgive me, Ostap, for bringing this terrible misfortune upon you. I was engaged to him, but I've driven him away. Now I'm going back to Petersburg."

' "Why?" Ostap asked softly.

' "O my dear one, my heart!" said the woman. "They'll never leave us in peace to be happy together."

' "It must be as you wish," said Ostap. "I'm a simple man, I'm only a blacksmith. For me it's happiness just to think of you."

'The woman took the rose, she kissed Ostap and she slowly rode away. He stood watching her from the threshold. Twice she stopped. Twice she made as if to turn back, but in the end she rode on, while the starlight played over the hills and the shooting stars fell into the steppe, as if the sky itself were weeping.'

At this point in the story Grandfather always paused. I sat holding my breath.

'Did they never see each other again?' I finally asked in a whisper.

'No,' said Grandfather. 'They never did. Ostap began to go blind. He decided to walk to Petersburg while he could still see something. But when he got there he learned that the woman had died. Perhaps she couldn't bear to live away from him. Ostap found her grave in the graveyard. He looked at it and his heart stood still, for upon the white marble tombstone he saw the steel rose. The woman had asked that it should lie there for ever. Ostap took to playing the lyre, and he must have died somewhere on the road under a fence, or under a cart in a market place. May he rest in peace!'

Ryabchik, a shaggy dog with burrs stuck to his muzzle, sat at Grandfather's feet, listening and yawning. I nudged him indignantly, but instead of taking offence he nuzzled against me, thinking it a game and licking me with his hot tongue.

Ryabchik had hardly any teeth left. He had broken them the year before when we were leaving Gorodishche for the autumn and he hung on to the carriage wheel, refusing to let go.

It was partly to my grandfather that I owed the romanticism and the susceptibility to new impressions which turned my childhood into a succession of collisions with reality. But painful as they were, I remained grateful to him, for I knew that a life of nothing but sober common-sense, however good for others, would never have suited me. One man's meat is another man's poison, as Grandfather said.

Poor Grandfather could not get on with my grandmother. He spent his time in hiding from her. The only attraction she owed to her Turkish blood was her handsome but forbidding appearance.

She was a tyrant and a nagger. A short pipe full of glowing tobacco always between her teeth (she used up more than a pound of the strongest black Turkish tobacco a day) she ran the house, keeping on it an eye which no trace of disorder ever escaped.

On Sundays she put on a black satin and lace dress and sat on the low stone ledge in front of the house, puffing at her pipe and watching the rapid little river flowing past. Now and then she would laugh loudly at her thoughts, but no one ever ventured to ask her what they were.

The only thing we liked about her was a bar of a hard pink substance rather like soap which she kept in her chest of drawers and on rare occasions proudly took out and allowed us to smell. It smelt very faintly of roses.

My father told me that a valley near my grandmother's native town of Kazanlyk was known as the Valley of Roses, and that the pink substance was impregnated with attar of roses which came from this valley.

What could be more romantic! It puzzled me that anyone born in so poetic a place could be as harsh and hard-hearted as my grandmother.

3
Carp

Staying on in Gorodishche after my father's death, I was reminded of the many times in my childhood when, happy and carefree, we used to arrive from Kiev for the summer holidays.

The train pulled into Belaya Tserkov in the evening. My father hired one of the drivers who waited in front of the station, and he got us to Gorodishche in the middle of the night.

Half asleep I heard the monotonous jangling of the springs, then the noise of the water by the mill and the barking of dogs. The horses snorted and the wicket gate creaked. The damp darkness smelled of weeds.

Aunt Dosia carried me, drowsing, into the cottage with its many-coloured rugs on the floor. The cottage smelt of milk warm from the cow. Close to my face was the rich embroidery on Aunt Dosia's snow-white sleeves.

In the morning I woke up to see the hot sun striking on the white-washed walls. Red and yellow hollyhocks swayed outside the window. A nasturtium looked in with a furry bumble-bee inside it. I watched it anxiously as it buzzed crossly, backing its way out. Waves of light reflected from the river rippled endlessly across the ceiling. The river rushed noisily, close to the house.

'Here they come,' said my Uncle Ilko's voice. 'Naturally, the sun is up, so what else can you expect! Dosia, get the cakes and the cherry brandy.'

I jumped up and, barefooted, ran to the window. Slowly advancing along the causeway across the river came a procession of old men in broad-brimmed straw hats, their sticks tapping on the stones and their medals clanking on their smocks.

Carp

These were the venerable elders of the neighbouring village of Pilipchi, coming to greet us in accordance with tradition. Walking at their head was the pock-marked mayor Trofim with his copper badge of office round his neck.

The house filled with bustle. Aunt Dosia shook out a cloth over the table, sending a breeze through the room. Mama hurriedly sliced salami and piled dishes with cakes. My father pulled the corks out of bottles of home-made cherry liqueur, and Uncle Ilko set out the glasses.

Then Mama and Aunt Dosia rushed away to change while the men went out on the porch to welcome the elders who were approaching, as solemn and ineluctable as fate.

At last they arrived and, having silently embraced my father and my uncle, sat down on the low stone ledge, all sighing in unison—after which the mayor would clear his throat and pronounce the traditional phrase:

'I have the honour to congratulate you, Georgy Maximovich, upon your safe arrival in our quiet countryside.'

'Thank you,' said my father.

'Just so . . .' the old men all said together, sighing with relief. 'That's so, of course . . .'

'Yes,' said Trofim, glancing through the window at the bottles glinting on the table.

'That's the way it is,' added an old soldier with a bulbous nose, who had fought under Nicholas I.

'Naturally,' butted in a small and inquisitive old man called Nedolya. He was the father of twelve daughters whose names he was beginning to forget in his old age. He could get as far as five by counting them on his fingers—Hannah, Parasya, Gorpyna, Frosya, Olyosya—but after that he got muddled and had to begin again.

'Yes, indeed,' said the elders and fell silent.

At this point my grandfather Maxim Grigoryevich came out of the house and they all got up and bowed. My grandfather bowed in return. They resumed their seats, sighed, grunted and sat looking silently down at their feet. At last my uncle, deducing from some sign imperceptible to the rest of us that the meal was ready to serve, said:

23

'Well, thank you, kind folks, for your conversation. Please come inside and let us eat what God has sent us.'

Indoors, the elders were greeted by Mama who had put on an elegant summer dress. They kissed her hand and, following the custom, she kissed their brown wrinkled hands in return. Aunt Dosia, rosy-cheeked and prematurely grey, pretty in her shawl with crimson flowers on it, bowed from the waist.

After a glass or two of liqueur Nedolya, tortured with curiosity about everything we had brought with us from Kiev, began his questionnaire:

'What's this? What's it for? What is it called?'

This was a flat-iron heated by methylated spirit, my father would explain, and that was a freezer for making ice-cream, and that over there was a folding mirror. Nedolya nodded admiringly:

'Fancy! There's a thing for everything.'

'That's so, of course,' the elders agreed as they drank up.

In Gorodishche summer came into its own—a hot summer with terrifying storms and the rustling of trees, and cool draughts of water from the river, with fishing and blackberrying, and enchanting, leisured, unexpected days.

The island with my grandfather's house on it was of course the most mysterious place in the world.

There were two deep lakes at the back of the house. The water was dark, and the ancient willows on the banks made the landscape permanently gloomy.

Climbing up the hillside beyond them was a dense and tangled thicket of nut trees. The thicket opened out on to meadows with flowers in them as high as your waist, and so scented that on hot days they gave you a headache.

On the far side of the meadows you could see the smoke rising from the chimney of my grandfather's hut where it stood beside the beehives. And beyond it lay an unexplored region of rocks of red granite covered with creepers and wild strawberries.

The rocks had warm pools of rain-water in their hollows, where wagtails came to drink, and cheeky bumble bees flopped in and spun and buzzed, vainly calling for help.

The rocks ended in a sheer drop to the river. We were forbidden to go near it, but sometimes we would crawl to the edge and look

Carp

down. At a vertiginous depth below us, the water hurtled, tense and transparent. And below its surface were narrow quivering outlines of fish, slowly advancing against the current.

Climbing up the slope on the other side was Countess Branit-skaya's centuries' old forest. Its solid green was almost impenetrable to the sun. Only once in a while would a solitary shaft reveal the fabulous density of the undergrowth. Like shining dust-motes, birds would dart into the beam. They chased each other up and down it and dived into the foliage as into water.

But I liked the two lakes best of all.

Every morning when my father went fishing he took me along.

We would go out very early, picking our steps across the heavy wet grass. Willow branches, catching the first sun, made patches of tranquil gold among the dark, as yet nocturnal trees. The carp splashed in the quiet enclosed waters of the lake, where the clumps of duckweed, water-lilies and millefoil hung as though suspended above the blackness of an abyss.

Engulfed in the mysteries of this world of vegetation and water, I could happily have sat beside the lake from sunrise until sunset.

My father would silently cast his lines and light a cigarette. The smoke drifted across the lake and became entangled in the branches on the bank.

I filled the pail I had brought with water from the lake, threw in a few handfuls of grass and sat waiting. The scarlet floats were motionless. Then one of them would begin to tilt, making light ripples, and suddenly sank and swiftly drifted aside. My father reeled in and the line tautened, the rod bending into an arc, while a turmoil of splashing and gurgling broke out in the haze over the lake. The ripples rocked the water-lilies, water-beetles scurried off in all directions, and at last out of the enigmatic depth there came a quivering flash of gold. It was impossible to make out what it was until my father landed the heavy carp and it lay on its side on the trampled grass, panting and gently stirring its fins. Its scales had the wonderful smell of its underwater kingdom.

I put the carp into the pail. It turned about among the drifting tufts of grass, unexpectedly thrashing its tail and spattering me with spray. I licked my lips and longed to drink out of the pail, but my father would not allow it.

It seemed to me that the water in the pail with the carp and the grass in it had the same smell and taste as the rain-water we so avidly drank after a thunderstorm, in the conviction that, as Nechipor had assured us, it would make us live to be a hundred and twenty.

4
Pleurisy

The storms began on midsummer day and went on all through July. They besieged the island with enormous many-coloured clouds which flashed and thundered, making the house quake and frightening Aunt Dosia into fits.

My memory of my first, childish love affair is connected with one of these thunderstorms. I was only nine at the time.

On the Feast of St. John the Baptist the peasant girls from Pilipchi descended upon our island, like a flock of bright-feathered birds, and observed the custom of 'floating the wreaths'. The wreaths were made of wild flowers and had a wooden crosspiece in the middle with a candle attached to it. At twilight the candles were lit and the wreaths were sent drifting down the river.

The wreaths told the girls their fortunes: the one whose candle floated the farthest without going out would be luckiest. The most fortunate of all was the girl whose wreath drifted into the whirlpool and continued slowly to revolve in the eddy of the deep pool, which was invariably still so that the candle on it burned with a particular brightness, sputtering so much you could hear it from the bank.

The grown-ups were as fond of this custom as were the children —all except Nechipor who would grunt scornfully: 'Rubbish! What's the sense of it?'

One of the girls who always came to the 'floating' was Hannah, my cousin; she was sixteen. She braided black and orange ribbons in her splendid reddish plaits, wore a necklace of unpolished corals, and had shining green eyes. When Hannah smiled she lowered her eyes and would only raise them again slowly, as if her eyelids were too heavy to lift. Her cheeks were always burning.

I used to hear Aunt Dosia and Mama speaking of her with pity, but I could never discover why as they always stopped talking as soon as I came up.

One midsummer's day I went with Hannah to watch the wreaths. On the way she asked me:

'What will you do when you grow up?'

'I'll be a sailor.'

'Oh, you mustn't!' she said. 'Sailors get drowned. You'll make some girl cry her eyes out for you.'

I wasn't listening. I was hanging on to her hot sunburned hand, telling her about my first visit to the sea.

Early that spring my father had had to go on a three-day business trip to Novorossisk and had taken me with him. The sea appeared to us in the distance like a dark blue wall. I could not imagine what it was until finally I saw the wide green bay and the lighthouse, and heard the sound of the breakers, and the sea invaded me like the memory of a confused but magnificent dream.

There were two black warships with yellow funnels anchored in the harbour: *The Three Bishops* and *The Twelve Apostles*. My father and I went to visit them. I was fascinated by the oily warmth of the engine room, and by the sunburned officers in resplendent white uniforms with gold-hilted daggers. But it was my father who astonished me. Never had I seen him so gay and full of life as when he chatted and laughed with the officers. We even went into the cabin of one of the ship's engineers, and my father had a brandy with him, and they smoked pink Turkish cigarettes which had golden Arabic lettering on them.

Hannah listened to me, looking down at the ground. Feeling unaccountably sorry for her, I said that when I was a sailor I would take her to sea with me.

'As the ship's cook? Or to do the laundry?' she asked.

'No,' I said, fired by my schoolboy enthusiasm, 'you will come as my wife.'

Hannah stopped and looked sternly into my face.

'Will you swear it?' she whispered. 'Swear it by your mother's heart.'

'I swear it,' I said without a moment's hesitation.

She smiled, her eyes became as green as sea-water, and she kissed me hard on the forehead. Her lips were feverishly hot. We walked the rest of the way in silence.

Pleurisy

Hannah's candle was the first to go out. An enormous dark-grey cloud was rising over Countess Branitskaya's forest but we never noticed it—we were so busy watching the wreaths—until the wind struck and the reeds whistled and bent, and the lightning lashed in a blinding explosion of thunder.

The girls ran squealing into the shelter of the trees. Hannah ripped her shawl off her shoulders and tied it round me, then she seized me by the hand and we ran. But the downpour was catching up with us and I knew that we could never reach home in time.

The cloudburst overtook us not far from my grandfather's hut but we were drenched by the time we got to it. My grandfather was out.

We sat inside the hut, clinging to one another. Hannah chafed my hands. She smelled of damp chintz. 'Are you cold?' she kept asking me in a frightened voice. 'Oh, what shall I do if you should fall sick!'

I was indeed shivering with cold, and Hannah's expression alternated between love and despair.

At one moment she clutched at her throat and burst into a fit of coughing. I could see a vein throbbing under the smooth soft skin of her neck, and with a sudden longing that my mother were as young and as kind as Hannah, I flung my arms round her and buried my head in her shoulder.

'What is it?' she asked puzzled, stroking my head without ceasing to cough. 'Don't be frightened. It's all right. I'll look after you. The thunder won't hurt us.'

Then she gently pushed me away and pressed her sleeve to her mouth. It was embroidered with crimson oak leaves and I saw a blood stain spreading among them like another embroidered leaf.

'I release you from your oath,' Hannah whispered, looking up at me with a guilty smile. 'I was only joking.'

The thunder had rumbled over the edge of the earth, the downpour was over. The only sound was the quick patter of raindrops off the trees.

During the night my temperature went up and, two days later, young Doctor Napelbaum bicycled over from Belaya Tserkov and said I had pleurisy.

He went from us to Pilipchi to see Hannah and when he came back I heard him speaking next door to my mother.

'She's got galloping consumption,' he said. 'She won't live through the winter.'

Bursting into tears I shouted for Mama, and as I threw my arms round her I noticed that she had the same touchingly throbbing vein in her neck as Hannah. I cried all the louder, while Mama stroked my head and said:

'What is it? Don't be frightened. It's all right. I'll look after you.'

I recovered but Hannah died that winter—in February.

Next summer I went to visit her grave with Mama and placed a bunch of daisies on the grassy mound. Hannah used to wear such flowers in her braids. Unaccountably I felt embarrassed by the presence of Mama with her crimson sunshade, and at not having come alone.

5
Trip to Chenstokhov

My other grandmother, Vikentia Ivanovna, was a tall old Polish woman who lived in the town of Cherkassy on the Dnieper. She had many daughters and she lived in a wooden house with one of them, my Aunt Euphrosine who was the headmistress of the Cherkassy High School[9] for girls.

Vikentia Ivanovna always dressed in black and wore a black veil on her head. She first went into mourning after the suppression of the Polish mutiny of 1863, and she never gave it up. We were all convinced that she had been engaged to a proud Polish revolutionary who was killed in the uprising—someone altogether different from her surly husband, my grandfather, a retired notary public.

I remember him only dimly. He seldom came down from the small flat at the top of the house to which his wife had relegated him on account of his incurable addiction to smoking.

Occasionally we went up to his room. The air was thick, foggy with smoke. Packets of tobacco lay tumbled on the desk, spilling out their contents. My grandfather sat in his armchair, holding a cigarette in his shaking, heavily veined hand.

He never spoke to us. He only ruffled the hair on the back of our heads and gave us the shiny purple paper off his packets of tobacco.

We often came from Kiev to stay with my grandmother. In Lent she always went on a pilgrimage to one of the Catholic shrines in Warsaw or Vilno or Chenstokhov. Sometimes she took it into her head to visit an Orthodox shrine as well and would go to the Troitsko-Sergievsky Monastery or to Pochayev.

Her daughters and sons-in-law used to say jokingly that she would end by visiting famous Jewish rabbis and would finish her life on a pilgrimage to the tomb of the Prophet Mohammed in Mecca.

The worst collision between my grandmother and my father happened when I was eight. While he was away at a statisticians' conference in Vienna, my grandmother took me with her on a pilgrimage to Chenstokhov. Personally I was delighted. I could not imagine why my father was angry.

I remember the wonderful weather in Vilno, and the Chapel of Ostraya Brama where my grandmother went to Mass. The whole town was veiled in green and gold by the shimmer of budding leaves. At noon a cannon which had stood on Castle Hill ever since Napoleon, fired a salute.

My grandmother was very well read and gave me endless explanations about everything.

Her religious piety went astonishingly hand-in-hand with her progressive political views. She was equally enchanted by Herzen and by Henryk Sienkiewicz.[10] In her room, the portraits of Pushkin and Mickiewicz hung on the wall beside the ikon of Our Lady of Chenstokhov. She had given revolutionary students shelter in her house in 1905, and had hidden Jews when there was a pogrom.

From Vilno we went on to Warsaw. All I remember of it is the monument to Copernicus, and a café with waitresses in frilly aprons, where I first tasted 'upside-down-coffee'—more milk than coffee—and had cold sweet creamy meringues which melted in the mouth.

From Warsaw we went to Chenstokhov where the miraculous ikon of the Virgin is preserved in the monastery of Yasnaya Gora.

This was my first encounter with religious fanaticism. I was shaken and frightened by it, and my aversion to it remains with me to this day.

We arrived in the morning. The monastery stood on a hill, just over a mile away from the station. The pilgrims got out of the train, mostly Polish peasants and their wives, and a scattering of city folk in bowler hats. A stout, elderly priest and several servers in surplices were waiting for them at the station.

The procession formed on the road outside. The priest muttered a blessing and a prayer. The pilgrims fell to their knees and, singing psalms, crawled along the dusty road towards the hill.

They crawled on their knees all the way to the monastery church, a grey-haired woman with a white fanatical face and a wooden crucifix in her arms taking the lead.

The priest walked slowly and calmly in front. The pilgrims panted and sweated through the heat and the dust, casting reproachful glances back at those who fell behind.

I grabbed at my grandmother's hand. 'What are they doing it for?' I whispered.

'It's all right, don't be frightened,' she answered in Polish. 'They are penitents. They are praying the Lord God to forgive them their sins.'

'Let's go away,' I said, but she pretended not to hear me.

The monastery was a mediæval castle, with rusty Swedish cannon-balls embedded in the walls, green water in the moats, and trees rustling on the ramparts.

The drawbridge was down, we clattered across it in our cab and were immediately lost in a labyrinth of monastic courtyards, cloisters and alleyways.

A lay brother, with a cord round his waist, led us to the guest house. We were given a chilly room with a vaulted ceiling and the inevitable crucifix on the wall; someone had hung a chain of paper roses on the pierced feet of the metal figure of Christ.

The monk asked my grandmother whether she had any illness of which she wished to be cured. Grandmother, always nervous about her health, at once complained of pains in her heart. The monk took a handful of small silver hearts, arms, legs and even babies from the pocket of his habit and poured them in a heap on the table.

'Here are hearts,' he said, 'at five roubles, at ten or at twenty. They've already been blessed. You have only to say a prayer and hang one on an ikon of Our Lady.'

My grandmother bought a plump little heart for ten roubles.

She gave me tea, told me we were going to a Solemn Mass at the monastery church that night, and lay down on her bed and fell asleep. I sat looking through the narrow window. A monk in a shiny and faded habit walked past. Then two Polish peasants sat down in the shadow of the wall, got some bread and garlic out of their bundles and began to eat. They had blue eyes and strong teeth.

I got bored and tiptoed out of the guesthouse. Grandmother had forbidden me to speak Russian inside the monastery. This scared me as I only knew a few words of Polish.

I lost my way and found myself in a narrow passage between high walls. Dandelions grew in the cracks between the flagstones. Lanterns were fixed on metal brackets to the walls, but they can rarely have been lighted for in one of them I spotted a bird's nest.

A narrow gate in one of the walls stood half open. I looked out. An apple orchard, dappled with sun, spread over the slope of the hill. I walked in warily. A faint but melodious peal came from the belfry.

A young Polish peasant woman was sitting under an old apple tree suckling her baby. The baby wrinkled its face and cried. A pale-faced, oversized young peasant in a new felt hat stood next to her. A sky-blue satin ribbon was sewn to the hat and a peacock feather stuck into the ribbon. He stood motionless, his eyes fixed on his toes.

A bald-headed little monk with gardening shears in his hands was sitting on a tree stump beside them; he looked up at me and said:

'Praised be Our Lord Jesus Christ.'

'For ever and ever,' I answered in Polish as my grandmother had taught me.

The monk turned away to listen to the woman who, gently brushing back a strand of fair hair which kept blowing in her face, was wailing:

'When the baby was four months old, Mikhas shot a stork and brought it into the house; I cried. I said: "What have you done, you silly fool? Don't you know that for every stork that's killed, God takes away a child. Why did you shoot it, Mikhas?" '

The boy in the felt hat stared at his feet as impassively as before.

'And ever since then,' the woman went on, 'the baby has been having fits and choking and going blue in the face. Will Our Lady cure him?'

The monk silently looked away.

'Ah! What grief!' said the woman clawing at her throat. 'Ah! What grief!' she cried, pressing the baby to her breast.

The baby panted and its eyes bulged.

I thought of the toy silver babies the lay brother had shown my grandmother and, feeling sorry for the woman, wished I could tell her to buy one and hang it on an ikon of Our Lady of Chenstokhov. But I had not enough Polish for such a complicated piece of advice, and I was afraid of the monk, so I went away.

When I came back to our room, my grandmother was still sleeping. I lay down on my hard bunk without undressing and also fell asleep.

Grandmother awakened me in the middle of the night. I washed with cold water in the big china bowl on the washstand. I was shivering with excitement. Lanterns were drifting past the windows and there were footsteps and the multiple pealing of bells.

'The Cardinal is saying Mass tonight,' said my grandmother. 'He's the Papal Nuncio.'

We went to the church, finding our way with difficulty in the dark.

'Hold on to me,' said my grandmother as we reached the unlit porch.

We groped our way in. I could see nothing. There was not a candle, not a chink in the solid blackness penned in by the walls of the church and filled with the breathing of hundreds of people. The darkness had a sweetish smell of flowers.

Feeling the worn metal floor under my feet, I took a step forward and immediately stumbled against something.

'Keep still,' whispered my grandmother. 'There are people lying on the floor, you'll step on them.'

She recited a prayer while I waited anxiously, holding her arm. The people who lay on the floor sighed, and a mournful rustling echoed round the walls.

Abruptly, in the oppressive darkness, the organ broke into its throbbing thunder, shaking the walls, and hundreds of candles burst into flame. I cried out, dazzled and alarmed.

The great golden curtain in front of the ikon of the Chenstokhov Madonna slowly swung apart. Six old priests in lace-edged surplices were kneeling before it with their backs to the crowd and their arms stretched up. Only the tall thin Cardinal in his purple cassock with its broad violet sash stood upright, also with his back to the congregation, as if listening to the dying chords of the organ and the sobbing of the crowd.

I had never before seen anything so theatrical or so incomprehensible.

After the service, Grandmother and I went into a long vaulted passage. It was beginning to get light. People were kneeling in prayer along the walls. My grandmother sank to her knees and made me kneel beside her. I didn't like to ask her what all these wild-eyed people were waiting for.

The Cardinal appeared in the distance and swiftly and lightly advanced along the passage. His cassock billowed, brushing the faces of the people. They caught at it and kissed it with passionate humility.

'Kiss the cassock,' my grandmother whispered to me.

But I wouldn't. Pale with resentment, I stared straight into the Cardinal's face. There must have been tears in my eyes, because he stopped, put his dry little hand on my head and said in Polish:

'A child's tears are a prayer to the Lord.'

I looked at him. He had a dark-skinned hatchet face. A dim glow seemed to light it up. The black eyes narrowed expectantly.

I was obstinately silent.

The Cardinal turned sharply away and swept on as lightly as before.

My grandmother seized my hand in a painfully tight grip and led me out.

'Exactly like your father,' she said when we were in the court-yard. 'Exactly! What will become of you! Oh, dear Mother of God!'

6
Pink Oleanders

Pink oleanders in green tubs stood on the verandah of my grand-mother's house in Cherkassy. I was fond of their greyish leaves and pale flowers. For some reason they made me think of the sea—a distant, southern sea washing a shore which blossomed with oleanders.

My grandmother had green fingers. There were always fuchsias flowering in her bedroom in winter. As for her garden, it was thick with burdock along the fences, but in summer it looked like one solid enormous bouquet. Its scent reached even into my grand-father's attic where it almost overcame the smell of tobacco, making my grandfather slam his windows angrily shut. He believed that flowers gave him asthma.

I used to think of flowers as people. Mignonette was an im-poverished girl in a patched grey dress, whose fabulous origin was only betrayed by her wonderful scent. Tea-roses were young society beauties who had lost their rosy cheeks from drinking too much tea.

The border of pansies was like a fancy-dress ball. The pansies were gay, sly gypsies in black velvet masks—dancers in motley clothes, now blue, now purple, now yellow.

The daisies bored me. In their washed-out pink, they reminded me of the daughters of my grandmother's neighbour, a school-master named Zimmer, two little girls with tow-coloured hair and invisible eyebrows, who held up their skirts and bobbed every time you met them.

The most fascinating flower of all was, of course, the purslane—a creeper blazing with pure colours. It had soft juicy needles

instead of leaves, and if you pressed them the green juice spurted
into your face.

The garden acted upon my imagination with extraordinary force.
It must have been there that I first conceived my passion for travel.
I used to imagine a far-away country which I felt certain that I
would some day visit. It was an undulating plain filled with grasses
and flowers as far as the eye could reach. The towns and villages
were submerged in the vegetation, and the coaches of the express
trains which crossed this region had thick layers of pollen clinging
to their sides.

I told Mama and my brothers and sisters about it: but they none
of them showed the slightest understanding. Instead, my eldest
brother called me a dreamer, in fact, he turned it into a scornful
nickname which was to stick to me.

The only person who perhaps understood me was my Aunt
Nadya, the youngest of my grandmother's daughters.

She was twenty-three at this time, had a beautiful contralto
voice and was being trained as a singer at the Moscow Conservatoire.

She used to come home at Easter and for the summer holidays.
The moment she arrived the quiet spacious house was filled with
noise and bustle. Aunt Nadya, slender and graceful, with her
tousled fair hair and her fresh half-open lips, played with us children,
shouting with laughter as she tore about and skidded on the polished
floors.

Her grey eyes were flecked with gold and they laughed at everything—any joke or merry word, or just at Anton the cat who watched
us enjoying ourselves with a fastidiously disapproving expression on
his face.

Mildly critical, Mama used to say: 'Nadya takes nothing seriously.'

Aunt Nadya's irresponsibility was proverbial in the family. She
was always losing her gloves, her powder or her money, but she
never allowed anything to upset her.

The piano stood open from the moment she arrived until after
she returned to her cheerful, hospitable Moscow. Sheets of music
littered the chairs, the candles smoked, the piano rumbled. Sometimes I woke up in the night to the sound of her pure deep voice
singing the Barcarolle:

> *Sail, my gondola*
> *Lit by the moon. . . .*

Pink Oleanders

While in the morning I was often wakened by Aunt Nadya bending over me, her soft hair tickling my face as she sang almost in a whisper:

> *Wake up! Get up!*
> *The robins are chirping,*
> *The roses are blooming*
> *For you. . . .*

When I opened my eyes, she kissed me and immediately disappeared. A moment later I would hear her waltzing in the hall with her brother Kolya, an army cadet, who sometimes came for Easter from Petersburg.

Then I would jump out of bed in anticipation of a happy, turbulent, unpredictable day.

When Aunt Nadya sang, even my grandfather opened his door to listen from the landing and afterwards asked my grandmother:

'Where on earth does she get her gypsy blood from?'

My grandmother always assured him that Nadya wasn't a gypsy but a Pole, and quoted examples from Polish history and literature to show that Polish women were often endowed with just such a cheerful, extravagant, devil-may-care nature.

'Exactly!' my grandfather said provocatively, banging his door. 'Exactly,' he repeated loudly after it was shut, as he sat down to roll a cigarette.

One year, Easter was late and the gardens in Cherkassy were already in bloom when we arrived by river-boat from Kiev. Aunt Nadya joined us a few days later.

I always looked forward to Easter but not to the days before it, when I was made to grind almonds and whisk white of egg with a spoon until my arms ached.

The house became unbearable; women scuttled about with their skirts tucked up, washing the ficus and rhododendron plants and scrubbing the floors, beating the carpets and the upholstery, polishing the handles on the doors and the windows. We were chased from room to room all day long.

After the cleaning came the ritual of the cooking. Grandmother made dough for the Easter cakes known in our family as 'satin ladies'. The yellow bubbling dough was put in a tub and wrapped in an eiderdown, and until it had risen, no one was allowed to run, shout or bang the doors. If a cab drove past the house my grandmother shuddered with alarm—the slightest commotion could make the dough 'settle', and then it was goodbye to the tall, round, airy cakes covered with icing and smelling of saffron!

In addition to the satin ladies, Grandmother baked a variety of biscuits with almonds and raisins, known as 'mazurkas'. Even my grandfather got restless when the baking tins came out of the oven and the house filled with their delicious smell. Opening his door, he would peer down into the drawing-room where the long marble topped table was already covered with a heavy damask cloth.

On the morning of Holy Saturday the house finally became a haven of cool cleanliness and quiet. After a breakfast of weak tea and dry biscuits, we ate nothing more until Lent ended on the following day after the Easter Mass. We rather enjoyed feeling a little hungry. There was a faint ringing in our ears as the long day drew to its close, and my grandmother's insistence on our keeping quiet put us in a thoughtful mood.

At midnight we went to church. I was dressed in a sailor suit with long trousers and brass buttons, and my hair was brushed painfully hard. Looking at myself in the mirror I saw a terribly excited, flushed little boy and felt very happy.

Aunt Euphrosine came out of her apartment. She alone had taken no part in the preparations for Easter. She was always ailing, hardly ever spoke to anyone, and only smiled gently at our chatter.

Now she appeared in a dark blue dress with a gold watch-chain round her neck and a handsome silk rosette pinned on her shoulder. Mama told me that the rosette was a distinction she had been awarded as a girl for her exemplary conduct at her boarding school.

Mama was in her grey party frock and my father in a black suit with a white waistcoat.

My grandmother would come out looking handsome and imposing, all in black silk, with an artificial heliotrope pinned to her corsage. Her smooth white hair showed through her lace veil, her skirt rustled and her movements were graceful—she always became younger on that night.

She would light the lamp before the ikon and draw on her black lace gloves, while my father held her mantle with its broad satin ribbon fastenings.

'I take it you are not coming to Mass?' she asked him with chilly courtesy.

'No, Vikentia Ivanovna,' my father replied smiling. 'I'll go and lie down for a bit. They'll wake me up before you are back from church.'

'Oh well,' said my grandmother, twitching her shoulders to adjust her cloak. 'My only hope is that God has ceased to pay any attention to your jokes.'

'That's what I fervently count on too,' said my father politely.

Grandmother went upstairs for a moment, to say goodbye to my grandfather. As she was coming down, Aunt Nadya rushed into the hall. She was invariably late.

Hurrying, in her white dress of light silk with a train and puffed sleeves, she did not so much walk in as alight like a thin, graceful, shimmering bird. She was breathing fast and a yellow rose fluttered on her breast.

It seemed as if all the light and joy of the world were shining in her eyes.

My grandmother stopped on the stairs and pressed her hand-kerchief to her eyes. The sight of her youngest daughter's beauty moved her to tears. Clearly, she worried about Aunt Nadya's future and wondered if she was tough and practical enough to stand up to the difficulties of life—perhaps it was this that made her cry.

That night, my father was awake when we returned from church. He had opened the windows of the drawing-room which looked out on the garden. It was very warm.

We sat down and had breakfast. The night was all around us and the stars shone straight into our eyes. The twittering of a sleepless bird came from the garden. We spoke little and sat listening to the pealing of the church bells, now swelling and now dying away in the darkness.

Aunt Nadya was pale and looked tired. I had noticed as we came in that my father, when he helped her off with her cloak, had handed her a telegram.

She had blushed and crushed it in her hand.

Immediately after breakfast we went off to bed. I awoke late to the clinking of cups in the drawing-room where the grown-ups were having coffee.

At dinner Aunt Nadya said that she had had a telegram from the nearby little town of Smela, from her friend Lisa Yagorskaya.

Lisa had invited her over for the day to their house outside the town.

'I'd like to go tomorrow,' said Aunt Nadya looking at my grandmother. 'And I'd like to take Kostik.'

I blushed with joy.

'All right, darling,' said my grandmother. 'Mind you don't catch cold, either of you.'

'They'll send a carriage to meet us,' said Aunt Nadya.

It was an hour by train from Cherkassy to Smela. Lisa, plump and cheerful, met us at the station in Smela and we set off in a carriage and pair through the clean, pretty little town. At the foot of the steep green hills the river Tasmin had flooded its banks and now flowed from one quiet lake to another, its slow current making a streak of silver through them. It was very hot. Dragonflies darted about over the water.

As we drove through a deserted park on the edge of the town, Lisa told us that Pushkin had been fond of walking in it. I could not believe that Pushkin had actually been in this place; that I was actually in a place where Pushkin had been. At that time Pushkin seemed to me a wholly legendary being. How could any part of his brilliant life have come anywhere near this Ukrainian backwater?

'Over there is Kamenka,' said Lisa. 'That was once the Rayevsky's estate. He used to stay with them a lot and that's where he wrote a wonderful poem.'

'Which poem?' asked Nadya.

Lisa recited it. I could not understand all of it, but the power and music of the poetry, the evening light on the park, the ancient lime-trees and the clouds drifting above them, all combined to put me in a magical mood, and the whole of this day has remained in my memory as a quiet celebration of spring.

We were driving up a wide avenue when Lisa told the coachman to stop, and we got out and walked to the house along a footpath lined with hedges of dog-rose.

Suddenly at a turning we saw coming towards us a man with a sunburned, bearded face and without a hat. He had a double-barrelled gun over his shoulder, and a brace of duck dangled from his hand. His jacket was unbuttoned and his strong brown chest showed underneath.

Aunt Nadya stopped dead and I noticed that she went very pale.

Scratching his hands on the thorns, the man broke off a big branch of dog-rose and presented it to Aunt Nadya. She cautiously grasped the spiky branch and gave him her hand, which he kissed.

'You smell of gunpowder,' she said. 'And your hands are bleeding. You must have the thorns taken out.'

'It's nothing,' he said smiling.

He had very even teeth. Now that I saw him close to, I realised that he was still a young man.

We walked on. The man was talking very strangely and about everything at once—his journey from Moscow two days earlier, and how wonderful the country was, and how he had to leave in two days' time to take his pictures to an exhibition in Venice, and how a gypsy who was Vrubel's model had cast a spell on him and how he was altogether a lost soul whom only Aunt Nadya could save by her voice.

Aunt Nadya was smiling. I was watching the man. I liked him a lot. I realised that he was an artist. He really did smell of gunpowder, and his hands were smeared all over with sticky resin. Occasionally a drop of blood from the black bills of the ducks splashed crimson on the path.

The artist had cobwebs in his hair, and pine-needles, and even a dry twig. Aunt Nadya took him by the elbow, stopped him and removed the twig.

'You really are incorrigible,' she said, adding with a sad smile: 'You're nothing but a schoolboy.'

'Oh, but do understand,' he mumbled imploringly, 'I was pushing my way through a thicket, I got torn to bits, but the smell of it! And the red pine-needles and the cobwebs and the dry white pinks, how lovely it all was!'

'That's what I love you for,' Aunt Nadya said softly.

The artist seized his gun and fired both barrels into the air. A puff of bluish gunpowder smoke drifted up. Dogs started to bark and rushed out at us. A hen broke into a terrified squawking.

'I salute life,' said the artist. 'It's a hell of a marvellous thing to be alive.'

We came up to the house with the dogs yapping excitedly round us.

The house was white, with a pillared porch and striped awnings at the windows. An elderly little woman—Lisa's mother—came out to meet us. She had silvery curls, a pale mauve dress and a lorgnette. She screwed up her eyes at Aunt Nadya and, clasping her hands, exclaimed at her beauty.

There was a cool breeze blowing through the rooms, filling the awnings and sweeping copies of *Russian Word* and *The Thought of Kiev*[11] off the tables. The dogs wandered about everywhere and raced off into the garden, yapping and bumping into each other at the slightest suspicion of a noise from outside.

Patches of sunlight shifted with the breeze and picked out, here the castor on the leg of the piano, there a gilt picture frame, or the light straw hat which Aunt Nadya had tossed on a table, or the blue barrels of the gun which the artist had put down on the windowsill.

As we were having coffee in the dining-room he told me how he had fished in the middle of Paris, off the *quay of the Seine*, opposite the Cathedral of Notre Dame. Aunt Nadya watched him with a gentle, amused smile, and Lisa's mother kept saying:

'Really, Sasha! When will you grow up?'

Afterwards he took Aunt Nadya and me by the hand and led us to his room. There were paint brushes and squeezed tubes of paint lying about and the room was in great disorder. He swept up a few shirts, canvases and shoes, shoved them under the sofa, filled his pipe with oily tobacco from a blue tin, lit it, and ordered us to sit down on the windowsill.

We did as we were told. The sun was uncomfortably hot on our backs. The artist went up to a picture which hung on the wall, covered with a cloth, and removed the cloth.

'There it is,' he muttered wretchedly. 'It's a mess, as you can see.'

The painting was a portrait of Aunt Nadya. I knew nothing whatever about painting. I had heard my father and Uncle Kolya arguing about Vereshchagin and Vrubel,[12] but I had never seen a good picture in my life. Those on my grandmother's walls were boring landscapes of gloomy trees and stags beside a stream or still-lifes of brown duck hanging head down.

When the artist uncovered the portrait I laughed with sheer pleasure—he had caught the essence of Aunt Nadya's radiant springtime beauty, the golden cascades of sunlight in the park, the breeze drifting through the house and the greenish reflections of leaves in the rooms.

Aunt Nadya sat looking at it for a long time, then she lightly ruffled the artist's hair and went swiftly from the room without saying a word.

'Well, thank God,' he sighed. 'That means I can take it to Venice.'

In the afternoon we went out in a rowing boat on the Tasmin. The shadow of the woods lay on the water like a green crenellated wall. Deep below it, young water-lily leaves could be seen reaching for the surface.

In the evening, before we started for home, Aunt Nadya sang in the low-ceilinged hall, accompanied at the piano by the artist whose fingers, still covered with resin, kept sticking to the keys:

> *First meetings, last meetings,*
> *The dear sound of a beloved voice . . .*

Then once again we drove in the carriage and pair, returning to Smela. The artist and Lisa saw us off. The horses' hooves rang on the hard road. A damp breeze and the croaking of frogs came from the river. A single star shone very high up.

At the station Lisa took me to the buffet to have an ice, while the artist and Aunt Nadya sat on a bench in the station square. The buffet had, of course, no ices, and we went back to find them still sitting as before, lost in their thoughts.

Aunt Nadya went back to Moscow soon after this, and I never saw her again. In carnival week the following spring she drove in a sleigh to Petrovsky Park, sang in the open air and caught a chill which developed into pneumonia. She died just before Easter. My grandmother, Mama, and even my father went to her funeral.

I missed her terribly, and I cannot forget her to this day. She remains for me the everlasting embodiment of youth, kindness, spontaneity and joy.

7
Chinese Elderwood

The small soft white balls rolled about inside the box. I dropped one into a bowl of water. It swelled, opened out, and turned into a black elephant with red eyes, or an orange dragon or a rose with green leaves.

These fabulous Chinese balls made of elderwood were a present from my godfather and uncle, Iosif Grigoryevich, or, more simply, Uncle Yusia; he had brought them from Peking.

'An adventurer, pure and simple,' my father used to say of him, but with a certain envy rather than with disapproval.

What he envied Uncle Yusia was that he had been all over Africa, Asia and Europe—not as a well-behaved tourist but as a cónqueror, noisy, rowdy, insolently daring, and with an insatiable thirst for every sort of improbable deal in every corner of the world, from Shanghai to Addis Ababa and from Meshed to Kharbin.

Every one of the deals ended in a crash.

'I should go to the Klondike,' Uncle Yusia used to say. 'I'd show those Americans!'

What it was he intended to show the gold-seekers of the Klondike remained unknown. But it was perfectly clear that he would indeed have shown them something that would have made his name resound all the way from the Yukon to Alaska.

Perhaps he was born to be a famous explorer such as Nikolai Przevalski or Livingstone. But life in the Russia of those days—my father called them 'untimely'—had warped him. In him the noble passion for travel had taken the form of haphazard and purposeless globe-trotting. All the same, I am indebted to him, for his stories made the world a desperately interesting place and I have kept this feeling about it all my life.

Chinese Elderwood

My grandmother Vikentia Ivanovna regarded Uncle Yusia as a form of 'divine retribution' and treated him as the black sheep of the family. When I was naughty she warned me: 'Mind you don't become a second Uncle Yusia.'

Poor Granny had no idea that his life seemed to me utterly splendid and that my one dream was to become a 'second Uncle Yusia'.

Whether in Cherkassy or Kiev, Uncle Yusia would always turn up suddenly and as suddenly vanish, to reappear in another twelve or eighteen months with his deafening ring at the door and fill the house with his raucous voice, his coughing, his swearing and his contagious laughter. And each time he would be followed by the cab driver dragging enormous suitcases filled with rare things.

Uncle Yusia was tall, bearded, he had a broken nose and fingers of steel—they could bend a silver rouble—and a glint of cunning in his deceptively quiet eyes.

With no fear of 'God or Satan or death', as my father used to say, he yet went all to pieces if a woman cried or a child was upset.

The first time I saw him was after the Boer War.

He had joined the Boer Army as a volunteer. This courageous and unselfish action had greatly raised his stock with the family.

We children were tremendously excited by the war. We were sorry for the Boers fighting for their independence, and we hated the English. We knew every detail of the battles being fought at the other end of the world—Ladysmith, Bloemfontein, Diamond Hill. Our heroes were the Boer generals De Witt, Joubert and Botha. We scorned the haughty Lord Kitchener and made jokes about English soldiers going into battle in red coats. We were intoxicated by a book called *Peter Maritz, a young Boer from the Transvaal.*

We were not alone in this. The whole civilised world was tensely watching the unequal struggle in the plains between the Vaal and the Orange River, and even the organ grinders in Kiev, who had so far always played 'Parting', now had a new song: 'Transvaal, Transvaal, my country burning in flames.' For playing this we gave them the five-kopeck pieces we had saved up for ice-cream.

For boys like myself the Boer War was the undoing of the exotic dreams of our childhood. Africa now turned out to be quite unlike the vision we had had of it from the stories in 'Around the World' or from Gorodetsky's house in Vankovsky Street.

The grey walls of this house, built to look like a castle, were decorated with sculptures of lions, crocodiles, giraffes, rhinos, antelope and other African animals. Carved elephant trunks hung down to the pavement and served as drainpipes. Water dripped from the jaws of rhinoceroses, and stone boa-constrictors reared their heads from dark recesses in the walls.

The owner of the house, an engineer, was a passionate hunter. He had shot big game in Africa and had decorated his house with animals in memory of his expeditions. The grown-ups thought him a bit crazy, but we loved his house and it had shaped our picture of Africa.

But now, small boys though we were, we realised that a great struggle for human rights was being waged on the huge black continent which we had imagined to be filled with wise elephants trumpeting in the steaming jungle and hippopotamuses quietly snorting in the slimy ooze of the great uncharted rivers for, until then, Africa had been for us only a land for explorers, for Stanleys and Livingstones.

We were sorry to lose our Africa, the one we had explored in our dreams—the one of lion hunts, dawns over the Sahara, rafts on the Niger, and whistling arrows and the furious chattering of monkeys in the gloom of impassable forests. There, danger had ambushed us at every step and in our imagination we had more than once died of fever or wounds behind the log walls of a fort, breathing the poisonous exhalations of the swamps, listening to the whine of a solitary bullet, our moribund eyes fixed on the last glimmer of the Southern Cross in the black velvety sky.

How often had I died regretting the shortness of my life and my failure to cross the mysterious continent from Algiers to the Cape of Good Hope and from the Congo to Zanzibar!

We could not, of course, completely efface this Africa from our memories—it was much too alive. Hence my wordless, ecstatic amazement at the appearance in our prosaic Kiev house of my Uncle Yusia, bearded, burned by the African sun, wearing a broad-brimmed Boer hat and an open-necked shirt and with a cartridge clip in his belt.

I dogged his footsteps and gazed into his eyes—eyes which had seen the Orange River, Zulu kraals, British cavalrymen and storms on the Pacific.

All this happened when Kruger, the unwieldy old President of the Transvaal, came to Russia to ask for help. Uncle Yusia arrived with him. He only stopped in Kiev for a day and went on to join the President in Petersburg.

Uncle Yusia was convinced that Russia would come to the assistance of the Boers. But from Petersburg he wrote to my father: 'Overriding considerations of State have forced the Government to an ugly decision: we have refused help to the Boers. So it's all over and I am going back to the Far East.'

My maternal grandfather had not been wealthy. He had not been able to afford an education for his many children—five daughters and three sons—except by sending the boys to the Kiev Cadet Corps where the teaching was free.

There my Uncle Yusia went with his two brothers, and all was well with him for four years but in his fifth year he was transferred from Kiev to the 'penal' corps at Volsk on the Volga. A cadet could only be sentenced to Volsk for a 'grave crime'. So evidently such a crime had been committed by my uncle.

The kitchen of the Kiev Cadet Corps was in the basement. A lot of buns had been baked before a holiday and left to cool on the kitchen table. Uncle Yusia got hold of a pole, fixed a long nail to it, used it to fish out several dozen buns through the open window, and laid on a feast for his class.

He only spent two years in Volsk. In his third year he was expelled from the Corps and reduced to the ranks for striking an officer: the officer had stopped him in the street and shouted at him for some trifling fault in his turn-out.

Uncle Yusia was given a soldier's greatcoat and a rifle and sent off on foot to join an artillery regiment stationed in Kutno near Warsaw.

He crossed the country from east to west in winter, reporting to the local garrison commanders on the way, begging his food in the villages and spending the nights where he could.

He left Volsk as a hot-headed boy, he arrived in Kutno an embittered soldier.

In Kutno he was eventually commissioned as an ensign, but his military career was dogged by the worst possible luck. He was transferred from the artillery to the infantry and his regiment was sent to Moscow to do guard duty during the coronation of Nicholas II. His particular unit was on duty on the quay of the Moskva outside the Kremlin.

Early on the morning of the coronation he saw his men rushing down to the river bank where a violent scuffle had broken out. Clutching his sword, he hurried after them.

A terrifying creature with a copper head was rolling about in the mud, entangled in tubing. The soldiers had knocked it down and piled on top of it, and it was clumsily kicking out at them with its enormous leaden boots. One of the soldiers squeezed a ribbed rubber tube near the copper head, and the monster, giving a hoarse rattle, ceased to resist. My uncle realised that the monster was a diver and shouted at the soldiers, but by the time they had unscrewed the helmet the diver was dead.

Neither my uncle nor his men had been warned that divers from Kronstadt were that morning searching the bed of the river for terrorists' bombs.

After this incident Uncle Yusia was discharged from the army. He went to Central Asia, and for a time worked as organiser of camel caravans travelling between Uralsk, Khiva and Bokhara. There were as yet no railways linking Central Asia to Russia: the track ended at Uralsk, where all the goods had to be re-loaded on to camels and sent on by caravan.

In the course of his trips Uncle Yusia made friends with the two brothers Grum-Grzhimailo, who were exploring Central Asia, and went hunting tigers with them. He sent a tiger skin to my grandmother, but the tiger had such a ferocious expression that she immediately wrapped it up in mothballs and hid it in the cellar.

Uncle Yusia was fond of instructing us on how to kill jackals by sneezing at them. When spending the night in the desert, he used to lie down with his head on the knapsack which contained his food and pretend to go to sleep. The jackals crept up with their tails between their legs. When the boldest got its teeth into the knapsack and started cautiously pulling it out, my uncle gave an ear-shattering sneeze, and immediately, so he said, the timid jackal dropped dead of heart failure, without giving so much as a squeal.

We believed him because we heard him sneeze every morning

in preparation for the new day: the windows rattled and the cat, panic-stricken, hurtled about the room looking for shelter.

We found Uncle Yusia's stories more fascinating than the adventures of Baron Munchhausen. The Baron had to be conjured up by our imagination, whereas Uncle Yusia was there beside us, wrapped in a cloud of tobacco smoke and shaking the sofa by his huge laughter.

After he left Central Asia his life entered an obscure period. He roamed about Europe, gambled—so they said—in Monte Carlo, found himself in Abyssinia and came back with an enormous gold medal, for some reason conferred upon him by the Negus Menelik. The medal was like one of the large round badges of office worn by janitors.

Uncle Yusia continued to be restless until he discovered the attraction of the mysterious Far East. Manchuria and the region of Ussuria—seemed to exist expressly for such people as my uncle, for there they could live an expansive, rumbustious life, to the full extent of their will and resourcefulness, unthwarted by any 'asinine laws'.

This was the Russian Alaska—uninhabited, rich and dangerous. No better place on earth for Uncle Yusia could have been invented. The Amur, the virgin forest, gold, the Pacific, the Chinese, Korea and beyond—Kamchatka, Japan, Polynesia . . . A vast, unknown world thundered like surf against the shores of the Far East, disturbing the imagination of such men.

Uncle Yusia and his young wife, a religious ascetic—no one else, according to Mama, could possibly have stood him—went off to the Far East.

There he took part in the defence of Kharbin against the Boxers, in fights against the *hungusi* bandits, and in building the Chinese Eastern Railway, only interrupting his activities to go to the Transvaal.

After the Boer War he returned to Asia, not to Manchuria but to Port Arthur, where he worked as an agent for the Navy. He wrote to us that he had fallen in love with ships and felt sorry he had not become a sailor when he was young.

At about this time he lost his wife and found himself with two small daughters on his hands. A touchingly affectionate though clumsy father, he brought them up with the help of a devoted old Chinese servant whom he called Sam Drink Tea and to whom he was perhaps as attached as to his daughters. He was in general very fond of the Chinese and said they were a wonderful, kind, wise people whose only defect was their fear of rain.

As a former officer he was called up at the outbreak of the Japanese war. He packed his daughters off to Kharbin with Drink Tea.

After the war he came to visit us in Kiev, and this was the last time I saw him.

By then he was grey and staid, but the wild gay sparkle still occasionally flickered in his eyes.

He told us all about Peking, the gardens of the Chinese Emperors, Shanghai and the Yellow River. His stories left me with a curious vision of China fixed in an everlastingly clear, warm evening light. This may have been because Uncle Yusia no longer made things up, no longer rolled his eyes or roared with laughter, but spoke in a tired voice, continually flicking ash off his cigarette.

This visit took place in 1905. Uncle Yusia had little understanding of politics. He thought of himself as an old soldier, which he in fact was, honourable and loyal to his oath. When my father began one of his harsh, dangerous speeches, Uncle Yusia would fall silent and go out into the garden where he would sit smoking in solitude. He considered my father 'more leftist than the left'.

In the autumn of 1905 there was a mutiny in an engineers' battalion stationed in Kiev. An artillery battery joined the uprising. The rebels fought their way through the city, beating off the Cossacks who harassed them, and took up a position on the far side of the Demyevsky Gate.

From there the rebel battery opened fire on the Governor's Palace and on the barracks of the Cossacks. But so inaccurate was their aim that every shell went wide.

All that day Uncle Yusia was on tenterhooks, chain-smoking and swearing under his breath.

Finally he left the house. That evening the battery opened up again, breaking up the attacking Cossacks and laying down a fast, accurate barrage on the fort, the barracks and the palace. The authorities were thrown into confusion, and although the engineers had clearly lost the day, they were able, under cover of the barrage, to escape and scatter in the swamps and forests to the west of Kiev.

Chinese Elderwood

Uncle Yusia did not come home either that night or the next. He never came back at all. It was not until six months later that we heard from his daughter in Kharbin, who wrote that Uncle Yusia had settled down for good in Japan and begged us to forgive him for his abrupt disappearance.

Much later still we learned that Uncle Yusia, an old artilleryman, had found it unendurable to hear of the wretched marksmanship of the mutineers and on leaving the house had joined them and taken over the command of the battery.

He had naturally had to flee, and had gone to Japan where he died soon afterwards in Kobe, of cardiac asthma and incurable homesickness.

In the weeks before his death this huge, violent man would cry at the slightest reminder of Russia. In his last, seemingly half-jesting letter, he asked us to send him the most precious thing he could think of—a dried leaf from a Kiev chestnut tree.

8
Svyatoslavsky Street

Our trips to Cherkassy and Gorodishche were the holidays of my childhood. The 'weekdays' were those passed in Kiev where we spent the long winters in our gloomy, uncosy flat in Svyatoslavsky Street.

The street, lined with monotonous blocks of flats built of the yellow local brick which was also used for the pavements, ended in an enormous waste-lot furrowed with ravines. There were several such lots in the city. We called them 'wastelands'.

All day long 'dirt-carts' loaded with soil and gravel filed past our house on their way to the wasteland. They tipped their loads into the furrows to level the ground in preparation for building.

The soil was always spilling from the carts, and the street was always muddy—this was one of my reasons for disliking it.

We were strictly forbidden to play on the wasteland. But occasionally we boys made up a gang and went all the same. We took a police whistle with us, just in case . . . It seemed to us as reliable a weapon as a revolver.

At first we used only to stand on the edge of a ravine, looking apprehensively down at the glint of broken glass and the dogs who rummaged among the rusty tins in the litter without taking any notice of us.

Then we became bold enough to go down through the pall of dirty yellow smoke which hung over the gully. The smoke came from the hovels and dug-outs at the bottom. The hovels were put together out of anything that had come to hand—bits of plywood, old tin, broken packing cases, chair seats, mattresses with their springs sticking out of them. Dirty sacking was hung up in place of doors.

Ragged, dishevelled women sat round the fires in the ravine. They snapped at us or begged money for vodka. Only one of them, a shaggy grey-haired old woman with a leonine face, smiled at us, showing her one remaining tooth.

She was an Italian beggarwoman, well known in Kiev, who went from yard to yard playing the accordion. For a little extra she would play the 'Marseillaise'. On such occasions a boy was posted as look-out at the gate to watch for the policeman who patrolled the street.

Not only did she play the 'Marseillaise' on her accordion—she bawled it in her furious raucous voice. Sung by her, it sounded like an angry call to arms, a malediction from those who dwelled in the wasteland.

There were other familiar faces we used to come across. There, for instance, was Yashka with his white vodka-bleary eyes, who begged on the steps of the Vladimir Cathedral, everlastingly whining his one and only tag: 'Kind sirs, take pity on my crippled-dippled condition.' Seen on his home ground, he was very different from the snivelling misery who sat in the church porch. Tossing his vodka down his throat, he would cheerfully pound his chest and sing bawdy songs.

Then there was the bald old man who sold toothbrushes in Fundukleyev Street near the François Café, next to the hurdy-gurdy man with his parrot.

The hovels had clay ovens beside them, belching smoke through the broken samovar pipes stuck into their tops.

The organ grinder was never at home in the daytime but his daughter was there, a barefooted girl with an earthy complexion and fine smouldering eyes, who used to sit on the ground outside, peeling potatoes, her leg bound up in a rag.

She was double-jointed and had been a 'tumbler', going from door to door with her father—a wisp of a child in blue tights who performed her acrobatic tricks on a small square of carpet she put down on the ground. But since the accident which had damaged her leg, she could no longer 'work.'

Sometimes I would find her reading, always out of the same book. Judging from the illustrations, I guessed it to be Alexandre Dumas' *The Three Musketeers*.

'What are you hanging about for?' she used to shout at us. 'Have you never seen how people live?'

But after a while she got used to us and stopped shouting. One day the undersized organ grinder, her father, ran into us in the ravine and told her:

'Let them be. Let them see what our half of the world has to put up with. They may find it useful later on when they are students.'

At first we always went in a gang, but later, as I got to know the people in the wasteland, I went alone.

For a long time I kept this a secret from Mama, but in the end the organ grinder's daughter gave me away. I had lent her *Uncle Tom's Cabin* and didn't come to fetch it because I was ill. She got worried about me and brought the book to the flat. Mama opened the door to her, and so it all came out. Mama's icy silence and tight lips told me all I needed to know.

That evening I heard my parents talking about me in the dining-room next door. Mama was upset and cross, but my father said there was nothing terrible about it, I wasn't easy to spoil, and he would rather I made friends with these unfortunate people than with the sons of Kiev merchants and officials. Mama objected that at my age I ought to be protected from distressing impressions.

'What you don't realise,' said my father, 'is that these people respond to being treated decently with a devotion you would never find in our circle. I don't see why his impressions should be distressing.'

'Perhaps you are right,' said Mama after a silence.

When I got well she brought me *The Prince and the Pauper* by Mark Twain and said:

'There . . . Take it to the organ grinder's daughter . . . I don't know what her name is.'

'Lisa,' I said shyly.

'Well, take it to Lisa. As a present.'

From then on, no one made any more fuss about my visits to the wasteland. I no longer had to filch the sugar for my new friends from the sideboard, nor the pignuts for Mitya their half-blind parrot. I asked Mama for whatever I wanted and she never refused me.

One day in the early autumn I saw the organ grinder standing in our yard without his parrot. The organ was wheezing out a polka: 'Come along, my darling angel, come along and dance with me.' The organ grinder was listlessly turning the handle and scanning the windows and balconies, waiting for the coppers in their twists of paper to start falling to the ground.

I ran out to him and he told me without ceasing to turn the handle:

'Mitya's sick. Sits like a hedgehog. Eats nothing—not even your nuts. Must be a goner.'

He took off his dusty black hat and wiped his face with it.

'It's a hard life!' he said. 'An organ grinder by himself, without Mitya, can't even earn his vodka, let alone his bread. Who will help me with the "lucky dip" now?'

For five kopecks, the parrot would pick out a blue, red or green slip with a prediction printed on it. For some reason, the slips were called 'luck'. They were kept, rolled up into spills, in an empty cartridge box. Before pulling one out, Mitya would stamp up and down on his perch, screeching unhappily.

The language of the prophecies was obscure. 'You were born under the sign of Mercury and your stone is the emerald, which signifies diffidence and the arrangement of worldly affairs to your liking in the years which are grey with age. Be on your guard against blondes of either sex, and avoid going out in the streets on the Feast of St. John the Baptist.'

Sometimes the sentence was shorter and more sinister: 'To-morrow at dusk' or 'If you want to stay alive, don't look back.'

A day later Mitya died; I put him in a cardboard shoe box and buried him in the wasteland. The organ grinder got drunk and disappeared.

I told Mama about the death of the parrot. My lips were trembling but I managed not to cry.

'Get your coat on,' Mama said sternly. 'We're going to Burmistrov's.'

Burmistrov was an old man who kept a dark, stuffy little shop on the Bessarabka. He was hard of hearing, his beard was green with age and he looked like a gnome, but he sold the most wonderful things—fishing rods, bright-coloured floats, fish tanks, goldfish, birds, ants' eggs and even transfers.

Mama bought an old green parrot with a lead ring on its leg. I carried it in a cage we borrowed from Burmistrov. It contrived to bite my finger to the bone; I had it bandaged at a chemist's but I was so excited that I felt almost no pain.

I longed to take the parrot to the wasteland at once but Mama said:

'I'm coming with you. I must see this place for myself.'

She went home to change. I was ashamed at the idea of her dressing up to call on ragged paupers but I said nothing.

In a few minutes she came out in an old dress darned at the elbows and with a shawl over her head. For once she was without her elegant kid gloves and her shoes had trodden down heels.

I looked at her gratefully and we set off.

Mama climbed valiantly down into the ravine, walked through the crowd of dishevelled women struck dumb with amazement, and didn't even once raise her skirt to avoid the mounds of rubbish and cinders.

When she saw us coming with the parrot, Lisa's grey face turned a deep red and, to my astonishment, she curtsied to Mama. Her father was still out with his friends, drowning his sorrows in the pubs on the Demyanovka.

Lisa took the parrot, blushing more and more and saying again and again:

'Oh, why did you? You shouldn't have done it!'

'Can he be taught to pull out the lucky slips, do you think?' Mama asked.

'Of course! It won't take a couple of days,' Lisa said happily. 'But you shouldn't have done it! Good Lord! The money you must have spent!'

When my father was told, he grinned:

'That was very philanthropic of you, my dear—the result of your sentimental upbringing.'

'Good Lord!' my mother exploded. 'Do you always have to contradict yourself? You really are extraordinary! You'd have done exactly the same in my place.'

'No, I'd have done more.'

'Oh, would you?' Mama's voice was threatening. 'All right! We'll see!'

I didn't realise that he was deliberately provoking her.

Next day Mama sent Lisa a black dress which had belonged to my sister, and a pair of brown shoes of her own.

But my father was not to be outdone. He waited until the organ grinder turned up with his new parrot.

He was wearing a red scarf round his neck and his nose shone with vodka and joy. The hurdy-gurdy played everything it knew: 'Yearning for the Fatherland', 'The Waves of the Danube', 'Bitter Parting' and 'Oh, the box is full to bursting'—a march, a waltz, a polka and a song. The parrot picked out lucky slips, and the coppers came showering from the windows.

Finally he slung his organ on his back and set off, bent double as always, but up the stairs to our door instead of down the street.

His hat in his hand and almost brushing the floor, he thanked Mama and kissed her hand. My father invited him inside. The organ grinder leaned his organ against the wall and, picking his steps, followed my father to his study.

My father gave him a brandy, said he realised how hard and unrewarding must be his lot, and offered him a job as watchman on the South-West Railway. He would have his own little house and a garden.

'I'm sorry, Georgy Maximovich, and I hope you won't judge me too harshly,' the organ grinder said, blushing. 'But I'd be bored to death. It seems it's my lot to be an organ grinder.'

He went off. Mama said nothing but she couldn't hide her satisfaction.

A few days later, without warning, the police evicted all the squatters from the wasteland. The organ grinder and Lisa disappeared—they must have moved to another town.

But before this happened I had time to pay them one more visit. The organ grinder had invited me to 'an evening' at his house.

A plate of baked tomatoes and brown bread, a bottle of cherry brandy and some grubby, thick striped sticks of rock had been set out on an upturned packing case.

Lisa had on a new dress and her hair was in tight braids. She watched me jealously to make sure I was 'eating as much as at home'. The parrot slept, a leathery shutter let down over each eye. The organ heaved an occasional musical sigh without anyone touching it. The organ grinder explained that this was because air was trapped in a pipe inside it.

This was in September. Twilight was coming on. No one who

hasn't seen a Kiev autumn can have any conception of the gentle beauty of these hours.

The first star lights up in the sky. The luxuriant autumnal gardens are still, waiting for the night and for the shooting stars which they will catch in their dense foliage as in a hammock and lower to the ground so softly that no one will wake up or know.

Lisa took me to our door, thrust a sticky pink sweet into my hand and fled down the stairs, while I stood trying to make up my mind to ring the bell and face the scolding I would get for being so late.

9
Winter Scene

My father gave me a pair of 'Halifax' skates for Christmas. Nowadays children would laugh if they could see them, but at that time there were no better skates in the world than those that came from Halifax.

'Where *is* the city of Halifax?' I asked everyone. Where was this city covered with snow where all the little boys went about on skates? Where was this wintry country populated by retired sailors and happy schoolboys? No one could tell me.

My eldest brother Borya said Halifax was not a city at all—it was the name of the inventor of these particular skates. My father said he thought Halifax was a town—yes, it was a little town off the north coast of America, on the island of Newfoundland which was not only famous for its skates but also for its dogs.

The skates lay on my table. I looked at them and thought about Halifax. I saw it so clearly in my mind that I could have drawn a detailed plan of its streets and squares.

I could sit over my Malinin and Burenin arithmetic book—I was working for my entrance examination to the High School—and think about Halifax for hours on end.

This addiction was a great worry to Mama. She was greatly concerned about it, and said that penury and death in a ditch lay in store for moony little boys like myself.

The gloomy prediction, 'You'll die in a ditch', was very widely used in those days; for some reason death in a ditch was regarded as particularly shameful.

I heard it often, but still more often Mama told me that I had a 'dislocated mind', that I was 'different from other people' and that she was afraid I would never be a success at anything.

My father was furious whenever he heard this, and would say:

'I don't care what kind of a failure he is—let him be a tramp or a pauper so long as he doesn't grow up into one of those damned Kiev philistines.'

In the end I myself became a little shy and wary of my imagination. It seemed that I was wasting my time over trifles while everyone around me was busy with serious things: my brothers and my sister went to school and worked hard at their lessons, my father was on the managerial staff of the South-West Railway, and Mama did her sewing and ran the house. I alone lived in my own world, taking no part in their interests and with nothing to show for mine.

'I wish you'd go out and skate instead of sitting at home mooning,' said Mama. 'You really are a funny boy. Just look at yourself.'

I went skating. The winter days were short and dusk often found me still at the rink. A brass band struck up. Little coloured lights were lit. Schoolgirls in fur coats skated in circles, swinging from side to side, their hands tucked away in their muffs. Schoolboys skated backwards or 'pistol-fashion', one leg bent at the knee and the other stretched straight out. This was regarded as the height of style and I greatly envied them.

I came home flushed and tired. But my heart was troubled, for even after skating I still felt the same dangerous inclination to 'moon', 'daydream' and 'make things up'.

At the skating rink I often met my sister Galya's friend Katya Vesnitskaya who was in the senior form at the Fundukleyev High School for girls. Katya too had Halifax skates, but hers were black and burnished.

My eldest brother Borya, who was gifted in mathematics and went to the science school,[13] flirted with Katya and the two of them used to waltz on the ice.

A large space was cleared for them by the other skaters who stood round in a ring, the small urchins who darted about on home-made skates were cuffed out of the way, and the slow, gliding dance would begin.

Even the carroty-haired Czech bandmaster Kovarshic turned his back on the band and watched the dancing, a pleased smile wreathing his red face.

Katya's long braids swung in time to the waltz, getting in her way, and she tossed them forward, while her half-shut eyes glanced disdainfully at her enthusiastic public.

I watched Borya with malicious joy. His skating was less good than Katya's. Occasionally he even skidded on his 'Yacht-Club' skates of which he was so proud.

Little did I think that Katya's life would take an even more unexpected turn than it did in my daydreams.

One of the sons of the King of Siam, Chakrabon, had been a cadet at the Corps des Pages in Petersburg.

When he was near Kiev on his way home, he caught pneumonia. The Prince was brought to Kiev, lodged in the Tsar's palace and put under the care of the best Kiev specialists.

He recovered but was in need of a rest before continuing his long journey and stayed on for another two months. Every effort was made to distract him from his intense boredom—he was taken to balls at the Merchants' Club, charity galas and raffles, the circus and the theatre.

At one such ball Prince Chakrabon saw Katya Vesnitskaya. She was waltzing as she did at the skating rink, with her braids flying and her arrogant deep-blue eyes half-closed. The Prince, a short, slant-eyed young man with hair gleaming like polish, was enchanted. He fell in love. He left for Siam, but soon returned to Kiev incognito, proposed to Katya and was accepted.

There was a terrible commotion among the Kiev schoolgirls. With one voice they declared that not for anything would they, in Katya's place, have married an Asiatic, even though he was the son of a king.

Katya went off to Siam. Soon afterwards the King of Siam died of some tropical disease. His two eldest sons caught the same disease and died in their turn.

Katya's husband was the next heir. He had had very little expectation of succeeding his father, but he now found himself on the throne. Thus Katya Vesnitskaya became Queen of Siam.

The courtiers hated their foreign queen. Her very existence violated all the traditions of the court and when electricity was laid on in Bangkok at her insistence their cup filled to overflowing. They decided to assassinate the queen who had spurned the ancient customs of the country. So they ground the glass of broken electric bulbs down into the finest of powders and added it to her food; within six months Katya died of intestinal hæmorrhage.

The King put up a monument on her grave. A tall black marble elephant, with a golden crown on its head and its trunk hanging despondently, stands up to its knees in the dense grass, and beneath the grass lies Katya, the young Queen of Siam.

Afterwards whenever I found myself at the skating rink I thought of the band playing the waltz 'The Summer is Gone', and of Katya brushing the snow from her forehead with her mittens, and of her burnished skates which came from Halifax, a city populated by simple-hearted, kindly sailors in retirement. Had you told these good old men the story of Katya, they would first have gaped at you in astonishment, and then flushed with indignation at the wickedness of the courtiers, and finally sighed and shaken their heads at the perversity of human fate.

In the winter we used to go to the theatre.

The first play I was taken to was *The Storming of Ismail*. I took a dislike to it when I noticed a bespectacled man in shiny velvet trousers who stood in the wings beside Suvorov and at a given moment shoved him so hard in the back that the General flew out on to the stage crowing like a rooster.

To make up for this, the second play I saw—Rostand's *La Princesse Lointaine*—utterly bewitched me. It had everything to stir my imagination—the deck of a ship with enormous sails, knights, troubadours and a princess.

I fell in love with the Solovtsovsky Theatre, its small boxes and its sky-blue velvet upholstery. When the play was over I refused to budge until after the lights were put out. The darkened auditorium smelling of scent and orange peel fascinated me so much I only wished I could hide and spend the night in it.

I could not as a child distinguish between drama on the stage and in life, so that I genuinely suffered and was even physically ill after every performance.

The theatre fanned my passion for reading. I had only to see *Madame Sans-Gêne* to throw myself upon every book I could find about Napoleon. The period and the people I had seen on the stage came to life and were at once full of extraordinary interest and charm.

Winter Scene

It was not only the plays I enjoyed, I loved the corridors with their tarnished mirrors in gold frames, the mother-of-pearl opera-glasses, the dark cloakrooms smelling of furs, the impatient trampling of the horses waiting outside the entrance.

During the interval I would run to the window at the end of the corridor and look out. It was pitch-dark, only the snow was pale on the trees. From this I swiftly turned to the festive hall with its lights gleaming on women's hair and jewels, and the curtain across the stage softly stirring in a warm draught. I did this again and again, looking from hall to window and from window to hall— I found this occupation delightful.

The opera I disliked because the first one I was taken to was *Daemon* by Rubinstein:[14] the 'daemon' was a fat, greasy, coarse faced actor who sang in a superciliously sloppy way. He had hardly any make-up on and looked an absurd little pot-bellied figure in his long black spangled muslin shirt and with wings tied on to his shoulders. I couldn't stop giggling and Mama never took me to the opera again.

In winter Aunt Dosia came from Gorodishche to stay with us. Mama enjoyed taking her to the theatre. After a sleepless night, and several hours before the performance, Aunt Dosia would put on an ample brown satin dress embroidered with yellow flowers and leaves, and a matching scarf round her neck. A tiny lace handkerchief crushed in her hand, she rustled about the house— until finally it was time to go, then she got into the cab with Mama, looking ten years younger than usual and a little scared. Like all Ukrainian countrywomen she covered her head with a black kerchief dotted with pink roses.

Everyone stared at her in the theatre but she was much too busy watching the play to notice.

The plays she was taken to were usually Ukrainian, such as *Natalya from Poltava*, or *The Cossack from beyond the Dvina*, or *Shelmenko the Coachman*. Once in the middle of the performance she got up and shouted at the villain:

'Shame on you! How dare you, you wretch! Stop it at once.'

The audience rocked with laughter. The curtain came down. All next day Aunt Dosia wept with shame and kept apologising to my father; we didn't know how to cheer her up.

It was with Aunt Dosia that we went to the cinema for the first time. In those days it was called 'Illusion' or *Cinématographe*

Lumière. The first *séance* was held at the Opera House. My father was delighted with the illusion and welcomed it as one of the splendid novelties of our era.

A wet sheet was stretched across the stage. Then the chandeliers were put out, an ominous livid light played on the sheet and black spots scurried about on it. A smoky shaft pierced the darkness just above our heads, sizzling alarmingly as if a whole boar were being roasted behind our backs.

'Why does it crackle like that, this illusion?' asked Aunt Dosia. 'You don't think we'll all be burnt like chickens in a coop?'

After a lot of blinking, a title came into focus: 'Eruption on the Island of Martinique. Travel Picture.'

The screen quivered and an erupting volcano appeared as through a dust storm. Staggered by the sight, the audience roared.

We were next shown a comic film about life in a French barracks. The drummer beat his drum. The soldiers woke up, jumped out of bed and began to pull on their trousers. A rat fell out of a trouser leg. It ran about the barrack room, and the terrified soldiers, their eyes bulging improbably, climbed on to their beds and up the windows and doors. On this the film ended.

'A Punch and Judy show,' said Mama. 'The side-shows at the Contract Fair[15] are more interesting.'

My father remarked that this had been precisely the reaction of unimaginative people to Stephenson's steam engine, and Aunt Dosia, trying to make peace, said:

'I don't really care for this illusion. But it's not for us women to judge.'

The side-shows at the Contract Fair were indeed very interesting. We loved the Fair and looked forward to it all through the winter months.

It was held at the end of the winter in Podolye, in the old Exchange building and the wooden booths around it.

Usually the thaw had set in by the opening day and was turning the roads to mud. The sharp smell of the wares carried a long way —a smell of barrels, leather and calico, and of ginger and mint cakes.

I particularly liked the merry-go-round, the toys and the panopticon, but almost everything was delightful.

Oily blocks of vanilla and chocolate *Khalva* crunched under the salesmen's knives. Translucent chunks of sticky pink and lemon

Turkish Delight melted in our mouths. Huge platters were piled with pyramids of the sugared pears, plums and cherries produced by the famous Kiev confectioner Balabukha.

Roughly carved and painted wooden soldiers paraded on the sacking spread over the muddy ground—Cossacks in tall hats and wide trousers with crimson piping, drummers with fierce goggling eyes, trumpeters with tassels on their trumpets. Clay mouth-organs lay tumbled into heaps.

Hawkers jostled through the crowd, offering 'divers'. This wonderful toy was a small shaggy black devil who spun and dived in a glass tube filled with water.

We were deafened by the noise—hawkers yelling, metal-rimmed wheels clanging, the bells of the Bratsky Monastery ringing for Lent, mouth-organs shrilling and children squealing on the merry-go-round.

For a few kopecks extra, the merry-go-round turned so fast that all you saw was a confusion of grinning horses' heads and coloured skirts, ties, boots, ribbons and kerchiefs. Occasionally a glass necklace broke in mid-air and shot its beads like bullets at the crowd.

The panopticon scared me a little, especially the wax figures.

The murdered French President Carnot lay smiling on the floor in his dress coat with decorations pinned to it. Blood like red vaseline crept down his starched shirt-front. He seemed to be pleased at making so effective a corpse.

Queen Cleopatra stood clutching a black adder to her firm greenish breast.

A red-eyed mermaid floated in a zinc bath. The dim light of an electric bulb was reflected in her grimy scales. The water in the bath was muddy.

A boa constrictor slept on an eiderdown in an open trunk covered with wire netting. Now and then it rippled its muscles and the crowd shied away from it.

Surrounded by foliage made of painted wood shavings, a stuffed gorilla was whisking off into the jungle, a swooning girl with flowing golden hair slung over its back.

For three kopecks you could shoot the gorilla and rescue the girl. If you hit the target, the rag doll hit the floor in a cloud of dust.

A chintz curtain was then drawn across the scene. After a few moments the gorilla reappeared, as fierce as ever, whisking off with the same girl into the same jungle.

Another reason why we liked the fair was that it heralded Easter and our visit to Cherkassy, followed by the always wonderful Kiev spring.

10
The Midshipman

The spring began when the Dnieper overflowed its banks. You had only to climb the Vladimir Hill on the edge of the town for a great expanse of bluish sea to open out before you.

But this was not the only flood in Kiev—the city was inundated with sun, freshness and warm, scented winds.

The sticky cone-shaped poplars on Bibikov Boulevard burgeoned, filling the surrounding streets with a smell of incense. The chestnuts put out their first, creased, transparent leaves covered with a reddish down. By the time their yellow and pink candles were in flower, spring was at its height, and the damp smell of new grass and the whispering of newly unfolded leaves poured over the garden walls into the streets.

There were caterpillars on the pavements even in the Kreshchatik. The wind swept fallen petals into drifts. Butterflies and maybugs flew in at the windows of the trams. Nightingales sang at night. The fluff off the poplars eddied on the flagstones like the surf of the Black Sea, and dandelions blossomed in the gutters.

Striped awnings were lowered over the wide-open windows of pastry shops and cafés. Vases of lilac sprinkled with water stood on the tables of the restaurants, and young girls searched its clusters for five-petalled blooms, their faces shadowed to a creamy ochre by their summer hats.

In spring I vanished for whole days into one or other of the Kiev parks. There I played and did my homework and read, coming home only to eat and sleep.

I knew every corner of the huge Botanical Gardens with its gullies, its lake and the dense shadow of its ancient avenues of lime-trees.

But my favourite park was the Marinsky Park in Lipki, near the Palace. It overlooked the Dnieper, it had fountains playing on its lawns, and its walls of white and purple lilac, three times a man's height, swayed and hummed with their multitude of bees.

The parks stretched in a wide belt along the tops of the red cliffs overhanging the Dnieper. The famous view from the Merchants' Park over the Podol was the pride of Kiev. A symphony orchestra played in the Park throughout the summer, and there was nothing to distract you from listening to the music except the hooting of the steamers.

The farthest of the parks along the bank was Vladimir Hill. It had a statue of Prince Vladimir holding up a large bronze cross in his hand. Electric bulbs had been attached to it and at night the fiery cross blazed in the sky above the Kiev heights.

So beautiful was the city in spring that I could never understand Mama's passion for driving out on conventional Sunday excursions to the near-by places of interest. I was bored by the summer cottages of Pushcha Voditsa, indifferent to the stunted Boyarka woods haunted by the poet Nadson, and disgusted by Darnitsa because of the trampled grass littered with cigarette butts at the foot of its pine-trees.

One day I was sitting with my sister Galya in Marinsky Park, reading Stevenson's *Treasure Island*. Galya was also reading; her summer hat lay beside her on the bench, its green ribbon stirring in the wind.

Earlier it had rained but now the rain had nearly stopped and only a few drops pattered off the lilacs.

Galya was a short-sighted and extremely trusting girl whose equanimity it was almost impossible to upset.

A child with bows in her hair and a skipping rope had stopped in front of us and was distracting me by her skipping. I shook the lilac tree. A small shower descended noisily on to the child and Galya. The little girl stuck out her tongue at me and ran away; Galya only brushed the drops off her page and continued to read.

It was at this moment that I saw the man who for years to come was to poison my mind with dreams of an unattainable destiny.

A tall midshipman with a calm, sunburned face came striding lightly down the path. A straight black cutlass hung from his shiny belt. Black ribbons with bronze anchors on them fluttered in the breeze. His uniform was all black, the vivid gold of the insignia alone relieving its austerity.

In our land-locked Kiev where we hardly ever saw a sailor, he was a visitor from the remote and legendary world of sailing ships, from the Frigate Pallada, from the world of all the oceans, all the ports, all the winds, all the fascination of the life of those who toil at sea. His antique black-hilted cutlass had come to Marinsky Park straight out of Robert Louis Stevenson.

The midshipman walked past, the sand crunching under his feet. I stood up and followed him. Galya was too short-sighted to notice my disappearance.

The man was the embodiment of all my ocean-going dreams. I had often imagined the sea, stormy or misty or calm in the gold evening, and myself on a distant voyage, with the whole world swiftly shifting and changing before my eyes like the patterns in a kaleidoscope. Good gracious, if someone had only thought of making me a birthday present of so much as a bit of rust off an anchor! I would have treasured it like a jewel.

The midshipman looked round. Inscribed on the narrow ribbon of his cap was the mysterious word 'Azimuth'. I learned later that this was the name of a training ship of the Baltic fleet.

I followed him down street after street. He saluted infantry officers with a careless grace which made me ashamed of our land-lubbing soldiery.

After looking back several times he finally stopped at a corner of a street and beckoned me over.

'Tell me, boy,' he said with an amused smile, 'why have I got you in tow?'

I blushed and couldn't get out a word.

'I know, he wants to be a sailor,' he guessed, for some reason referring to me in the third person.

'I'm short-sighted,' I said despondently.

He put his lean hand on my shoulder.

'Let's go to the Kreshchatik.'

We walked side by side. Not daring to look up I could only see the dazzling gloss on his stout, polished boots.

When we got to the Kreshchatik, he took me to the Samadeni Café and ordered two pistachio ices and two glasses of water. The waiter put them down on a small three-legged table with a marble top. The marble was very cold and had figures scribbled all over it: the stock exchange brokers used to gather in the café and work out their profits and losses on the tables.

We ate our ices in silence. The midshipman drew from his wallet the photograph of a magnificent corvette fully rigged and with a large funnel. Handing it to me, he said:

'Take this to remember me by. It's my ship. I sailed in her to Liverpool.'

Then he firmly shook my hand and walked out. I stayed on until the sweating businessmen in boaters who sat at the next table began to stare. Then I stumbled out and ran all the way to Marinsky Park. There was no one on the bench. Galya had gone. I realised that the midshipman had felt sorry for me and learned for the first time that pity leaves a bitter aftertaste.

For years after this I was tormented by the longing to be a sailor. I yearned for the sea. I had only had that one glimpse of it, when I spent a few days with my father in Novorossisk, and that had only whetted my appetite.

I used to sit for hours over an atlas, tracing the outlines of seaboards, looking up obscure little ports, capes, islands and estuaries.

I invented a highly complicated game. I made up a long list of ships with glamorous names such as Sirius, North Star, Chingkhan, Walter Scott; I added to it day after day, and I became the owner of the largest fleet in the world.

Needless to say, I sat in my own shipping office, the air thick with tobacco smoke, the walls bright with posters and sailing schedules, the wide windows facing the quayside. The yellow masts of steamships reached to the windows, poplars whispered cosily outside the walls, and smoke from the funnels blew in freely, mixing with the smell of new sacking and old brine.

I worked out the most astonishing routes for my ships. There was not a corner of the world they left unvisited. They even called at the island of Tristan da Cunha.

I switched them from route to route. I followed their sailings and knew unerringly where each of them would be on a given day—the *Admiral Istomin* was today loading bananas in Singapore while the *Flying Dutchman* was unloading grain in the Faroes.

There were many things I needed to know in order to conduct an undertaking on so vast a scale, and I pored over guides and nautical almanacks and whatever else had the remotest connection with the sea.

That was when I first heard Mama mention meningitis.

'I only hope it doesn't end by giving you meningitis,' she said one day.

But I had heard that meningitis was a disease which struck children who learned to read before they were old enough, so I only laughed at Mama's fears.

What it actually ended in was my parents' decision that we should all spend our summer holiday by the sea.

I realise today that Mama was hoping to cure me of my infatuation. She believed that, after dreaming of it so passionately and for so long, I would, as usually happens, be disappointed by the reality. She was to some extent right, but not altogether.

II

Paradise

One day Mama solemnly announced that we were all going to spend the whole summer by the Black Sea. We would leave the following week and stay in the little town of Gelendzhik near Novorossisk.

A better place to discourage my passion for the sea and for the south could not have been imagined.

Gelendzhik in those days was a dusty, sultry little town with barely a blade of grass in it. The vegetation for miles around had been destroyed by the prevailing north-east winds; nothing but thorn and stunted acacias with hard little flowers grew in the gardens. The tall mountains reflected the heat. A cement factory belched smoke at the end of the bay.

Yet the bay itself was lovely. Jellyfish, like pale blue and pink flowers, swam in the warm, clear water. Spotted flounders and pop-eyed bullheads lay on the sandy bottom. Red seaweed, the floats of fishing nets, bits of dark-green bottle-glass worn smooth by the waves, all these were washed up on the beach.

The sea kept its attraction for me. It was only more simple, and therefore more beautiful, than in my elaborately ornate fantasies.

In Gelendzhik I made friends with an elderly boatman called Atanas, a Greek who came from the town of Volo. He had a new lugger, white with a red keel and a latticed deck scrubbed to a white sheen.

Atanas used to take the summer residents out in his lugger and, as he was known to be very experienced and reliable, Mama would sometimes allow me to go alone with him.

Usually we only sailed in the harbour, but on one occasion he took me out into the open sea. I shall never forget my terror or my delight when the bellying sail leaned over so far that the waves were scudding on a level with the gunwales. Great, noisy breakers came at us, translucently green and spitting cold, salty spray.

I grabbed at the sheets and wished I were back on shore, but Atanas only clamped his pipe between his teeth, humming to himself, and after a while nodded at my new Caucasian shoes:

'That's a very smart pair you've got. How much did your mother pay for them?'

My legs were trembling. I made no reply. Atanas yawned and said:

'Never mind. It's only a little shower, and a warm one at that. You'll have a good appetite for your dinner. They won't keep telling you to eat a spoonful for Mama and a spoonful for Papa.'

He turned the lugger with casual assurance. It shipped water and made for the harbour, diving and leaping. The waves raced from the stern with a menacing roar. My heart stood still.

Suddenly Atanas broke into song. I stopped shivering and listened, puzzled by the words.

> *From Batumi to Sukhumi*
> *Ai-vai-vai!*
> *From Sukhumi to Batumi*
> *Ai-vai-vai!*
>
> *A little boy ran, lugging a box*
> *Ai-vai-vai!*
> *The little boy fell and broke the box.*
> *Ai-vai-vai!*

To this tune we furled sail and were borne towards the pier where Mama stood waiting for us, white as a sheet. Atanas lifted me up, stood me on the jetty and said:

'He's got his sea legs now, Madam. He's a regular old salt.'

Another day my father hired a carriage and we went for a drive to the Mikhailov Pass.

At first the flinty road wound its way up barren, dusty slopes. Bridges spanned ravines which had not a drop of water in them. The same grey cotton-wool clouds clung all day to the tops of the mountains.

I was terribly thirsty. Our Cossack driver said that if I waited till we got to the pass I would find all the water I could drink, but I didn't believe him. The dry, waterless mountains filled me with alarm. I looked back regretfully at the dark strip of sea we were leaving behind. One couldn't drink it but at least one could bathe in it and it was cool and wet.

The road climbed higher and higher. Suddenly I felt a cool breath on my face.

'Here we are, right at the pass itself,' said the driver, stopping the horses and getting out to put brake-shoes under the wheels.

Over the ridge we could see densely wooded hills rolling to the horizon, with only here and there a red granite rock rising above the green, and, very far in the distance, a peak blazing with ice and snow.

'It's sheltered from the north-easter, it's a real paradise, this bit of the country,' said the driver.

The road began to go downhill, and immediately we were in shadow. Sounds of water, of bird calls and of leaves ruffled by the midday wind came from the impenetrable forest around us.

The farther we went the denser was the forest and the darker the shadows on the road; it was now bordered by a very clear small stream, which had a bed of coloured pebbles, and purple flowers growing along its bank; the current caught at their stems, shaking and bending them but unable to tear them from their stony ground and sweep them away with it into the gorge.

Mama scooped a cupful of water and gave me a drink; it was so cold that the outside of the cup misted over.

'You can smell the ozone,' said my father.

I took a deep breath. I didn't know what the smell was but I felt as if I were being wrapped in armfuls of rain-drenched leaves.

Creepers plucked at our hair. Small shaggy flowers, half hidden among the wayside stones, peered curiously at the carriage and at the grey horses, stepping out gravely, their heads held high as if on parade, in order to keep themselves from tearing downhill and spilling us out into a ditch.

'Look, there's a lizard,' said Mama.

'Where?'

'Over there. You see the nut tree, and to the left of it a red stone? And higher up a flowering bush—that's an azalea by the way—well, it's just to the right of the azalea, where there's that

76

beech tree lying on the ground. Near that shaggy reddish root and those tiny blue flowers—just there. See it?'

I spotted the lizard after making a fascinating tour of the nut tree, the azalea and the roots of the beech tree.

'So this is what the Caucasus is like,' I thought.

'It's a paradise,' the driver said again, turning off the highway into a narrow cutting through the wood. 'We'll stop in a moment and have a bathe.'

The cutting became so narrow that the branches on either side slapped our faces and we had to get out and continue on foot. The carriage followed us at a walking pace.

At last we came to a clearing. Tall clumps of dandelions made islands in the juicy grass. We found an old empty barn overshadowed by beeches. It stood on the bank of a noisy little torrent. The water eddied over the stones and ran on, hissing and bubbling.

The driver unharnessed the horses and he and my father fetched firewood, while we washed in the stream, after which our faces felt even hotter than before.

We wanted to walk on at once, upstream along the river bank, but Mama spread a tablecloth on the grass, got out the provisions and said she wasn't letting us go anywhere until we had something to eat.

I choked over my ham sandwiches and cold rice pudding, only to find that I needn't have hurried. The copper kettle obstinately refused to boil, presumably because the water from the stream was as cold as ice. Then it spluttered and boiled over so suddenly that it put out the fire.

We gulped our strong tea and pestered Father to hurry up and come into the forest with us. The driver told us to watch out for wild boar, for there were a lot of them in the woods. If we came upon small pits dug in the ground, we would know it was a place where the boar slept at night.

Mama became alarmed for us—she wasn't coming, as walking made her breathless—but the driver reassured her by saying that a boar would never attack a man unless it was thoroughly teased and provoked.

We went off upstream. Pushing our way through the woods, we kept stopping to look and point, now at trout flashing in a granite bowl scooped out by the stream, now at enormous green, whiskered beetles, or at a frothing, grumbling waterfall, or at clumps of mares tail taller than ourselves, or at thickets of peonies and carpets of wood anemones.

Borya stumbled across a small dusty pit. It was shaped like a baby's bath. We walked cautiously round it. It obviously served as the night quarters of a boar.

Father had gone on ahead. He shouted to us and we caught up with him forcing our way through buckthorn and past huge, moss-covered boulders.

He was looking at a curious arrangement of stones overgrown with brambles. Four smoothly hewn boulders stood upright and a fifth covered them like a roof. They made a sort of house. One of the walls had an opening in it, but so small that not even I could get through. There were several other such buildings nearby.

'They're dolmens,' said my father. 'The Scythians built them as burial chambers. Or perhaps not as burial chambers. Scholars are still arguing about what they were meant for, and how they were built.'

I was convinced that the dolmens were the dwellings of a long extinct race of dwarfs. But I said nothing about it to my father because Borya was with us and he would certainly have made fun of me.

We went back to Gelendzhik, feeling burned out by the sun and drunk with fatigue and forest air. I was almost asleep when a hot breath struck my face and I heard the distant rumble of the sea.

After this I became the owner of yet another magical kingdom—the Caucasus. I went mad over my Lermontov, the tribesmen, Shamil.[16] Again Mama was upset.

Now in my old age I am grateful for my childhood enthusiasms. They taught me a lot. Fortunately they didn't turn me into a noisy pest. I was shy and didn't bother the grown-ups too much with my excitements.

12
The Forest of Bryansk

I was to join the preparatory form of the First Kiev High School in the autumn of 1902. My brother Vadim was already at school, and what he told me of it filled me with terror. I wept and implored my mother not to send me.

'You don't really want to be a private pupil, do you?' she asked in a worried voice.

Private pupils studied at home and only took their yearly examinations at school. Both my brothers had given me nightmare descriptions of their fate. A higher standard of work was expected of them, they were deliberately failed in their exams and humiliated in every way. And they had no one to turn to—no one would even prompt them.

I pictured these wretches, tired out by cramming, with pinched, tearful faces and protruding ears burning with anxiety. It was a pitiful sight and I gave in:

'No, I don't want to be a private pupil.'

'Crybaby, Mummy's darling,' shouted Borya from his room.

'Don't you dare to bully him,' said Mama angrily.

She considered Borya heartless and was always wondering where he could have got his callousness from. It was obviously from our Turkish grandmother. All my other relations were of an exceptionally sensitive, affectionate and unpractical disposition.

My father knew all about my fears, anxieties and fits of weeping, and, as usual, he found an unexpected cure for my troubles. After a slight brush with Mama, he decided to send me to stay with her brother, my Uncle Kolya.

This was the same Uncle Kolya who as a cadet used to come to Cherkassy, and had been so fond of dancing with Aunt Nadya.

Now he was an army engineer, married, and stationed in Bryansk, near Orel, where he worked at an antiquated ordnance factory which produced gun-carriages and was known as 'the Arsenal'.

Uncle Kolya had taken a cottage in Ryovna, an old and neglected estate in the Forest of Bryansk, and had invited us all to stay for the summer. My parents had accepted but were unable to go until after my brothers' and my sister's examinations, so I was sent ahead.

'He should learn to be on his own,' said my father. 'The kindest thing you can do for a timid little boy like Kostik is to let him get used to it.'

I knew he had written to my uncle, but not what he had said. Mama, furtively wiping her eyes, packed a suitcase with everything I could possibly need, including a list of helpful instructions.

A second class ticket to Sinezerki was taken for me; it was the station nearest to Ryovna and about six miles from my uncle's house.

Everyone, even Borya, came to see me off. Papa tipped the guard.

'Don't you worry about him, Madam,' the guard said to Mama. 'I'll deliver him safe and sound. You'll see, he'll be as right as rain.'

Mama asked the passengers in my compartment to keep an eye on me, and not to let me get out on the way. They agreed willingly. Furiously embarrassed, I kept tugging at her sleeve.

At the second bell, everyone kissed me, even Borya, though he seized the occasion surreptitiously to give me a 'pear'—a painful flick of the thumb on the back of the skull.

Then everyone got out, except Mama who couldn't tear herself away and held on to my hands, saying:

'Be a good boy, now. You will, won't you? A good, sensible boy. And be very careful.'

She looked searchingly into my eyes. The third bell went. She gave me a last hug and hurried to the door, her skirts rustling. She jumped out just as the train was moving. My father caught her and shook his head.

I stood at the closed window, watching her as she walked swiftly, ahead of the others along the platform, and it only now occurred to me how pretty she was, how small and how kind.

I stood at the window long after both Mama and the platform had vanished from sight. Sidings, goods trains and shrill shunting-engines swept by, and the Catholic church in Vassily Street, newly built in the Gothic style, slowly pirouetted past. I was afraid to turn, in case the other passengers noticed my tear-stained face. Then I remembered that a telegram announcing my arrival had been sent to Uncle Kolya. A stirring of pride at having been rated worth a telegram cheered me a little, and I looked round.

The compartment was upholstered in red velvet. It was small and cosy. Dusty patches of sunlight moved, all at the same time, from one corner to the other and back. The train was breaking out of the labyrinth of suburbs, and the track was snaking from side to side.

I was in a compartment reserved for ladies. Mama had insisted on it. I cautiously examined the passengers. One, a lean dark Frenchwoman, gave a succession of rapid nods, smiled, showing horsy teeth, and offered me a box of crystallised fruit. I wasn't sure what I ought to do but I thanked her, took one and held it, my hands getting more and more sticky.

'Pop it into your mouth,' said a girl of about sixteen, in a brown school uniform and with laughing Tartar eyes. 'Gobble it up, don't think about it.'

The Frenchwoman, evidently her governess, spoke severely to her in French. The girl made a face, and the governess broke into a long angry tirade. Without waiting for it to end, the girl got up and went into the corridor.

'Look at these young people nowadays!' said a fat old lady with a mouth like a doughnut, and a bag of doughnuts lying on her lap. 'I sometimes wonder what they're coming to.'

'Yes, yes,' nodded the Frenchwoman. 'Nothing but disobedience! Nothing but caprices!'

The old lady raised her eyes to the ceiling and sighed so deeply that even the governess looked at her with curiosity.

I wanted to look out, so I went into the corridor, where I found the schoolgirl standing in front of an open window.

'Hallo, Vitya,' she said. 'Come along, we'll watch together.'

'I'm not Vitya,' I said, blushing.

'Never mind. Come along.'

I climbed on the radiator and hung my head out. We were crossing a bridge over the Dnieper. I could see the Kiev Lavra[17] against the background of Kiev in the distance, and the shallows of the Dnieper where it silted up against the pylons of the bridge.

'Beastly old witch!' said the girl. 'But you needn't be scared of her. She's quite a nice old thing really.'

My journey completely exhausted me because I spent the whole of it, except at night, watching through the open window. But I was happy. For the first time I experienced the serenity of travel, a time when you have nothing on your mind, and nothing to do except look at the rye-fields, the woods, the little stations with barefooted peasant women selling milk on the platform, the rivers, the signalmen, the station-masters in red caps, the geese, and the children who run after the train, shouting: 'Throw us a kopeck, Uncle!'

The way to Bryansk was long and roundabout. It went through Lvov and Navlya. We got to Sinezerki only on the third day.

The train was in no hurry, it stopped for a good long rest at each station, puffing and panting beside the water tower. The passengers leapt out and dashed off, to fill kettles with hot water at the buffet, or to buy roast chicken and wild strawberries from the peasant women. Then everyone calmed down. Long after the time scheduled for departure, the station lay in the grip of a somnolent stillness, the sun pouring out its heat, the clouds drifting and trailing their shadows, while the passengers dozed in their carriages. Only the engine sighed and dripped oil and boiling water on the track.

Finally the head guard, in his canvas jacket, came out of the station-master's office, wiping his moustache, put his whistle to his lips and blew a long, loud blast. The engine puffed but made no answer. He strolled up to it and blew again. Still there was no response. Not until the third or fourth blast did the train emit a brief displeased hoot and move on.

I leaned out of the window because I knew that just beyond the signal box there would be a slope covered with clover and harebells, and after that would come a forest. Whenever we went through a forest, the noise of the wheels grew louder and was caught up by an echo, as if a lot of blacksmiths were cheerfully hammering away on every side.

I was seeing Central Russia for the first time. I liked it better than the Ukraine. It was wilder, emptier, more spacious. I liked the forests, the roads overgrown with weeds, the conversation of the peasants.

In our compartment, the old lady slept all day, the governess had recovered her temper and was crocheting lace, while the school-girl hung out of the window and skilfully ripped leaves off the branches of trees as we swung past.

Every two hours she got out a basket of provisions, made a solid meal, and forced me to share it. We ate hard boiled eggs, roast chicken and rice pasties and drank tea.

After that we again leaned out, getting light-headed with the scent of flowering buckwheat. The shadow of the train ran clattering over the fields, while the carriage was flooded with such a brilliant orange sunset that all you could see in our compartment was a fiery haze.

We arrived at Sinezerki at dusk. The guard lifted my suitcase out on the platform. I had expected either Uncle Kolya or his wife, Aunt Maroossya, to be there to meet me, but there was no one. My fellow passengers got worried but there was nothing they could do.

The train stopped at Sinezerki for only one minute. I stayed beside my suitcase, feeling sure that Uncle Kolya had only been delayed and would turn up at any moment.

A bearded peasant in a jacket and a black peaked cap, with a whip stuck in his boot, stumped up to me. He smelled of horse's sweat and of hay.

'You must be Kostik,' he said. 'I've been waiting for you. The Captain—that's your uncle—gave orders to deliver you safe and sound. Let's have your suitcase. Come along.'

This was the final test my father had prepared for me. In his letter to Uncle Kolya, he had asked him not to meet me at the station.

The driver—his name was Nikita—still muttering something about the Captain, my uncle, settled me in his cart on soft hay covered with sacking, untied the horses' nosebags, climbed on, and we set off.

At first we drove through the darkening fields, then the road began to climb a wooded slope. Sometimes the cart rolled over a wooden bridge with black swamp water gleaming below. There was a smell of marsh and of sedge. A lifeless red moon rose over a stunted thicket, a bittern cried, and Nikita said:

'It's wild, wooded country round here—not many people about. There's plenty of bark and water. It's the most scented region in the whole Province of Orel.'

We drove into a pine wood and started down a steep bank with a stream at the bottom. The trees blotted out the moon and it grew dark. I heard voices on the road. It was all a little frightening.

'Is that you, Nikita?' my Uncle Kolya's voice came out of the darkness.

'Whoa!' Nikita yelled desperately, holding back the horses. 'Of course it's us, who else would it be? Whoa there, you devils, may you fry in hell.'

Someone grabbed at me and lifted me out of the cart; in the vague remnant of the afterglow I could see my uncle's laughing eyes and glittering teeth. He kissed me and handed me over to Aunt Maroossya.

She ruffled my hair and laughed her deep, chesty laughter. She smelt of vanilla—she must have been baking pastry.

We got into the cart and drove off; Nikita walked alongside.

We crossed an old, black bridge over a deep, clear river with islands of reeds on it, then a second bridge. A fish gave a loud splash. At last the cart scraped a stone gate-post and entered an avenue of trees so dark and so tall that their tops seemed to be tangled up among the stars.

Deep in the park, under the shelter of these impenetrable trees, we stopped before a small timber house with lighted windows. Two dogs, one white and one black—Mordan and Chetvertak—jumped up at me, yapping and trying to lick my face.

All through that summer I stayed at Ryovna, an old Potemkin estate, among the woods, the rivers and the gentle peasants of Orel, in an ancient park so vast that no one knew where it ended and where the forest began.

This was the last summer of my real childhood. After this I became a schoolboy. Then my family fell apart. I was left alone early, and before I had left school was earning my living and feeling completely grown-up.

It was during this summer that I became attached, for life and with all my heart, to the countryside of Central Russia. There is no other country I know of, which has the lyrical power and touching and compelling beauty of this melancholy, calm and spacious region. It is hard to measure the strength of an attachment. You get to love every blade of grass warm with sun or heavy with dew, every mouthful of water from a well in a wood, every sapling shivering in the windless air beside a lake, every cock crow, and every cloud in the high, pale sky.

And if I sometimes feel like living to be a hundred and twenty, as Nechipor predicted I would, it is because a lifetime is not enough to experience all the beauty and healing power of this countryside.

My childhood was nearly over—and it's too bad that only the grown-ups know how nice it was to be a child. In childhood, everything was different. Everything was more vivid—the sun brighter, the smell of the fields sharper, the thunder louder, the rain more abundant and the grass taller. And our hearts were bigger, our griefs more poignant, and our country—that soil of our birth which is the greatest gift we have in life, to tend, care for and protect with our whole being—was more enigmatic.

13
The Swarm

Unlike other boys, I had never felt envious of the Officer Cadets who wore white shoulder straps with yellow badges on them and stood to attention in front of generals. Nor had I envied the boys at the High School, although their grey cloth greatcoats with silver buttons were considered very splendid.

When I first put on long trousers and a uniform jacket in the autumn of 1902, I merely felt uncomfortable, self-conscious and for a time estranged from myself—as if the boy in the heavy cap, whom I saw in the mirror, were someone else. The reason I took a particular dislike to the stiff blue cap with its enormous badge was that it made the ears of all the boys in my form stick out. Boys with perfectly normal ears had only to put on their caps, and their ears protruded, as though on purpose for Inspector Bodyansky to grab them as he shouted in his terrible voice:

'Late again, *misérable*! Go and stand in the corner and reflect on your wretched fate.'

So as soon as Mama bought me my cap, I copied my brothers by removing the metal hoop which stiffened it from inside, and ripping out the satin lining. The more disreputable the hat, the smarter, according to school tradition, was the wearer. 'Only a sucker-up or a swat would go about in a new cap,' said my brothers.

You were supposed to sit on your cap, wear it in your pocket and use it for knocking down chestnuts. Thus it gradually assumed the battle-worn look which was every schoolboy's pride.

Having also provided me with a deerskin satchel, a pencil case, ruled exercise books and the slim text-books used in the preparatory form, Mama took me to school.

Grandmother Vikentia Ivanovna was staying with us at the time.

She made the sign of the cross on my forehead, and hung a small cross on a cold chain round my neck. With shaking fingers she undid the collar of my black jacket, thrust the cross inside my shirt, and turned away, pressing a handkerchief to her eyes.

'Go along now,' she said in a muffled voice, giving me a gentle push, 'work hard, and be a good boy.'

I went with Mama, but kept looking back at the house as if I were seeing it for the last time.

We were then living in Nikolsk-Botanical Street. It was shady and quiet. Tall chestnut trees stood pensively round the house. By now they were beginning to drop their crinkling, five-pointed leaves. The day was sunny, very blue and warm but with cool shadows—a normal autumn day in Kiev. My grandmother stayed at the window and kept nodding to me, until we turned off into Fundukleyev Street.

When we reached Nicholas Square and I saw the yellow school buildings through the trees, I burst into tears. I suppose I realised that my childhood was over, that now I would have to work, and that my work would be hard, long and very different from my peaceful days at home.

I stopped, buried my face in my mother's skirt, and sobbed so hard that the pencil case rattled in my satchel, as if asking what was the matter with its new owner. Mama removed my cap and wiped my tears away with a scented handkerchief.

'Stop it now,' she said. 'Do you think I am happy about it myself? But we have to do it . . .'

'We have to do it'—I think nothing I had ever heard before had struck me with such force as these words uttered by Mama.

The older I grew the more often did I hear the grown-ups say that a man must 'live as he has to and not as he chooses or fancies'. For a long time I refused to accept this and kept asking them: 'Why can't a man live as he wants to and not as other people want him to?' I was told that I didn't know what I was talking about, and once Mama said to my father: 'It's all because of this anarchist upbringing you've been giving him.' My father drew me close to him, pressed my head against his white waistcoat and said lightly:

'They don't understand us in this house, Kostik.'

When I had stopped crying and quietened down, we entered the school. A wide iron staircase, polished to the sheen of lead by countless feet, went up to where an uproar like the angry buzzing of a beehive could be heard.

'It's only the break,' said Mama.

We climbed the stairs. For the first time, Mama let go of my hand. Two senior boys came running down. They made way for us, and one of them said behind my back:

'Another miserable little swarmer arriving!'

Thus I joined the restless and defenceless company of prep-form boys, known scornfully to our elders as 'the swarm'. The reason they called us the swarm was that, small and nimble, we swarmed about under their feet during break.

We crossed the white Assembly Hall with its portraits of Emperors on the walls. I particularly remember Alexander I, a green cocked hat pressed to his thigh and reddish sidewhiskers bristling from his pussy-cat face. In spite of the cavalrymen in plumed hats who galloped on the hills behind his back, I didn't take to him.

We crossed the Hall and went into the study of Inspector Bodyansky, a corpulent man in a uniform frock coat as roomy as a lady's dressing gown.

He laid a podgy hand on my head, thought for a long while, and said:

'Work hard or I'll gobble you up.'

Mama forced a smile. Bodyansky summoned the proctor Kazimir and told him to take me to the preparatory class.

Mama gave me a nod and Kazimir, taking me by the shoulder, led me along several endless corridors. He gripped me tightly, as if he were afraid I would break loose and run back to Mama.

There were lessons going on in the classrooms. The corridors were empty and quiet. The silence was particularly striking after the frantic uproar during the break. The dust of the commotion still hung in the air, floating in the beams of sunshine from the garden. The gardens of the First Kiev High School were a famous, huge, century-old park.

I glanced at it through the window and felt like crying again. The chestnut trees were speared through and through by the sun. The poplar leaves, their green turning to pale mauve, stirred in the breeze.

Even then, as a small boy, I already loved gardens and trees.

The Swarm

I didn't break off branches or destroy birds' nests, perhaps because Grandmother Vikentia Ivanovna was always telling me that 'the world is very beautiful and people ought to live and work in it as in a garden.'

Kazimir saw me getting ready to cry and, digging a sticky sweet out of the back pocket of his worn but neat frock coat, gave it me, saying with a Polish accent:

'Eat it during break.'

I thanked him in a whisper and took it.

All through my first week at school I spoke in whispers and was too afraid ever to raise my eyes. Everything intimidated me—the bearded and frock-coated teachers, the vaulted ceilings, the echo in the passages, and the Director whose name was Bessmertny—an ageing Adonis with a golden beard and a brand new frock coat.

He was in fact a mild, enlightened man, but we somehow expected him to be frightening, perhaps because he sat under a portrait of the Surgeon Pirogov, in a lofty room with moulded ceilings and a crimson carpet. He hardly ever came out of it. We stopped and bowed when we saw him, whereas the other masters were greeted in passing.

The echoing passages, through which Kazimir led me, were patrolled by Supervisors 'Twerp', 'Melon', 'Snuff' and Platon Fyodorovich (the only one whom the boys were fond of); they wandered up and down and peered into the classrooms through the glass panels at the top of the doors. My preparatory classroom was part of Platon Fyodorovich's territory, and this saved me from a lot of unpleasantness at the beginning.

It was the supervisors' job to watch the behaviour of the boys and to report their many misdemeanours to the Inspector.

Various punishments followed—detention for one or for two hours 'without dinner' (in other words the anguish of sitting in an empty classroom after the lessons were over), or a bad conduct mark or, as a last resort, an invitation to the parents to call on the Director. This frightened us more than anything.

In the senior forms there were other punishments as well: rustication, expulsion with the right to apply to another school and —worst of all—expulsion with a 'wolf's ticket' which closed the doors of every secondary school to the offender.

I only saw one senior schoolboy expelled with a wolf's ticket.

It was said that he had slapped the face of the German teacher Yagorsky, a rude man with a green complexion. Yagorsky had called him a blockhead in front of the class. The boy demanded an apology. Yagorsky refused. Then the boy hit him. This was why he was expelled with a wolf's ticket.

The day after he was expelled he came back to the school—none of the supervisors liking to stop him—walked into the classroom, pulled out a revolver and pointed it at Yagorsky.

Yagorsky jumped up, shielded himself with a newspaper and scuttled down the room between the desks, trying to hide behind the backs of the students. The boy shouted 'Coward!' turned, went out on the landing, and shot himself through the heart.

The landing was outside our door. We heard a sharp crack and the rattle of glass, then something falling and rolling down the stairs. Our form master dashed for the door and we followed him.

The freckled schoolboy was lying on the stairs. He lifted his hand and clutched at a banister, then his fingers opened and he lay still, looking at us with a puzzled smile.

The supervisors were bustling round him; then the Director hurried up and, kneeling beside the boy, undid his jacket; that was when we saw the blood on his shirt. Ambulance men were already coming up the stairs, in their brown uniforms and peaked caps. They quickly put the boy on a stretcher.

'Remove the children immediately,' said the Director. But probably our form master didn't hear him, at any rate, we stayed on.

Yagorsky, his shoulders hunched up, came out of his classroom and made for the teachers' common room.

'Get out,' the Director suddenly called after him.

Yagorsky turned.

'Get out of my school,' the Director said in a low voice.

And Yagorsky ran, cowering, down the passage.

Next day Mama wanted to keep me at home but in the end changed her mind. At school we were released after the second study-period. We were told that those of us who wanted to, could go to the funeral.

So we all went, small and frightened in our long overcoats and with our stiff satchels.

It was a cold, foggy day. The entire school followed the coffin.

The Swarm

Walking on the Director's arm was a grey, poorly dressed woman—the mother of the dead boy.

I could as yet make little of such a happening, all the same I realised that life was giving us our first lesson in comradeship. We went up to the grave in turn and threw in handfuls of earth, as though promising always to be kind and fair to each other.

But all this happened much later, long after that first day at school, when Kazimir brought me to my classroom and presented me to my form master, Nazarenko. Nazarenko was a man with a voice of thunder and the blue, waving beard of an Assyrian king. The seniors called him Nebuchadnezzar and swore that he worked for the Secret Police.

All that first year we miserable new boys spent in his class, he tormented us with his bellowing voice, his jeers, his bad marks, and his stories of the operation he had had for an ingrowing toe-nail. I both feared and hated him. Most of all I hated him for his stories about the toe-nail.

I took my seat at a low desk, its top scored all over with a pen-knife. I found it almost impossible to breathe. The room had an acid smell of ink. Nazarenko was dictating: 'One day the swan, the crayfish and the pike . . .' Perching on a branch outside the window was a sparrow with a yellow maple leaf in its beak. I longed to change places with it. The sparrow looked at the class-room through the window, emitted an appalled twitter and dropped the leaf.

'New boy!' roared Nazarenko. 'Get your exercise book, take down the dictation, and don't gape, if you don't want to go without your dinner.'

I got out my exercise book and started to write. A tear splashed on my blotter. Seeing it, my neighbour, a dark, cheerful looking boy called Shmukler, whispered to me:

'Try swallowing your spit, you'll feel better.'

I swallowed but I felt no better. It was a long time before I could draw a deep breath.

Thus began my first year at school. What I chiefly remember of it is the dust and scuffle during break, the everlasting fear of being called to the blackboard, my inky fingers, the weight of my satchel, and—like the echoes of a lost world—the melodious tinkle of trams outside the windows, the distant wheeze of a street organ and, reaching us from the railway station, the hooting of locomotives. Out there, the big trains chuffed off on their way through the woods and the fields of stubble—while we bent over our desks, stifling in the chalk dust which Nazarenko swept with a dry sponge off the blackboard.

Opposite our classroom was the narrow door of the physics room. We often looked inside it during break. The benches were arranged in an amphitheatre and rose almost to the ceiling.

The boys from the senior forms, who took physics, inevitably found us swarming under their feet in the corridor and this annoyed them. One day, a tall pale senior boy gave a long-drawn-out whistle, and immediately, each of the others grabbed one of us, and dragged him into the physics room. There they took their seats on the benches, holding us firmly between their knees.

At first we were pleased and stared with curiosity at the black discs, glass retorts, brass spheres and other mysterious paraphernalia on the shelves. Then the first bell went on the landing. We struggled to get out, but instead of letting us go, the seniors only tightened their grip, and dealt with the more unruly of us by administering the hard flick of the thumb against the skull, known as the 'pear'. This was very painful.

The second bell clanged. We fought, we wept, we implored, but the seniors were inexorable. The pale youth stood at the door.

'Mind you get the timing right,' the others shouted to him.

We were bewildered. We howled with fright. At any moment the third bell would go. Nazarenko would burst into our empty classroom. His rage would be terrible. Not all our floods of tears would mollify it.

The third bell went. We roared in every audible key. The pale youth raised his arm, then signalled the appearance of the physics master at the far end of the passage. He approached unhurriedly, nervously aware of the uproar.

The physics master was so fat that he had to squeeze through the narrow door sideways; it was on this that the seniors' calculation was based. As soon as he had wedged himself in the door, the pale youth waved his arm, we were set free, and in our demented state— dazed, blind, weeping and yelling—hurtled back to our classroom.

The Swarm

We ran full-tilt into the terrified master. For a moment an eddy of small cropped heads seethed in front of the door. Then we ejected him like a cork and, swarming between his legs, made for our room. Luckily Nazarenko had been detained in the teachers' room and had seen nothing.

The seniors only got away with this treacherous trick once. After that we were more careful. As soon as we saw them coming, we shut ourselves up in our room, and barricaded ourselves in with our desks.

This entertainment, which cost us so many tears, had been thought up and organised by the tall pale youth, whose name was Bagrov. A few years later, he shot Stolypin during a performance at the Kiev Opera House, killed him and was hanged.

At his trial Bagrov behaved with calm and showed little interest in the proceedings. When the sentence was read to him, he said:

'It makes not the slightest difference to me whether I live to eat another two thousand beefsteaks or I don't.'

There were many arguments among the grown-ups as to whether Bagrov had been a genuine revolutionary, or an agent of the Secret Police which had itself organised the assassination in order to please the Tsar (Nicholas hated Stolypin who dominated him by his will-power). My father claimed that no genuine revolutionary would have been capable of Bagrov's cynical pronouncement when he was on the verge of death.

14
Water from the Limpopo

Bottles filled with yellowish water, corked and sealed with sealing wax, stood in rows on the classroom table. They had labels, inscribed in an uneven elderly hand: 'Nile', 'Limpopo', 'Mediterranean'.

There were bottles of water from the Rhine, the Thames, Lake Michigan, from the Dead Sea and the Amazon, but however long we looked at them they all remained equally yellow and uninteresting.

We pestered our geography master Cherpunov to allow us to taste the water from the Dead Sea—we wanted to see if it really was as salty as we were told—but he always refused.

Short, slit-eyed and with a grey beard almost down to his knees, he was nicknamed Merlin.

He was always bringing curious objects with him to illustrate his lessons, but the bottles were his favourites. He told us that he had himself got the water from the Nile in Cairo.

'Just look,' he would shake the bottle, 'look at all that sediment. Nile water is richer than gold. The culture of Ancient Egypt was based on mud. Markovsky, tell the class what is meant by culture.'

Markovsky stood up and said culture was the cultivation of wheat, raisins and rice.

'An idiotic answer, but there's something in it,' commented Cherpunov, turning to his other bottles.

He was very proud of the one from the Limpopo, which had been sent to him as a present by a former pupil.

Cherpunov devised his own visual aids to geography. He would draw three *A*'s on the blackboard, one inside the other, put a *B* inside the smallest *A* and say:

'Now remember, the big A stands for Asia, Arabia is in Asia, Aden is in Arabia and the British are in Aden.'

We immediately memorised this for life.

The seniors told us that Cherpunov had arranged a small geographical museum in his flat but would allow no one to see it. It was said to include a stuffed humming bird, a collection of butterflies, a telescope, and even a nugget of gold.

These stories inspired me to start a collection of my own. It was, of course, a modest one, but in my imagination it was priceless, unique. Each object, whether a dead praying mantis or a button off a Rumanian soldier's uniform, had a colourful legend attached to it.

One day I came across Cherpunov sitting on a bench in the Botanical Gardens. The bench was still wet from the rain. He was poking the ground with his stick.

I took off my cap and bowed.

'Hallo,' he said, holding out his hand. 'Come and sit down. I hear you're making a collection. What have you got in it?'

I shyly gave him the list of my simple treasures. He grinned.

'Most commendable. Come and see me on Sunday morning. I'll show you mine. Perhaps one day you'll be a geographer or an explorer—as you seem to be so interested in these things.'

'With my mother?' I asked.

'What about your mother?'

'Shall I come with my mother?'

'No—why?—come by yourself. Mothers don't understand about geography.'

Next Sunday I put on my uniform and went to call on Cherpunov. He lived in a small cottage in the suburb of Pechersk. Lilac bushes grew so thickly round it that they made it dark inside.

It was a day in late autumn. The lilac bushes, still green, stood dripping in the mist. Steamers hooted on the Dnieper at the foot of the hill, saying goodbye to Kiev and going off to their winter quarters.

I climbed the front steps, pulled the brass handle of the old-fashioned bell and heard it tinkle inside.

Cherpunov, in a warm grey jacket and felt shoes, opened the door.

The house was filled with marvels.

Standing in the hall, I saw in an oval mirror the reflection of a small boy, red with embarrassment, struggling with stiff fingers to undo the buttons of his greatcoat—I didn't at once realise it was myself. As I persevered with the buttons, I looked at the frame. It was a wreath of pale glass flowers, leaves and bunches of grapes.

'That's Venetian glass,' said Cherpunov, helping me with the buttons and hanging up my coat. 'Have a good look at it. Touch it if you like.'

I cautiously touched a glass rose. It was almost opaque, as if dusted with powder, but a shaft of light from the next room shone through it with a crimson glow.

'It's like Turkish Delight!'

'Idiotic, but there's something in it,' muttered Cherpunov.

I blushed so that my eyes smarted. He patted my shoulder.

'Sorry, that's only a saying I have. Well, come along. You'll have tea with us.'

I started to say no, but he took me by the elbow and led me into the dining-room. It was less a room than a garden. To reach my place, I had to shift the leaves of a philodendron plant and some long branches dangling from the ceiling, with aromatic red cones on them. Palm leaves fanned out on the table. Vases of pink, yellow and white flowers crowded the window-sills.

I sat down, but immediately jumped up again as a slight young woman with shining grey eyes came rustling swiftly into the room.

'That's the boy I told you about, Masha,' said Cherpunov, 'the son of Georgy Maximovich.'

The girl held out her hand. A bracelet tinkled on her wrist.

'Are you really going to show him everything, Pyotr Petrovich?' she asked him, glancing at me with an amused smile.

'Yes, as soon as we've had tea.'

'Then I'll take a walk into town while you are doing it. I want to get a cake at Kircheim's, and one or two other things.'

'As you wish.'

She poured out tea with lemon and put a plate of Vienna rolls in front of me.

'You'd better tuck in. You'll need your strength.'

After tea Cherpunov lit a cigarette. He flicked the ash into a seashell edged with the palest of pink petrified foam. There were two of them on the table. 'These come from New Guinea,' he told me.

'Well, goodbye,' said the girl in a loud voice, getting up and going from the room.

'Well, now,' Cherpunov watched her go, then pointed to a portrait which hung on the wall. It showed a man with an emaciated bearded face.

'Do you know who that is? He was a great Russian, Miklukho-Maklaï.[18] He was a traveller and a humanist. I don't suppose you know what a humanist is, but it doesn't matter, you'll understand later. He was a great scholar, and he believed in man's essential goodness. He lived all by himself among the cannibals of New Guinea, unarmed and slowly dying of fever. Yet he managed to do so much good to the savages, he showed them so much patience and kindness, that when our corvette, *The Emerald*, finally came to pick him up and take him back to Russia, they crowded on the beach, wailing and stretching out their hands and calling him back: "Maklaï! Maklaï!" So remember: with kindness you can achieve anything.'

The girl came back and stood in the doorway. She had a small black hat on her head and was pulling on her left glove.

'Incidentally, what is poetry?' Cherpunov suddenly asked me. 'No, I don't expect you to answer. You can't define it, anyway. But take this shell. It comes from Maklaï's island. If you look at it long enough, it suddenly occurs to you that there was once a morning when the sunshine fell on it in such a way that it will stay on it for ever.'

The girl sat down and began to take off her glove.

I was staring at the shell. For a moment I really thought I had dropped off to sleep and was seeing a slow dawn and the pink flash of the sunrise over the translucent waste of ocean waters.

'If you hold the shell to your ear,' Cherpunov's voice came from a long way off, 'you can hear a rumbling—I can't tell you why. No one can tell you. It's a mystery. Anything the human mind is incapable of grasping is a mystery.'

The girl took off her hat and put it on her lap.

'Try it,' said Cherpunov.

I pressed the shell to my ear and heard a sleepy murmur, as of surf breaking on a very distant shore. The girl held out her hand:

'Let me try. It's a long time since I've listened to it.'

I gave her the shell. She held it to her ear and smiled, half opening her lips and showing small and very white, moist teeth.

'Aren't you going to Kircheim's, Masha?' Cherpunov asked.

'I've changed my mind. It bores me to go to Kircheim's by myself. I'm sorry if I disturbed you.'

She left the dining-room.

'Well then, let's go on with our conversation, young man,' said Cherpunov. 'You see those black boxes, over in the corner. Bring me the top one, will you. Only be careful how you carry it.'

I picked it up and put it on the table in front of him. It turned out to be quite light.

Cherpunov raised the lid with deliberation. I looked over his shoulder and gasped. Lying on the black silk lining of the box was an enormous black butterfly; it was larger than a maple leaf and it shimmered like a rainbow.

'That's not how you must look at it,' Cherpunov said crossly. 'Look at it this way.'

He took hold of my head and turned it, now to the right, now to the left. The wings of the butterfly flashed white, gold, crimson and blue, as if it were blazing in a magic fire which burned without ever consuming it.

'It's an extremely rare butterfly from the island of Borneo,' Cherpunov said proudly, shutting the lid.

After that he showed me an astral globe, some old maps with the sign of the four Winds on them, and several stuffed humming birds with beaks as long as bradawls.

'Well, that's enough for today,' he said finally. 'You're tired. Come again any Sunday you like.'

'Are you always at home?'

'Yes. I'm too old now to go wandering about the world, so I do my travelling in my room.' He nodded at the bookshelves and the dead humming birds.

'Have you done a lot of travelling?' I asked shyly.

'Just about as much as Miklukho-Maklaï.'

I was struggling into the sleeves of my coat when the girl came into the hall. She had put on a short, close-fitting jacket, and her hat and gloves. A short dark veil, lowered over her eyes, made them seem quite blue.

We went off together. Cherpunov stood watching us from the door.

'Do be careful, Masha, I beg of you,' he called after her. 'And don't be away too long.'

'All right,' she said without turning round.

We passed the Nikolsky Fort with its bronze lion heads over the gateway, walked across Marinsky Park where I had once had my encounter with the midshipman, and turned into Institute Street. The girl was silent. So was I. I was afraid of her asking me some question I would have to answer.

'What did you like best in the collection?' she asked finally.

'The butterfly,' I said after some thought. 'Only I'm sorry for it.'

'Really? Why?'

'Well, it's so beautiful and practically no one ever sees it.'

'What else did you like?'

In the Kreshchatik she stopped outside Kircheim's and asked me if I was allowed to go into pastry shops to have cocoa and cakes. I didn't know if I was or not, but I remembered that I had once been to Kircheim's with Mama and Galya and that we had in fact had cocoa, so I said I was certainly allowed to go to Kircheim's.

'Good. Let's go.'

We sat at a table at the back of the shop. The girl moved a vase of hydrangeas out of the way and ordered two cups of cocoa and a fruit tart.

'Which form are you in at school?'

'The second.'

'And how old are you?'

'Twelve.'

'I'm twenty-eight. When you are twelve, of course, you can believe anything.'

'What do you mean?'

'Do you invent games, and tell yourself stories?'

'Yes.'

'So does Pyotr Petrovich. I don't, it's a pity. I wish you'd put me into yours. We could play together.'

'Play at what?' I asked, getting interested.

'I don't know. Cinderella perhaps. Or at running away from a sorcerer. Or we might invent a new game and call it the Butterfly from the Isle of Borneo.'

'Good,' I said, my imagination taking fire. 'We'll go to a magic forest and look for a well of living water.'

'At the risk of our lives, of course.'

'Of course.'

'We'll bring the water away in our cupped hands,' she said, raising her veil. 'And when one of us gets tired, the other will take over, only we'll have to be very careful not to spill the water as we make the change.'

'But a few drops will get spilled all the same. And where they fall . . .'

'Big bushes of white flowers will spring up!' she interrupted. 'And what do we do next?'

'We sprinkle the butterfly with the water and it comes to life.'

'And turns into a lovely maiden,' she laughed. 'Well, it's time to go. I expect they're waiting for you at home.'

She came with me as far as Fundukleyev Street and there we parted. I looked back and saw her crossing the Kreshchatik. She looked back at the same moment, and smiled and waved her small gloved hand.

At home, I told no one about having been to Kircheim's, not even Mama who wanted to know why I wasn't eating my dinner. Obstinately silent, I kept thinking about the girl who puzzled me completely.

Next day I asked one of the seniors who the girl was.

'Are you actually telling me you've been to Cherpunov's flat?'

'Yes.'

'And you saw his collection?'

'Yes.'

'Wonders will never cease! The girl is his wife. She's thirty-five years younger than he is.'

I didn't go to see Cherpunov next Sunday because he was ill and had stayed away from school since the middle of the week. A few days later, as we were having tea in the evening, Mama asked me whether I had met a young woman at Cherpunov's.

I said I had and blushed.

'Can it be true?' said Mama, looking at my father. 'They say he was so good to her. She was like a princess in a golden cage.'

Water from the Limpopo

Papa said nothing.

'You've had your tea, Kostik,' said Mama. 'Go to your room. It's nearly your bed time.'

I refrained from listening at the door, although I longed to know what had happened to Cherpunov.

I heard all about it at school. His wife had left him and gone off to Petersburg. The old man was breaking his heart and refusing to see anyone.

'Serves Merlin right,' said my classmate Littauer. 'Never marry a young wife.'

We were fond of old Cherpunov, and very indignant at Littauer. We paid him out at the end of break. As our French teacher, Serremout, came bursting into the classroom, we all yelled in chorus: 'Littauer! Tauer! Auer! Er!' Serremout, who always got hold of the wrong end of the stick, ordered Littauer out of the room and gave him a bad conduct mark.

Cherpunov never appeared at the school again. He had given up his job.

A year later I met him in the street. His face puffy and yellow, he was dragging himself along with difficulty, leaning on his stick. He stopped me, asked me how I was getting on with my work, and said:

'You remember my butterfly from Borneo? I haven't got it any more.'

I said nothing. He looked at me searchingly.

'I gave it to the University. I gave away all my collection of butterflies. Well, goodbye, keep well. I'm glad we met.'

He died shortly afterwards. I remembered Cherpunov and the girl for a long time. An obscure anxiety came over me whenever I thought of her bracelet, and of the way she smiled and waved to me as she crossed the Kreshchatik.

Years later when I was in my top form at school, our teacher of psychology, as he was talking about the creative power of the imagination, suddenly asked us:

'Do you remember Cherpunov?'

'Yes, of course.'

'Well, I can tell you now that there was never anything in his bottles except ordinary water from the tap. You'll ask me why he lied to you. He rightly believed that he was stimulating your imagination. He attached great value to it. I remember him telling me that it was all that distinguished man from the beasts. It was imagination, he said, that had created art, it expanded the boundaries of the world and of the mind, and communicated the quality we call poetry to our lives.'

15
The First Commandment

Our new divinity master, Canon Tregubov, had a cassock of a different colour for each day of the week—grey, blue, purple, black, brown, green and off-white. You could tell which day it was by the colour of his cassock.

On the very first day he came to teach us in our third form, he shattered one of the age-old traditions of the school. Whether because of the charity incumbent on them by virtue of their office, or because neither they nor their pupils took the subject seriously enough, divinity teachers invariably gave everyone top marks. Tregubov changed all that.

'Altukhov, recite the First Commandment.'

'I am the Lord thy God, thou shalt have no other gods before Me,' rattled off Altukhov and grinned.

'Sit down,' said Tregubov and gave Altukhov a nought. 'Borimovich, recite the First Commandment.'

Borimovich paled, recited no less correctly than Altukhov, and also got zero.

All the boys were called in alphabetical order and every one, from A to Z, received a nought. Such a thing had never happened to us before, and it boded very ill indeed.

When he finished handing out noughts, Tregubov leaned back in his chair, stroked his beard and said:

'You have no respect for punctuation. You have been penalised accordingly. Your attitude to Holy Scripture is slipshod and frivolous. After the words "I am the Lord thy God" there is a comma—why? Because you must make a pause in order to bring out the significance of what follows. You rattle off the words of the sacred text as if you were shelling peas. You should be ashamed of yourselves.'

He spoke without raising his voice, his eyes narrowed, his academician's badge glinting on his cassock.

The divinity teacher whom Tregubov had replaced was a toothless old man who was hard of hearing. We knew exactly where we were with him. It didn't matter what rubbish we reeled off so long as we did it in a flat monotonous drone. After two or three minutes of this he fell asleep, and we amused ourselves in our various ways, taking care not to awaken him. The boys in the back row played beggar-my-neighbour and fried small fishes on matchsticks. Those in front read *The Adventures of the Famous American Detective Nick Carter*. Two minutes before the bell for break we dropped a batch of books on the floor or we all sneezed loudly in unison.

Tregubov came down on us like an avenging Lord of Hosts. He even looked something like the figure of the Lord of Hosts in the dome of the Cathedral—huge, with a bushy beard and beetling eyebrows.

Not only were the boys afraid of Tregubov, but so were the teachers. He was a zealous monarchist, a member of the State Council and a persecutor of free-thinkers. Equal in rank to the Kiev Metropolitan, he reduced to dumb terror the shabby country priests who were sent to him for a dressing-down.

He was fond of taking part in the public discussions on religious philosophy fashionable at the time, and appeared at them, smelling of eau-de-Cologne and speaking with a smooth sugary eloquence.

We hated him with the same cold hatred he bestowed on us. But we learned his texts so that we never forgot them.

We cut his lessons on any pretext we could find. Our safest refuge on such occasions was the room in which the Roman Catholic divinity class was being held at the same time. Only there did we feel safe. This was the territory, as it were, of the Roman Catholic Church and of the Pope of Rome, Leo XIII. Tregubov's authority ended on the threshold of this dusty classroom: here it was Father Olendsky who was in charge.

Tall and stout, white-haired and with a black rosary on his wrist, he was never in the least surprised at the appearance in his doorway of an embarrassed Orthodox refugee.

'Are you playing truant?' he asked in a severe voice.

'No, Father. I just wondered if I could come to your class for a little while.'

'Oh, you did, did you,' Olendsky shook with laughter. 'Come here.'

The boy came up and Olendsky gave him a resounding smack on the head. This was a sign of absolution.

'Sit down,' he said. 'Over there, in the corner, behind Khorzhevsky' (Khorzhevsky was a very tall Pole) 'so that you can't be seen from the corridor and carried off and thrust into hell fire. Sit and read the newspaper. Here you are.'

He produced from the pocket of his cassock a copy of the *Kiev Post* folded in four and gave it to the truant.

'Thank you, Father.'

'Don't thank me, thank God. I am only a poor tool in His hands. It's He who has delivered you from the House of Bondage like a Jew from the land of Egypt.'

Tregubov knew, of course, that Olendsky was giving us shelter. But even he preferred not to take Olendsky on. The good-natured Father, when he met Tregubov became studiously polite and malevolent. Tregubov's dignity as a Canon of the Orthodox Church prevented him from getting into a wrangle with Olendsky. We profited by this to the best of our ability, and ended up by knowing the Catholic liturgy better than some of the Poles.

'Stanishevsky,' said Olendsky, 'recite the Magnificat.'

Stanishevsky got to his feet, straightened his belt, cleared his throat, looked at the ceiling and out of the window and finally confessed:

'I've forgotten it, Father.'

'You have, have you. Sit down. Who knows the Magnificat? Well? Holy Mother of God! What is this? Will any boy who knows the Magnificat raise his hand?'

If no Polish hand went up it sometimes happened that an Orthodox, in flight from Tregubov, would raise his.

'All right, you recite it,' Olendsky gave in. 'And if after that God doesn't punish the lot of you,' he turned to the Poles, 'you'll have to thank His exceeding mercy.'

'Come here,' said Olendsky.

The truant came up; Olendsky, reaching into the pocket of his cassock, produced a generous helping of sweets which looked like coffee beans and poured them into his hand. He then took a pinch of snuff, quickly recovered himself and told his favourite story about the day when he had said a Requiem Mass in Warsaw for Chopin whose heart had been returned to Poland in a silver casket.

After school, Olendsky walked back to his rectory, stopping children on the way to give them an encouraging smack on the head. The tall priest with the laughing eyes was a well-known figure in Kiev.

Divinity lessons were a permanent nuisance. What we enjoyed was the week's holiday we were given in Lent to make our confession and communion. For this we would pick a church in the suburbs, where the priests were not inclined to watch too closely whether a fasting schoolboy attended every Lenten service or not.

The holiday nearly always came in the grey and misty month of March. The snow was beginning to darken, and more and more often, the blue skies of approaching spring could be seen in the rifts between the clouds.

Jackdaws cawed on the bare poplars and pussywillows were sold in the market.

We longed to get under Tregubov's skin, but he seemed invulnerable.

Only once did we succeed in pitilessly avenging all the fears and pains he inflicted upon us.

When we were in the fourth form we heard from some of the old boys that Tregubov was afraid of rats. A brown rat was duly smuggled in and released while Tregubov was giving his lesson.

Zhdanovich let out a squeal and climbed on his desk.

'What's the matter?' Tregubov asked dangerously.

'A rat, Father,' said the trembling boy.

We all jumped up. The wretched rat tried to take refuge under Tregubov's feet. Tregubov, with unaccustomed lightness, sprang on to his chair, hitching his cassock to his knees and revealing striped trousers and laced shoes.

We flung our text books at the rat. It squealed and scuttled round the blackboard. Tregubov stepped from chair to table and threw his mark book at it.

'Open the door,' he roared in his deep canonical voice from the elevation of the table. 'The door! Let it out!'

We pretended to be too frightened. Then Tregubov yelled so that the window panes rattled:

'Platon Fyodorovich! Come here!'

The door flew open and the alarmed supervisor appeared, the proctor Kazimir crowding at his back. Finally Inspector Bodyansky arrived. Frowning and restraining a smile, he organised the expulsion of the rat.

Tregubov, still on the table, had let down his cassock and looked like his own statue twice life size. When the rat was finally driven out, he was helped down, handed his mark book, and swept with his customary manner from the room.

It occurred to him belatedly that the rat had not arrived in his classroom by chance. He insisted on an inquiry, but it led nowhere. The whole school was triumphant.

'Don't gloat over human weakness,' said Bodyansky. 'Better watch your own step, or I might start taking notice of some of you, gentlemen, who walk about with no badges in your caps, and leave you without your dinners.'

It was not until our last year at school that we managed to get rid of Tregubov.

By then I was living on my own in a room I rented from an infantry lieutenant who lived with his mother, a kind and taciturn old lady named Panna Kozlovskaya.

It was the autumn of 1910, dreary, cold, with leaden skies. The trees were sheathed in ice and rattled with leaves frozen on the branch. On such days I often had neuralgia and instead of going to school, stayed in my garret, lying in bed with my head in a shawl and trying not to groan for fear of disturbing Panna Kozlovskaya.

Gradually, as I got warm, the pain subsided. Without getting up I would start reading one of the yellow paper-backs from the 'Universal Library'. The fires crackled in the stoves. The small flat was quiet. Now and then a little snow drifted past the window. With the pain gone my head felt unusually fresh and everything pleased me—the colour of the dove-grey sky, the smell of logs and the snow on the window pane.

It was on one such day that Panna Kozlovska opened the door to the postman, took the newspaper, gasped, and hurriedly pattered to my room.

'Kostik,' she said, 'there's been a misfortune with Count Tolstoy . . .'

I leaped up, snatched the newspaper which smelled of kerosene, and read the first despatches about Tolstoy's flight and his illness.

I dressed and went out. It seemed to me that everything about the city should have changed the moment the staggering news came out, but everything looked much as usual. Carts loaded with fire-wood creaked along the streets, the bells of an old horse-drawn tram tinkled past, children were out with their governesses.

I went to school—I couldn't keep away. The desks were littered with newspapers. Our form master, Suboch, who taught us Latin, was late for the first time in his life. He came in, sank heavily into his chair, took off his pince-nez and for a long time sat hunched up, staring out of the window with his prominent short-sighted eyes. He seemed to be waiting. Finally he said to me:

'Be a good fellow and go along to the *Kiev Post*. They put out news bulletins. Find out what's happened. We'll wait for you.'

Such a thing was utterly unprecedented in the history of our class, but everyone immediately took it as the most natural thing in the world.

Platon Fyodorovich barred my way in the passage and asked me sternly where I thought I was going. I told him. He bowed his head and stepped back to let me pass.

When I came back I looked through the glass panel of the door before going in. Suboch was reading out loud. The class was breathlessly still. I opened the door and heard the familiar words of a passage from *Anna Karenina* . . .

For two or three days we somehow muddled through our lessons. Then, on another bitterly cold morning, I came out to find special editions of the newspapers with black borders on the front page, bewildered lost-looking people in the streets, and crowds of students in front of the university. They stood in complete silence. Every one had a black crepe arm band. Someone I didn't know pinned an arm band to the sleeve of my greatcoat.

I walked on to school. Posses of mounted Cossacks were slowly patrolling the streets. Knots of policemen stood in the gateways. I caught up with my classmates and saw that they all had arm bands like mine. In the cloakroom we took them off our coats and pinned them on our jackets. The school was unusually silent. Even the 'swarm' wasn't making any noise.

It so happened that just that day our first lesson was divinity. Tregubov walked in swiftly, not as on other days, crossed himself before the ikon and sat down.

Matushevich who was monitor left his desk and went up to him. Tregubov gave him a heavy look but said nothing.

'Yesterday at six in the morning, at the railway station of Astapovo,' said Matushevich making an effort to speak calmly and clearly, 'there occurred the death of the greatest writer in our country and perhaps in the world, Leo Nikolayevich Tolstoy.'

The desk lids slammed. The whole class stood up. In the deep silence could be heard the clip-clop of horses' hooves as a patrol rode past.

Tregubov leaned forward and clutched the edge of the desk but remained seated.

'Stand up, Father,' Matushevich said softly.

Slowly and clumsily, Tregubov rose to his feet. A few moments passed. They seemed hours to us. Then everyone quietly sat down. Tregubov picked up his mark book and went from the room. Stopping at the door, he said:

'You have forced me to honour the memory of an apostate who was excommunicated by the Church. That he was a great writer is beside the point. I am guilty of a crime against my office, and I will answer for it before God and my superiors. But from now on I am no longer your teacher. Goodbye. And God grant you wisdom.'

We were silent. Tregubov walked out.

When we next had a divinity lesson, it was taken by a young priest with the face of a poet, who loved literature and philosophy. We took an immediate liking to him for his youth, his sensitiveness and his discretion, and our friendship with him continued without a break for as long as we were at school.

16
Lime Blossom

Nowhere else have I seen such ancient lime-trees. At night their tops were lost in the sky and if the wind rose the stars darted in and out of the branches like fireflies. In the daytime it was dark under the trees, while up above, among the fresh leaves, there was the incessant fluttering, chattering and quarrelling of an immense population of birds.

'Soon the lime-trees will be in blossom. Then you'll see . . .' said Uncle Kolya.

He never told us what we would see, but we already knew that the old park at Ryovna would become a place of such magical beauty as only exists in a fairytale.

This was our second summer in Ryovna. We had come at the start of the school holidays and my father had joined us for his own leave.

The impoverished owner of the estate used to try to let several cottages in the park, but for most people it was too far from the towns and from the railway, so that we had the place virtually to ourselves.

It is almost impossible to convey its charm. Imagine a neglected park planted with lime-trees but overgrown with hazel and buck-thorn, with mossy benches among clumps of lilac bushes, and weed-grown avenues which all had names such as Diana's Grove, the Path of Sighs or Nightingale Ravine.

Here and there a sunny clearing opened out, thickly overgrown with wild flowers, then again you walked under the canopy of huge and, it seemed, thousand year old limes.

The park sloped down to the River Ryovna. Beyond it a dense forest shouldered its way uphill. A single dirt track led as far as a decrepit wooden chapel, which contained an ikon of Tikhon Zadonsky; after that it petered out in the dry grass.

Not one of us ever ventured to go farther than the chapel by himself—not even Volodya Rumyantsev, a student from the Petersburg Institute of Forestry, who was much the boldest of the summer residents.

The woods pressed against the walls of the chapel; they smelt of mould and ferns; owls flew out of them at dusk.

Once at night we heard a distant cry coming from the forest— it was a pedlar who had got lost as he was making his way on foot from the Svensk Monastery to the fair at Cherbinsk. The forest warden found him in the end and brought him to Ryovna. A lean little peasant with intensely blue eyes, he kept weeping and crossing himself.

One day we schoolboys took a compass with us and went with Volodya on an expedition into the woods.

We came across ravines, filled to the edge with brambles and wild hops, water muttering inaccessibly in their depths. Then we discovered a small river, so clear that it seemed to be made of glass, and looking down from its steep bank, saw clouds of minnows darting about over the bottom.

At last we found a rotting wooden cross beside a stream. A tin cup hung from the crossbeam, held firmly in place by the woodbine which had wound itself round it. We tore it away and scooped water up from the stream. It had a tang of rust.

Cranes, orioles and hawks circled above us. Blue-bottomed clouds passed overhead. Looking up at them we thought of how well this whole enigmatic forest region must be visible from up there.

Volodya kept assuring us that there was an abandoned Old Believers' Monastery hidden away somewhere in the woods. Wild bees had taken it over and, if only we could find it, the honey was ours for the taking.

But we never found the monastery, however hard we tried, climbing trees and scanning the ocean of leaves for a timbered roof with a slanting eight-pointed cross. In the treetops there was a warm breeze; our hands stuck to the resinous bark. Black-eyed squirrels leapt among the branches, and young green pine cones smelt of turpentine. But however much we craned our necks, peering as from a lighthouse and shading our eyes with our hands, we could see nothing except the forest and the drifting clouds which made our heads spin.

The clouds seemed very close to the tops of the tall pines. You felt like reaching out and touching their snow-white domes.

Above them there were pale ripples across the sky, spreading out into transparent plumes. Volodya said that they too were clouds, but so high up that they were not composed of watery vapour, but of crystals of ice. The plumes hung motionless in the cold inaccessible height.

The river at Ryovna was another place of mystery. It was overshadowed by willows, it divided round an island and was in places overgrown from bank to bank with water lilies and water-cress.

There were wooden dams across it at the level of the island. A derelict saw mill stood on the island, with hills of sawdust in front of the empty sheds. On hot days the smell of the wood shavings was overpowering.

The mill had worked off a water wheel, but now the wheel and the wooden gearing were broken and shaggy with cobwebs and had mushrooms growing on them as yellow as sulphur.

Above the dam were deep pools—the homes of enormous pike—the water in them black and slowly revolving.

Uncle Kolya and I had fixed up hooks and tin bait in them. In addition to the pike there were very large almost dark-blue perch living in the waterholes. We fished for them from the dam. Occasionally they would jerk the line away from us and drag it deep under. The bamboo rod shot like a golden arrow after them and usually surfaced below the dam, where we picked it up from a boat, together with the perch.

What else was there at Ryovna? There was an old house with a pillared porch, said to have been built by Rastrelli.[19] Swallows nested under the architrave. The empty stairways, halls and corridors were flooded with iridescent light—it came through convex window panes. Whenever anyone walked through the rooms the chairs creaked and the chandeliers tinkled.

No one lived in the house. Only on certain family occasions, such as the nameday of Mama and Aunt Maroossya (both were named Maria) was the ballroom with its musicians' gallery opened up and aired in preparation for a ball. Round lanterns were hung on the verandah and we had fireworks late at night in the park. The rockets shot through the dense foliage and released their coloured fiery balls which drifted slowly down illuminating the old house with a flickering reddish flame. The moment they went out the summer night surged back into the park, filling it with the distant croaking of frogs, the sparkle of stars and the smell of the blossoming lime-trees.

Uncle Kolya's fellow officers from Bryansk came to the ball, and we once entertained a Moscow tenor, Askochensky, who gave a concert in the ballroom.

'If only you would come to me again,' sang Askochensky, 'to where we were so happy, you and I, and hear the murmur of the trees and know it for the sighing of my heart.'

I thought that the song must have been written about our park. It had heard many declarations of love and seen the pale faces of lovers and their tears at parting.

'When melancholy sounds disturb your sleep,' sang Askochensky leaning against the piano, while Aunt Maroossya swiftly tucked in a strand of hair as she accompanied him, 'or when the wind moans on a stormy day, know that you hear the sobs of my despair.'

After the ball there was a supper at my Uncle Kolya's house. The candles in their round shades crackled with burning moths.

We schoolboys had wine poured out for us, like the grown-ups. It gave us Dutch courage and on one occasion we decided we would have a race in the dark—each of us running round the park in turn. To make sure that there was no cheating we agreed that each was to take some object with him which he would leave on the bench in Nightingale Ravine, and in the morning Uncle Kolya would check up on whether the condition had been honestly complied with.

The first runner was Pavlya Tennov, Aunt Maroossya's brother who was a student at the School of Medicine and Surgery. A lanky young man with a snub nose and curly beard who looked rather like Chekhov, he was exceptionally trusting, and as a result everyone played tricks on him. The object he was to leave in Nightingale Ravine was an empty wine bottle.

It was my turn next and I dashed off into the tree-lined avenue, branches covered with dew lashing me in the face. I had the feeling that someone was bounding after me in pursuit. When I stopped to listen there were stealthy footsteps in the undergrowth. I raced on and on and came to a clearing, the moon was rising beyond it. Nightingale Ravine lay at my feet, filled with impenetrable shadow and I leapt into the darkness as if diving. The river glittered and from beyond it came the desolate cry of a bittern.

I came to the bench and stopped. The smell of the lime blossom filled the night right up to the stars. In the stillness, it was hard to believe that there were guests nearby chatting and laughing on the brightly lit verandah.

We had agreed in advance to play a practical joke on Pavlya. I seized the wine bottle he had left and flung it into the river. It flashed, somersaulting; widening circles of moonlight rippled towards the bank.

Following the edge of the ravine with its damp smell of earth and of angelica, I finally turned panting into the wide avenue of lime-trees, and saw the lights shining ahead.

'Kostik! Is that you?' Aunt Maroossya called in a worried voice.

'Yes,' I answered, running up to her.

'What's this nonsense you're all up to?' She stood in the middle of the path, a light woollen shawl wrapped round her shoulders. 'Your mother is terribly anxious. Who invented this ridiculous game? Gleb, I suppose.'

'No,' I lied. 'We all thought of it together.'

Aunt Maroossya had guessed. The race had indeed been suggested by Uncle Kolya's ward, Gleb Afanasyev, a curly-headed schoolboy from Bryansk, whose inventiveness was inexhaustible. There was always a sly spark in his grey eyes; never a day passed without his thinking something up. As a result Gleb was automatically blamed whenever anything happened.

Next morning, when Uncle Kolya went to check, Pavlya's bottle was, of course, missing from the bench. We all teased him with having lost his nerve on the way to the Ravine and turned back after throwing away the bottle. He guessed what had happened and immediately threatened vengeance against Gleb.

Gleb loyally refrained from giving me away.

That same afternoon Pavlya ducked Gleb several times when they were out bathing, and soaked his trousers in the river after tying them in a knot. Gleb spent a long time undoing the knot with his teeth and afterwards looked a wretched sight in his crumpled trousers. This was particularly upsetting because there were two schoolgirls from Orel who were staying with their mother in Ryovna. Lyuba, the elder, was always reading in some remote corner of the park, her cheeks fiery red and her light hair permanently in disorder; we kept finding the black hair-ribbons she lost wherever she had been reading last. The younger sister, Sasha, was capricious and amusing and Gleb was in love with her. It was unthinkable that she should see him in his crumpled trousers. Feeling guilty towards Gleb, I induced Mama to press them. With his trousers smooth, he was at once restored to his usual flippant mood and appearance.

There was nothing special about that night race in the park, yet I long continued to think about it, remembering the waves of the lime blossom breaking against my face, and the cry of the bittern, and the whole of the night seething with stars and filled with the echoes of happiness.

There were times that summer when I felt there could scarcely be any room for unhappiness left in the world.

But I was disillusioned soon after the nameday ball, when I found a small bare-footed boy in a ragged cap standing outside our house. He smelled of berries and wood smoke, and had come to sell wild strawberries. He wanted ten kopecks for a jugful but Mama gave him twenty and added a piece of cake.

He stuffed the cake inside his shirt and stood silently looking at the ground and scratching one bare foot with the other.

'Who's boy are you?' asked Mama.

'Aniska's,' muttered the boy shyly.

'Well, why don't you eat your cake?'

'It's for Mum,' he said in a hoarse mutter without raising his eyes. 'She's ill. Strained her belly lugging firewood.'

'And where's your father?'

'He's dead.'

The boy sniffed, stepped back and made off at a run, clutching at the cake inside his shirt, and throwing frightened glances over his shoulder.

For a long time I could not forget that tow-haired boy, and I secretly criticised Mama. To me, it was clear that she had bribed her conscience with twenty kopecks and a piece of cake. I realised that something other than sops were needed in the face of the dark injustice of the world, though how to do away with that injustice—and I was meeting it increasingly often—I had as yet no idea.

We often heard my father and my uncle arguing at teatime about the future of Russia. Uncle Kolya maintained that the way to achieve the happiness of the people was by giving them education, my father believed that the revolution alone could bring it about. Pavlya too put in his word; he called himself a populist,[20] and had indeed narrowly missed being expelled from his medical school for a speech he had made at a students' meeting. Volodya kept quiet, but afterwards told us that neither my father and my uncle nor Pavlya understood a thing of what it was all about.

'And do you?' we asked him.

'Not a thing,' he replied cheerfully. 'I don't want to either. I love Russia and that's all there is to it.'

Volodya was the brother of my uncle's closest friend at the Arsenal, Captain Rumyantsev.

He was a little deaf and had a reddish beard in which there were always bits of hay—he slept in the hayloft. Despising all amenities, he used to roll up his student's jacket and use it in place of a pillow. He scuffled his feet, mumbled, and wore a faded blue Russian shirt tied with a black silk tasselled cord.

His hands were covered with burns from developing fluids—his hobby was photography. He was full of enterprise and he had got himself signed on by a Moscow firm of lithographers, Sherer and Nobholz: he spent his summer vacation travelling about to out-of-the-way places in the provinces, taking photographs, and they reproduced them as picture postcards which were sold at the book stalls.

We found his occupation fascinating. He often vanished for several days at a time and would come back telling us he had been to Yelets or Yefremovo or Lipetsk.

'That's the life, boys,' he said, sitting in the bath house, lathering his red beard. 'Two days ago I was swimming in the Oka, yesterday in the Moksha and today in the Ryovna.'

He infected us with his love of provincial Russia. He knew it inside out with its fairs, monasteries, famous country houses, local customs and traditions. He had visted Lermontov's birth place in Tarkhany, Fet's[21] house in the country near Kursk, the horse fair at Lebedyan, the Island of Valaam and the battlefield at Kulikovo.

Wherever he went he had friends who would put him up—usually some old lady who was a retired schoolteacher or post-mistress and who fed him on fish pasties and cabbage soup, in return for which he taught her canary to sing polka tunes, or left a packet of superphosphates for her geraniums—so that outsize scarlet blossoms should come out to the envy and amazement of the neighbours.

He never argued about Russia's destiny, but had always something to contribute on such matters as Tambov ham, or frozen apples from Ryazan or sturgeon from the Volga. On these subjects his knowledge was unbeatable. Uncle Kolya used to say jokingly that Volodya was the only man alive whom you could ask the price of a pair of bark shoes in Kinesham or a pound of swan's down in Kalyazin and be certain of your answer.

One day Volodya, who had been to Orel, brought us a tragic piece of news

We were playing croquet. We were all crazy about it and used sometimes to play until after dark, so that lamps had to be brought out on the lawn for us to finish the game.

Never did we quarrel so savagely as over croquet, especially with my brother Borya who was an excellent player and always became 'rover' early on; he would then start knocking our balls off the lawn, sending them so far out that sometimes they could never be found again. We stood round muttering furiously: 'A devil in your hand, a toad in your mouth.' Sometimes the spell worked and Borya missed a stroke.

We used to quarrel with Gleb as well. If Gleb was playing against Sasha he deliberately muffed his strokes—just to please the wretched girl. But if Sasha were his partner he performed miracles of skill and daring and invariably beat us. Usually, all the summer residents gathered on the lawn—even Uncle Kolya's dogs, Mordan and Chetvertak, who came to watch but prudently curled up behind the pine-trees, well out of the way of the balls.

That morning the lawn was as noisy as ever. We saw Uncle Kolya's carriage driving up, and someone said, 'Hullo, there's

Volodya,' but we were all so used to Volodya's comings and goings that no one paid any attention.

A moment later he was coming towards us, still in his dust coat and boots, carrying a newspaper and looking as if he was going to burst into tears.

'What's happened?' asked Uncle Kolya.

'Chekhov has died.'

Volodya turned abruptly and went back into the house.

We all ran after him. Uncle Kolya snatched at the paper, read it and, dropping it on the table, strode to his room. Aunt Maroossya followed him anxiously. Pavlya had taken off his pince-nez and stood rubbing the lenses with his handkerchief.

'Kostik,' said Mama. 'Go along to the river and call your father. He can leave his fishing for once.'

She spoke as if he could already have heard the news and was only prevented from reacting to it by his innate frivolity.

This annoyed me, but I went all the same. Gleb came with me. He was unexpectedly grave. 'Yes, Kostik . . .' he sighed deeply and said nothing more until we came to the river.

I told my father that Chekhov had died. He suddenly looked drawn and hunched up.

'Chekhov,' he said in a bewildered voice. 'Is it possible . . . I never thought I'd outlive Chekhov . . .'

We went home past the croquet lawn where the balls and mallets lay scattered about on the ground. The birds were noisy in the lime-trees. The sun shone through the branches and made patches of green on the grass.

I had already read some Chekhov and loved it. I walked on thinking that such people as Chekhov ought never to die.

Two days later Volodya went to Moscow for the funeral. We saw him off at Sinezerki station. He was taking a basket with him, full of flowers to put on the grave. They were ordinary wild flowers; we had picked them in the woods and fields and Mama had packed them between layers of damp moss and covered them with a damp cloth to keep them fresh. We felt sure wild flowers were the ones Chekhov preferred and had picked as many varieties as we could find—pinks, marestail, camomile, Solomon's Seal. Only Aunt Maroossya had cut some jasmin in the park.

The train left in the night. We walked from the station and

only got home at dawn. A new moon hung over the woods; its gentle light shone in the rain puddles. There was a smell of wet grass. A late cuckoo called in the park. When the moon set the stars came out but they were soon hidden by the dawn mist. It rustled, trickling off the bushes until at last a peaceful sun rose and warmed the earth.

17
School Days

One day when we were in our third form Inspector Bodyansky walked briskly into our classroom, dressed in his new uniform frock-coat and with a twinkle of cunning in his eye. We rose to our feet.

'On the occasion of the Imperial Manifesto granting civic liberties to the nation,' said Bodyansky, 'you are given a three days' holiday. Congratulations! Pack up your books and go home. But I advise you to keep out of the grown-ups' way at this time.'

We rushed out of school. The autumn that year was wonderful. The sun was still hot in October. The trees shone, powdered with gold and shedding hardly any of it on the paths. We were still in our summer coats.

Running out into the street, we saw crowds with red banners gathered outside the long building of the university. Speakers were addressing them from the steps. There were shouts of hurrah and hats were tossed in the air.

We climbed on the railings of Nicholas Square and also shouted hurrah and flung up our hats. They caught in the branches of the chestnuts. We shook them down together with a crackling rain of leaves and roared with laughter. We had already pinned red ribbons to our coats. In the middle of the square stood Nicholas I in bronze, pointing his toe and looking disapprovingly at all this disorder.

The shouting died down, the red banners were dipped and the revolutionary dirge was intoned:

'You fell as victims in the fateful struggle . . .'

The crowd knelt. We stood bareheaded and joined in the singing, though we didn't know all the words. Then everyone stood up and began to move past the railings. I caught sight of

Borya and of Markovich, a Montenegran student who was our lodger.

'Go home at once,' Borya told me. 'And don't you dare come out again by yourself.'

'Can't I stay with you?' I begged shyly.

'You'd be crushed to death. Off you go. You'll see all you want tomorrow.'

I very much wanted to march with the crowd in its gravely rejoicing mood, but Borya had already vanished.

Somewhere far ahead a band struck up the Marseillaise. I jumped down from the railings and mixed with the crowd. A girl in an astrakhan hat, probably a student, gave me her hand and we walked on together. I could see nothing ahead except people's backs. Up above, the roofs were lined with onlookers who were waving to us.

When we came to the level of the Opera House, we heard the clicking of hooves. I climbed a kerb stone and saw a chain of mounted police—they were backing, making way for the procession; a fat sergeant held his hand at the salute, smiling superciliously.

As soon as I jumped down, I could again see nothing, only the shop signs told me where we were. Now we were following Fundukleyev Street, past Kircheim's and Idzikovsky's book shop. I asked the girl where we were going.

'To the Town Hall. There's going to be a meeting. We are free as air now, do you realise that?'

'Yes.'

'Where do you live?' she asked me suddenly.

'In Nikolsk-Botanical Street.'

'Do your people know you've gone to the demonstration?'

'Everyone has gone to it,' I evaded.

We passed Balabukha's sweet shop and stopped. It was impossible to go any further. A dense crowd was jammed up against the walls of the Town Hall with its gilded figure of St Michael shining on the roof and its broad balcony across the frontage. There was a group of men standing bareheaded on the balcony. One of them began to address the crowd but I couldn't hear a word. I could only see the wind ruffling his grey hair.

A hand fell on my shoulder. I turned round and saw our classics teacher, Suboch.

'Konstantin Paustovsky,' he said sternly but with laughing eyes. 'What are you doing here? Go home at once.'

'He'll be all right,' said the girl. 'He's with me.'

'I didn't know,' he apologised.

The crowd backed and we lost sight of him. The girl took my hand and we pushed our way towards the pavement.

'Quiet, citizens!' ordered a hoarse voice near by.

The crowd grew very quiet. We had reached the pavement and the girl was pulling me towards the arched gateway of a yellow building I recognised as the post office.

I couldn't understand why she was holding me so tightly by the hand and pushing into the gateway. All I could see was people's backs and the pigeons wheeling overhead, catching the sunlight like pieces of paper. Tra-ta-ta-ta! Tra-ta-ta-ta! a trumpet blared in the distance. Then all was again silent.

'Comrade soldiers!' shouted the same hoarse, strained voice, and immediately after this there was a loud crack as of calico being torn across. We were showered with plaster.

The pigeons whirled away, leaving the sky empty. The sound of cracking came again and the crowd surged against the walls of the houses.

The last thing I saw before the girl pushed me inside the courtyard was a slight young student, with his greatcoat unbuttoned, leaping on the window ledge of Balabukha's shop and drawing a revolver.

'What's happening?' I asked the girl.

'They're shooting. The soldiers are shooting!'

'Why?'

She didn't answer. We were running through narrow yards and alleys, followed by the sound of screams, shots and running feet. The daylight had suddenly dimmed, misted over with yellow smoke. My heavy satchel rattled and banged on my back.

We came out into Proreznaya Street and ran on towards the Golden Gate. Two shiny ambulances swept by. People raced past us, panting and with pale faces. A Cossack patrol galloped up the street, the officer with a drawn sabre. Someone whistled shrilly after them but they rode on without stopping.

'Of all the filthy, mean tricks!' the girl kept saying. 'To hand out freedom at one moment and shoot people down the next!'

School Days

After making a long detour we reached Nicholas Square by way of St Vladimir's Cathedral and came out at the very spot where such a short while before I had hung over the railings, cheering and waving my cap.

I thanked the girl and told her that from here I could easily get home by myself.

After she had left I leaned against the railings and took off my cap. I had a terrible headache and I was very frightened. An old man in a bowler hat stopped and asked me if I was all right. I didn't answer, I was speechless. He walked on shaking his head.

I put on my cap and walked home. Dusk was falling. A crimson sunset was reflected in the windows. It was lighting-up time but for some reason the lamps remained unlit.

At the corner of our street, I saw Mama. She walked swiftly to meet me, put her arms round me, then asked abruptly:

'Where's Borya? Have you seen him?'

'Over there.' I pointed in the direction of the Kreshchatik.

'Go home,' she said, hurrying away.

I watched her out of sight and went slowly home. Our street was as deserted as usual. By now the lights were on in the windows and I saw the green-shaded lamp on the desk in my father's room. Lisa, our maid, was standing at the gate; she took my satchel and rubbed my face with her handkerchief, muttering:

'You're back, are you! It's enough to drive one crazy. Come along and wash.'

Only Galya and Dyma were at home. Galya was wandering about the rooms, stumbling into the furniture and saying over and over: 'Where are they all? Where have they all gone?' Dyma sat on the windowsill, listening to the noises outside. He hadn't managed to get to the demonstrations and was hoping to catch the sound of the firing.

I had a wash and Lisa brought me some hot milk. I couldn't stop shuddering.

'Did you see anyone shot?' asked Dyma.

'Ugh-ugh.'

'Leave him alone, can't you see the state he's in,' snapped Lisa.

At last Mama came home with Borya. He was covered with dust and had lost his cap; he was smiling oddly as though he were deaf. Markovich came in shortly after them; he said he had seen many wounded and dead.

Mama drew the blinds and told Lisa not to open the door to anyone without first making sure who it was. Then she packed me off to bed. Before lying down I pulled up the blind in my room and looked outside. The lamps were still unlit. It was as still as if the city were dead. A horseman galloped down the neighbouring street, then the silence closed in again.

I undressed and got into bed. Looking at the solid walls I told myself that our two storeyed house was like a fortress—no bullet could get through the thick masonry. The greenish tongue of flame before the ikon crackled softly. I dozed off. Just as I was falling asleep I heard the door bell, hasty footsteps, then my father's voice. He was pacing up and down the dining-room, talking incessantly.

Next morning Mama told me not to go outside the courtyard. I was annoyed and decided not to go out at all. Putting my greatcoat round my shoulders, I settled down on the balcony to do my homework, but I never got beyond the first two lines of the Nekrasov poem we had been set: 'It was autumn, the rooks had flown, the woods were bare, the fields deserted.' Everything distracted me. A fire engine clanged by. Then Staff-Captain Zadorozhny—a boor and a black reactionary[22] who lived in the other wing of the house—came out through the side door. He was wearing his grey army greatcoat with his sword belt over it and a revolver as well as his sword at his side. His wife—a tall woman as thin as a rake, with her hair dishevelled and dark circles under her eyes, followed him and stood on the doorstep, dressed in a flapping black silk kimono embroidered with peacocks.

Zadorozhny, 'the hero of Mukden' as my father laughingly called him, had recently come back from the Japanese War with two huge trunks stuffed with lengths of natural silk, kimonos and even a curved Chinese dagger.

'*Georges*,' his wife said in a high, affected voice, 'I really am very worried.'

'It's nothing, m'dear,' said the brave captain kissing her hand. 'We've just got to put an end to this nonsense.' And off he went without a backward glance.

The war with Japan was just over and we children felt as upset and as indignant as the grown-ups. We heard their conversations about the hopeless incompetence of the High Command, the 'bone-lazy' Kuropatkin, the treachery of Slessor, the surrender of Port Arthur, and the thieves and embezzlers in the Commissariat.

At the same time we heard them speak of the courage and endurance of the soldiers, and of how things could not go on as they were because the patience of the people was wearing thin.

What we felt as the most devastating blow was the sinking of the Russian fleet at Sushima. One day Borya showed me a piece of paper with some barely legible lines on it, stencilled in pale-mauve ink.

'Is it a proclamation?' I asked him. I had already seen revolutionary proclamations which had been pasted up on our walls at school.

'No, it's a poem.'

I could just make out the beginning:

> *Enough, O heroes of Sushima,*
> *You fell as the last victims.*
> *Our country's freedom is at hand*
> *Liberty is at the door.*

Liberty! My vague notion of it was taken from the allegorical picture in my father's study, of a wrathful but radiant young woman standing on a barricade, her strong breast bared, a red banner held high in one hand and a smouldering fuse she was putting to a cannon in the other. This was Liberty—and crowding behind her were men in workmen's overalls and with rifles, haggard but exultant women, schoolboys, and even a poet in a battered top-hat, all singing a rousing song which was presumably the 'Marseillaise':

'Citizens to arms! The day of glory has arrived!'

To the beating of drums and the blowing of trumpets, Liberty advanced in triumph, to be greeted by the stormy acclamations of the people wherever she arrived.

And marching behind her was a man with a revolver in his hand, and with the dark complexion and the burning eyes of the student Markovich—in fact, he looked remarkably like him.

One day I had looked into his room through the balcony door and found him humming a tune and cleaning a shiny black revolver; a handful of brass bullets lay on the open text-book on his desk.

As soon as he noticed me he covered the gun with a newspaper.

Next morning Lisa took the ikons off the walls and put them in the windows, facing the street, while Ignat the handyman chalked a big cross on the gate, bolted it and locked the front door. We were shut in a fortress.

Mama said a pogrom had started against the Jews, adding that it was 'on orders from Petersburg'. Lisa told us in a whisper that the looters had reached Vassily Street.

Borya went out with Markovich who was wearing boots and a leather belt with his student's uniform. Mama had tried to keep him at home but my father snapped at her and she let him go, kissing him and making the sign of the cross on his forehead. As they were going down the stairs she kept imploring Markovich to look after him.

'Where have they gone?' I asked my father.

'To join the Students' brigade—to defend the Jews.'

He too went out soon afterwards. Dyma and I were playing listlessly in the yard when, at about midday, we heard several shots. They began again in the afternoon and grew more frequent. A fire started in Vassily Street and charred pieces of paper blew into our yard.

Later on, my father brought home the mother of a Jewish doctor we knew—a bewildered old lady with her shawl slipping off her head, leading a speechless little boy by the hand.

Mama called Ignat into the kitchen and offered him ten roubles to take them in, but he refused the money:

'I simply can't do it. I've got Mendel the tailor and all his family as it is. They're all sitting in the lodge. You'd better make sure Zadorozhny's wife doesn't notice anything.'

Towards evening a short young fellow in a black peaked cap came to the gate. A greasy forelock hung over his eyes and his chin was plastered with sunflower seed shells.

Following him uncertainly were a tall clean-shaven old man in a boater, a hatless fidgety chap with a fat face and swollen eyes, a stout woman wrapped in a warm shawl and two boys who looked like pickpockets. The woman—we had often seen her at her stall in the Galitsky Market—had an empty sack over her shoulder.

'Open up!' shouted the youth, shaking the gate.

Ignat sauntered up from the lodge.

'Got any Jews here?'

'That's right. Lots of them—same sort as yourself.'

'We know you're hiding Jews,' screamed the youth, hitting the gate with a crowbar.

'You wait,' threatened Ignat. 'I'll get Colonel Zadorozhny to give you a talking to.'

'A fat lot I care for your Jerusalem colonels, I spit on them. We'll make mincemeat of your colonels.'

But at this point Zadorozhny's wife, who had been listening from her window, could contain herself no longer. Sweeping out of the house, she raced across the yard like an angry hen, the sleeves of her black kimono waving and flapping in the wind.

'You impudent scoundrel!' She spat through the bars of the gate straight in his face. 'How dare you insult an officer of His Imperial Majesty's Army, you dirty scarecrow! Vassily!' she screeched. 'Come here at once!'

A batman scurried out of the house. Taking in the scene he picked up an axe in the woodshed and made for the gate.

The youth leapt out of the way and fled down the street in terror, his companions trotting after him and the batman still shaking his axe at their backs.

'The idea!' Madam Zadorozhny enveloped herself in her kimono and stalked home. 'Every jumped up pip-squeak wants to claim he is a true Russian. Well, they won't get away with it—not this time!'

Thus the wife of the black-reactionary Captain drove the raiders from our door. My parents laughed about it for a long time afterwards.

When the youth with the forelock started to pound on the gate of the next house, Dyma and I went up into the attic. There was a contraption we had inherited from the children of the previous tenants but had never as yet used—we called it the 'Catapult'. It consisted of a thick rubber band nailed across the frame of the broken dormer window.

I picked up a hard yellow brick from the floor of the attic. Dyma placed it in position and held it squeezed inside the band. Then together we took aim at the youth, pulled with all our strength and let go.

The brick whistled across the yard, knocking leaves off the trees, and exploded at the feet of the old man—we had missed.

He staggered with surprise, leapt and ran, the youth clattering along the pavement after him.

'Get another brick,' Dyma shouted. But I was too slow and by the time I had brought it, the youth had vanished round the corner.

'You didn't pull straight,' said Dyma. 'That's what made us miss. You pulled sideways.' He always liked to hold a post-mortem.

Even though we had missed, we were proud of having shot our bolt from the 'Catapult'.

After dark I went across to the lodge with Lisa who was taking some gruel for Mendel and his family.

The windows of the lodge were blacked out. Ignat sat softly playing his accordion and singing a song of the Japanese War, 'The Hills of Manchuria':

'A dreadful night, the wind sighs in the trenches . . .'

Mendel was tacking a coat with white thread by the light of the small kerosene lamp. His family were asleep.

'That's right,' said Ignat. 'They're after you, they want to kill you, but don't you take any notice—you just go on doing your job. You have to earn your living, you don't want to starve.'

He went on with his song while Lisa stood inside the door listening, her cheek propped on her hand:

'Brightly shines the lonely moon upon the soldiers' graves . . .'

18
The Dark Room

I lit the small red lantern (it had an oil lamp inside it) and it glowed crimson in the narrow box room, lighting up the dusty rubbish on the shelves.

I began to develop my father's photographs. He had a small Kodak and was fond of taking snapshots, but after that the films usually lay for months in his desk drawer, until Mama cleared it out when she was tidying the house before a holiday and gave them to me to develop.

I enjoyed doing it, especially as I never knew what would turn up on the negatives. Besides, no one—not even Mama—dared to come in while I was at work. I was cut off from the world. Even the familiar household sounds—clattering dishes, clocks striking the hour, Lisa's piercing voice—were hardly audible in the little lumber room.

Hanging on the wall in front of me was the papier-mâché mask of a clown with a snub nose and very round red cheeks; it had a white top hat on, with a tuft of reddish tow sticking out from underneath.

In the red light of the lantern it came to life. The clown peered into the dark dish with the negatives. He even winked at me. He smelled of glue. Occasionally, when there was a moment of complete silence—as happens in even the noisiest households—I felt thoroughly uncomfortable alone with him.

Little by little I studied his character. I knew that he liked making fun of people, that nothing was sacred to him, and that he meant some day to pay us back for making him spend his life in the box room. Sometimes I even thought that, getting bored with the silence, he started to mutter to himself or to sing a curious little song:

> *Nonsense made jam*
> *Sitting on the fence*
> *On Sunday the rooster*
> *Was eaten by the hens.*

Yet the moment I opened the door and let the bluish daylight in, the clown was as dead as a doornail and covered with dust.

This time it was my father himself who had brought me the films.

He was just back from Moscow. It was the end of January 1906 and he had reached Moscow in the last days of the December rising. He told us about the barricades, the gunfire, the workers' brigades. In spite of the failure of the mutiny, he had come back from his visit excited, still flushed with the Moscow frost and convinced that the day was not far off when the whole country would rise up and fight for its long-awaited freedom.

'Do your best with them,' he told me. 'Some of the Moscow pictures are of great documentary interest. The trouble is, I don't remember which film is which.'

As he never bothered to mark his films, I could only take them as they came.

There were no pictures of Moscow on the first reel I developed —only snapshots of a short, thin man in a skimpy jacket and a bow tie; he stood in front of a wall on which there hung a long, narrow painting.

For a long time I couldn't make out what the subject of the painting was, then I saw an emaciated, hook-nosed face with enormous melancholy eyes, and with feathers flopping all over it.

'How are you getting on?' asked my father, coming to the door. 'Got to the Moscow pictures yet?'

'Not so far. All I've got is a little old man and a painting on a wall.'

'That's Vrubel. Don't you remember him? Mind you don't over-develop it.'

After he had gone I suddenly remembered. One morning at breakfast he had told Mama that Vrubel was spending a few days in Kiev and had asked him over to his hotel.

The Dark Room

'I can't think what you see in his painting,' said Mama. 'It's so decadent. I don't like artists who are obsessed. They make me nervous.'

All the same my father went to see Vrubel and took me along. The hotel was near the Golden Gate; we went up to the fourth floor —the landing had the characteristic coffee and eau-de-Cologne smell of a hotel morning—and we knocked at a low door. It was opened by a short little man in a worn suit; the suit was grey with yellow flecks in it, and so were the man's eyes, face and hair. I was introduced to Vrubel.

'Your son, is it?' He gripped me firmly by the chin. 'A real water-colour child.'

He seized my father's hand and led him to the table in the middle of the room, while I looked shyly round me. The room was a garret. A few water-colours were tacked to the dark wall-paper.

Vrubel poured brandy for my father and himself, emptied his glass and started to pace up and down, his heels tapping on the parquet—I noticed they were very high.

My father said something about how good the water-colours were.

'Junk,' said Vrubel.

He sat down.

'I don't know what's the matter with me, I keep scurrying round like a squirrel in a cage,' he said. 'How would it be if we took a drive to Lukyanovka?'

'To St Cyril's?'

'Yes. I'd like to have another look at my frescoes. It's a long time since I've seen them.'

My father agreed and we took a cab to Lukyanovka. We drove along Lvov Street, which was endless, then along Dorozhit-skaya Street which also was endless. My father and Vrubel were smoking.

I felt sorry for Vrubel—he kept twitching and jerking, his eyes darted about, he mumbled and lit one cigarette after another, throwing them away unsmoked. My father spoke to him as gently as to a child.

We dismissed the cab near the Church of St Theodore, walked through the suburban streets lined with gardens on either side, and came to the edge of a ravine overlooking the river. The road looped its way down and we could see the small onion dome of St Cyril's at the bottom.

'Let's sit down for a bit,' said Vrubel.

We sat by the side of the road with dirty grass all around us. The sky over the Dnieper was a faded blue.

'I'm in a bad way, Georgy Maximovich,' said Vrubel. He slapped his flabby cheek and laughed. 'I'm sick and fed up with lugging this carrion flesh around.'

A lot of what Vrubel said passed over my head and I would not have remembered it if my father had not repeated it, first to Mama, then to Uncle Kolya and several of their friends, and if they had not all been so sorry for Vrubel.

When we went into St Cyril's Church, Vrubel walked round it in silence, examining the frescoes he had once painted. They looked to me as if they were made of great blobs of blue, yellow and red clay. It was hard to believe that these enormous pictures had been done by this skimpy little man.

'That's painting all right,' said Vrubel as we were leaving the church.

It surprised me that my father, who never allowed me or my brothers to get away with a boastful word, accepted Vrubel's comment and even said that he agreed with him.

After Vrubel had left us at the corner of Reyter Street I said to my father I didn't think much of him.

'Why's that?'

'He's conceited.'

'You little donkey!' He slapped my back. 'Hold your shoulders straight.'

'Why am I a donkey?' I asked, offended.

'Well, first of all you must know that Vrubel is a very remarkable painter—some day you'll discover that for yourself. Secondly he is a sick man—he's unbalanced. And thirdly you'll have to learn one golden rule—never to make hasty judgments about people, or you're sure to make a fool of yourself. And now straighten your shoulders and don't think I've insulted you.'

Even when I made a print of it, the painting in my father's snapshot was difficult to make out. I only knew it was called 'The Demon'.

The Dark Room

It was not until 1911 that I saw the original at the Tretyakovsky Gallery in Moscow.

Moscow was steaming with cold. Clouds of vapour poured out of the open doors of taverns. Against the cosy Moscow snow-scene—the frosted trees along the avenues, the windows frosted with rime, the greenish glow of the gaslights—Vrubel's painting flashed with a diamond flame, like a jewel from the icy summits of the Caucasus. It filled the picture hall with the chilly breath of beauty and the majesty of human discontent.

I stood looking at it for a long time, realising as never before that the contemplation of such a painting is more than a visual pleasure—it dredges the mind for ideas one has never before suspected oneself of having.

I thought of Lermontov and imagined him walking in with a discreet jingle of spurs, tossing his greatcoat to the attendant in the hall, stopping in front of the picture and moodily gazing at his Demon.

It was about himself that he wrote with bitterness: 'I am as useless to the world as the blaze of a shooting star.' But my God, how wrong he was! How great is the world's need of the blaze of shooting stars—since man does not live by bread alone.

He thought of himself as in bondage to the world. He spent himself in the desert. But the desert blossomed, brought to life by his poetry, his anger, his anguish and his conception of joy. And he did after all confess to a nodding acquaintance with 'shy woodland flowers'. Perhaps the rarefied air above the summits sprinkled with the Demon's blood held something of their scent, and Lermontov and his Demon were only children refused by life what they so passionately begged of it—freedom, justice and love.

'Found those snapshots of Moscow yet?' asked my father's voice from behind the door.

It broke the spell, I forgot Vrubel and set to work on the negatives. Narrow Moscow streets were coming out, deep in snow and blocked by low barricades constructed of barrels, boards' paving stones and shop signs and manned by civilians with rifles and revolvers in their hands. Then came shelled buildings, the Gorbaty Bridge, the Zoo wreathed in smoke from burning houses, bullet-riddled tavern signs and overturned trams.

Everything was misted over with a winter haze, and there was nothing I could do about it—nothing would give sharpness to the photographs.

But the mist helped to convey the atmosphere of the mutiny. It seemed as if the photographs gave off a whiff of gunpowder and smoke.

Mutiny—the word had a strange sound in the Moscow of those days, a Moscow which had still preserved its patriarchal air. I had read about the Indian Mutiny, the Commune, the Decembrists —but the Moscow mutiny seemed to me the most romantic of all.

I got out a map of Moscow and my father showed me where the barricades had been set up and where the battles had been fought— Chistye Prudy, Presnya, Gorbaty Bridge, Samotyoka, Kudrinsky Square. From then on these very names had for me the fascination of places which had become a part of history within my own lifetime.

Everything about the background of the rising became significant—the shaggy Moscow winter, the tea houses where the rebels met, the curious intermingling of ancient Moscow with the new era to which the rising belonged—the cab-drivers in ragged caps, the gilded buns over bakers' shops, the market women selling hot pies, side by side with the whistling bullets and the shiny revolvers, the red flags and the strains of the *Varshavyanka*.

In all of it there was the poetry of struggle, the breath of freedom —though as yet seen dimly like the dawn of a winter day, all of it spoke of courage, faith and hope.

From all over their unending plains, Russians watched the glow of the Presnya fires, waiting for the outcome. The mutiny was like a winter storm—a presage of new, purifying storms and upheavals.

Today I can describe that intoxicating climate—at the time I could only feel it but not explain it.

The following afternoon I made prints of all the photographs and took them to my father. The lamplight fell on the familiar objects on his desk—the steel model of a steam-engine, the bronze of Pushkin with curly side-burns, the pile of satirical revolutionary magazines—new ones were appearing every day—and, in the place of honour, a picture postcard of Lieutenant Schmidt[23] in a black cloak fastened with metal lion-heads.

My father put down his newspaper, looked at the prints and said:

'Incredible country! Vrubel and the mutiny! All existing side by side and all leading to the same thing.'

'To what?'

'To a better future. You'll see a lot of interesting things in your life, Kostik—that's of course if you grow up to be an interesting person.'

19
Crimea

Two years later, when I was fourteen, Mama insisted on our spending the summer in the Crimea instead of going to Ryovna as usual. She chose the quiet little town of Alushta for us to stay at.

We went through Odessa. As all the hotels were full, we slept at the guest house of the Athos Monastery near the station. Pale young novices, with black patent-leather belts on their habits, served us a supper of nettle soup and dried fish. I adored everything—the soup, the glittering white city, the fizzy lemonade, and the port with its clouds of grey pigeons and white seagulls mixing as they wheeled over the ships.

Once again I was at the seaside, but the gentle landfall made it friendlier here than in the Caucasus.

An ancient steamer, the *Pushkin*, took us across to Yalta. The sea was dead calm. The deck railings were so hot that you couldn't put your hand on them. The vibration of the propeller made everything shake and tinkle in the saloon. The sun poured through the portholes and the open doors. I was amazed at its southern abundance of light. Everything sparkled with it. Even the rough canvas over the hatchway flickered like a flame.

The Crimea rose out of the bright blue sea like a Treasure Island, with lilac clouds on the tops of its mountains. The white port of Sebastopol sailed slowly towards us, greeting us with the midday salute of its guns and the blue crosses of St Andrew's flags.

The *Pushkin* spent a long time churning the water and making it bubble and hiss as it slowly turned in the bay. We dashed from starboard to port and back, trying to see everything. Over there was Malakhov Hill and the Bratsky Cemetery and here the Count's Wharf, and the Fort of Constantine thrusting into the breakers and the cruiser *Ochakov* surrounded by pontoons. Naval cutters swept by us, leaving a malachite wake.

I looked at it all spellbound. So it wasn't only in books—it existed in reality, this city where Nakhimov had died, where the bastions had been peppered with cannon balls, where Tolstoy had fought as a lieutenant in the artillery, and where Lieutenant Schmidt had sworn his oath of fidelity.[24] Here it lay, this city, in the blazing hot sun and the feathery shadow of its acacias.

The *Pushkin* only got to Yalta by nightfall, slowly drifting into the harbour, as into a summerhouse hung with strings of lights.

The first thing I saw when we got off at the stone landing stage was a swarthy pedlar with a cart; the light of a lantern hanging from a pole fell on the downy peaches and the large plums with their greyish bloom.

We bought peaches and walked to the Yalita Hotel, followed by porters cheerfully lugging our trunks.

Tired out, I went to sleep at once, hardly noticing either the centipede lying in wait in the corner of the room or the black cypresses outside the windows. For a few seconds I still heard the fountain tinkling in the courtyard, then sleep swooped down on me and gently rocking me as in a cabin, carried me away, to some far-off country as full of mysteries as the Crimea.

After Yalta with its elegant corniche, Alushta was at first disappointingly dull. Our villa was on the outskirts of the town, just beyond the Stakheyev quay.

The stony ground and the sweet-smelling thickets of thuya, the sea and the distant hills of Sudak—this was all Alushta had to offer us, but it was enough to reconcile me to the place and in the end I fell in love with it.

Galya and I used often to go and buy grapes from a neighbouring vineyard where they grew pink muscats and the sugary *shashla*. It was full of the singing of cicadas and the ground was yellow with flowers, each the size of a pinhead.

An elderly woman called Anna Petrovna, so sunburned that her grey eyes looked white, used to come out of her low white cottage and cut bunches of grapes for us off the vines. Sometimes, instead of going herself, she sent her daughter Lena, a seventeen year old girl, who wore her hair in a sunbleached wreath on her head and whose eyes were as grey as her mother's.

The grown-ups had nicknamed Lena 'the mermaid'. She often passed our villa at dusk, going down for a long swim in the sea and coming back with a towel over her shoulder, singing:

> *'In the wide blue sea*
> *In the azure ocean*
> *We'll forget the misfortunes*
> *And sorrows of life.'*

Galya made friends with Lena and discovered everything there was to know about her. Fond of questioning people about every detail of their lives, she did it with the determination of the myopic and the inquisitive.

It appeared that Anna Petrovna was a widow, a retired librarian from Chernigov, who had come to the Crimea on advice from the doctors because Lena had developed tuberculosis. In Alushta she married an elderly Ukrainian who died soon afterwards, leaving her his vineyard. Lena had quite recovered from her disease and now spent the winter at school in Yalta, only visiting her mother on Sundays.

Lena wanted to become a singer. Galya was trying to talk her out of it; she believed that the only worthy occupation for a woman was teaching and intended herself to become a village school-mistress. I was sick to death of Galya's views on this subject because she never stopped talking about her calling and insisting on the merits of her future profession, as if anyone had ever argued against it.

It annoyed me to hear her trying to turn Lena against the theatre, which I loved, and to spite her I used to give Lena enthusiastic accounts of the plays I had been to, such as *The Blue Bird*, *The Nest of Gentlefolk*, *Madame Sans-Gêne* and *Too Clever by Half*.

I foretold her a wonderful future. I liked to think of the slim, sunburned girl sweeping on to the stage in a pale satin dress with a long train, a crimson rose fluttering on her breast and her sunburn showing through her make-up.

I wove my daydreams around her, and she listened, faintly blushing, her head thrown back as if pulled by the weight of her hair, and now and then asking me:

'It isn't true, is it? Aren't you making it all up? Admit it—I won't be cross.'

She said 'you' to me, although she was three years older. In those days, only the closest of friends used to call each other 'thou'.

I could not 'admit it' because I genuinely believed in the truth of whatever I made up. My habit of believing my own stories was to cause me a lot of trouble, and the curious thing is that never, in my whole life, have I found anyone to understand it, or at least to make excuses for it.

But Lena actually believed everything I told her. She needed to believe it and if Galya and I stayed away for two or three days, she would come with a basket of grapes to the house shyly, telling Mama that her mother had sent them as a present, and snatching a moment to whisper to me: 'Why don't you come? It's horrid of you.'

My father stayed only a day or two in Alushta, he had business in Petersburg. Borya also went away—he had to sit for his entrance examination to the Kiev Technological Institute.

Mama was for some reason disturbed by my father's departure and ceased to take any notice of us. She was even glad to be rid of us when we vanished for days on end to the beach.

I spent my time up to the waist in water, catching crabs under the rocks, and ended up by getting pneumonia as a result of bathing at night. To add to my misfortunes, I was stung by a poisonous centipede.

By then it was August, near the end of the school holidays. It was time for us to return to Kiev but my illness upset our plans. Finally Mama sent Galya and Dyma home and herself stayed on with me in Alushta.

I was ill, seriously and for a long time. I couldn't sleep at night; it hurt me to breathe and I tried to take shallow, cautious breaths as I lay staring wretchedly at the white-washed walls. Earwigs crawled out of the cracks in the plaster. The light of the table lamp turned the shadows of the medicine bottles into prehistoric monsters stretching their necks to nuzzle at the ceiling.

The black window-pane reflected the lamplight. The sea whispered outside. A moth was beating its wings against the glass, trying to escape from the airless sick room with its medicinal smell.

Mama slept in the next room. I called her to give me a drink and to open the window for the moth to get out. When the moth was gone I quietened down.

But soon I could mysteriously see it alighting on the grass outside the window and almost immediately flying back into the room, this time as big as an owl. It settled on my chest with the weight of a stone which at any moment would crush my ribs.

Again I called Mama, begging her to drive away the moth. Her lips tight, she removed the hot bandage from my chest and wrapped me in a blanket.

I lost count of the nights filled with an incessant unaccountable droning and hot with the dry heat of the bed clothes.

Lena came to see me one afternoon. I didn't at once recognise her in her brown school dress with a black pinafore and black slippers, her fair hair hanging in two neat plaits on either side of her sunburned face.

She was leaving for Yalta and had come to say goodbye. While my mother was out of the room, she put her hand on my forehead; it was as cold as an icicle. Her hair brushed against my face and I could feel its warm fresh smell.

Hearing Mama coming back, she snatched away her hand. What Mama had come to say was that Lena had brought me some wonderful grapes.

'I only wish we had better ones,' said Lena without looking at her and speaking to me as if she were trying to tell me something important.

She left, running quickly down the stairs. There was no one in the house except ourselves, so that every sound carried clearly.

From that day on, I began to improve, but the doctor said that, even after I was up, I would have to remain in Alushta for at least a couple of months' convalescence; this would take us to October. At this, Mama made up her mind to send for Lisa to come up from Kiev and look after me. For some reason which she wouldn't tell me, she was very anxious to be home. Lisa arrived a week later and the very next day Mama took the coach to Simferopol.

Lisa gasped with astonishment at everything. She had never in her life been to the seaside or seen vineyards or cypresses. Mama had engaged her in Ryovna and brought her straight from the Bryansk forest to Kiev.

Crimea

I was beginning to get up but I wasn't yet allowed to leave the house. I spent my time reading on the glassed-in verandah where the autumn sun was still hot. I had found a copy of *Tristan and Isolde* tucked away in a chest of drawers, and I read this wonderful legend over and over, feeling a little more sad every time.

I then decided to write something of the same sort myself, and worked for several days on a story, but got no further than the description of a rocky shore and of a storm at sea.

Finally, at the end of September, the doctor allowed me to go out. I wandered about by myself in the deserted little resort. I liked going to the wharf when the sea was rough and the waves rolled under the wooden jetty, spouting through the cracks. One day I dropped in on Anna Petrovna. She gave me coffee and told me to be sure to come back next Sunday when Lena would be home. I spent the rest of the week thinking about Sunday.

I remember that Sunday as if it were yesterday, because of two events which took place that day.

I knew that Lena was arriving by the morning cutter and I waited for her on the jetty. But the moment the cutter showed round the cape, I took cover behind the kiosk which sold picture postcards of the Crimea, and there I stayed until the cutter had moored and Lena had come ashore, looking about her as though searching for someone, and slowly started for home.

I was terrified that she would see me. It was altogether ridiculous. She glanced over her shoulder once or twice, and even went back to stand in front of a poster on the quay, pretending to read it although it was hanging in tatters from its board.

Furtively I watched her. She was wearing a white woollen scarf on her head and looked whiter and thinner than I remembered her. Presently she dropped her eyes to the ground and stood frankly waiting. Finally she went away.

I walked home, torn with shame at my cowardice.

Was I to go and see Lena or not? I could eat no lunch and Lisa threatened to send a telegram to Mama, but as she could only just read I wasn't worried.

After lunch I at last made up my mind, threw my coat over my shoulders and went off. Lisa shouted after me to button up my coat but I paid no attention.

The leaves in the vineyard were by now dark crimson. As I

opened the wicket gate, a door slammed and Lena came running out of the house without her coat.

It was a very good day. I soon got over my embarrassment and sat telling stories about Ryovna, and Aunt Nadya, and the geography master Cherpunov. Lena kept surreptitiously piling grapes and greengages on my plate.

'You shouldn't have come out with your coat undone in this cold,' she told me after a while.

'You didn't have a coat on at all.'

'Oh well . . . I haven't had pneumonia,' she faltered and blushed.

Anna Petrovna peered over her spectacles, shaking her head. 'I wish you'd remember you are no longer a child, Lena, you are seventeen.' She spoke as if Lena were a woman whose frivolity was unbecoming to her age.

They both walked back with me to the villa, to see how I was managing without Mama. Lisa blushed as red as a beetroot with shyness but Anna Petrovna put her at her ease and she was soon telling her how disobedient I was and how I never buttoned up my coat. Anna Petrovna told her to come round if she ever needed anything, and Lisa was delighted. She had made no friends in Alushta. She occasionally came for a walk with me and picked herbs which she hung up to dry in her room; otherwise she spent her free time playing patience. She was an apple-cheeked girl with kind, fat-lidded eyes, and extremely credulous—she was always ready to believe any nonsense anyone told her.

After Lena and her mother had gone, I thought with misery of the long boring evening ahead and wished I could go straight back to the cottage in the vineyard, but I realised such a thing 'wasn't done'. Making up my mind to get on with my story, I lit the lamp and settled down to it. But what I wrote instead was my first poem. I only remember the first line:

'O pick the flowers with drooping stems . . .'

I was pleased with my verses and was intending to work late, when Lisa came in, said, 'What's the idea, spoiling your eyes! It's past your bed-time,' and blew out the lamp. I lost my temper, said I wasn't a baby and called her an idiot. She was so upset that she burst into tears and went off to her room sobbing:

'I'm going back to Kiev tomorrow, on foot. Then you can do what you like.'

When I made no comment, she said that tomorrow she would send a telegram to my mother about how badly I behaved—she had a passion for threatening me with telegrams. After muttering on and on in her room, she finally said: 'Well, God forgive you. Go to sleep. Hear the wind? It's blowing up for a storm.'

Above my head was a round-faced clock which invariably woke me up when it struck two in the morning. This time I awoke as usual but realised at once that something very strange was going on. A reddish light was flickering on the wall. My window looked out on the sea; outside the wind was howling more fiercely than ever. I sat up and looked: a crimson glow was swaying to and fro over the sea lighting the low-flying clouds and the storming water.

I began hurriedly to dress.

'Lisa,' I shouted. 'There's a fire out at sea.'

Her bed creaked as she got up.

'But what could be burning on the sea?' she asked.

'I don't know.'

'Then why have you got up?'

She was still half asleep and making no sense.

'I'm going to the beach,' I said.

'So am I.'

Outside, the cold wind came tearing round the house and wrapped itself round us. The glow in the sky had spread. Our Tartar handyman stood by the wicket gate.

'There's a ship on fire,' he said. 'Terrible thing! But what can one do!'

We ran down to the sea. A bell was clanging by the wharf. People were standing about on the quay. I lost Lisa in the darkness.

Fishermen in gumboots and oilskins were dragging a boat down the shingle. 'Passenger ship . . .' I heard in snatches through the wind, 'Couple of miles . . .' They climbed aboard in their wet capes and the boat rose on a crest and made for the open sea.

There was a touch on my arm. I turned and saw Lena beside me, her stern-looking face faintly illuminated by the glow of the fire.

Two white flares went up, one after the other.

'That's help coming,' said Lena. 'If it hadn't been for Mama,

I'd have gone with the fishermen in the lifeboat. I meant to go . . . When are you leaving, my dear?' she asked after a silence.

She had said 'dear' to me and it was so unexpected that my heart leapt.

'In about a week, I suppose.'

'Then I'll see you again. I'll try to come early.'

'Please come,' I said, feeling as though, with these alarming words, I had jumped off a precipice.

Lena pulled me back a little from the edge of the quay where we had been standing.

'What was I to do?' she asked softly. 'Mama was terrified, and she's been frightened enough in her life. She's here somewhere, by the wharf. You aren't cross with me?'

'What about?'

She made no reply.

'Lena,' called her mother's voice. 'Where are you? I can't see you. Let's go home.'

'I'm leaving by the early coach,' Lena whispered. 'Don't think of seeing me off, I don't want you to. Goodbye.'

She squeezed my hand and moved away. For not more than a few seconds I watched the white scarf on her head before it vanished in the darkness.

The red light on the sea was fading. A green search-light went on, low over the water. It came from the minesweeper *Impetuous* which was drawing near the burning ship.

was I impatient to be in bed and asleep, not to think of the amazing and wonderful thing which had just happened between me and Lena.

In the morning, when there was only a wisp of smoke in place of the glow, I went to the wharf to find out about the ship. People were saying that a bomb had exploded in the hold but that the captain had managed to beach the ship on some off-shore rocks.

After this I walked a long way down the Yalta road, where Lena's coach had passed only an hour earlier.

I sat down on the parapet, my back to the sea and my hands tucked into the sleeves of my overcoat. I thought about Lena and my heart beat painfully hard. I thought of the warm freshness of her hair and of her breath, and of the troubled look in her grey eyes with their faintly quivering, finely-drawn eyebrows. I couldn't understand what was happening to me. A terrible anxiety clenched my heart and I burst into tears.

My only longing was to see her, hear her voice, be near her always.

I had quite decided to walk straight on, all the way to Yalta, when a cart came creaking round the bend of the road. I hastily wiped my eyes and looked out to sea, but they filled again and all I saw was a blue dazzling shimmer.

I was chilled through and couldn't stop shivering.

The old man in a straw hat, who was driving by in his cart, pulled up and said:

'Get in, lad, I'll give you a lift to Alushta.'

I climbed in. 'Are you from the orphanage?' he asked over his shoulder.

'No, I'm at high school.'

As always in places we are sorry to leave, my last days in Alushta were extraordinarily sad and happy at the same time.

Fog rolled in from the sea. The sun seeped through it. Lisa fed the stoves with yellow acacia wood.

The trees shed their leaves; they were greyish and veined lilac, instead of golden as at home in Kiev.

The waves came silently out of the fog, broke on the beach and went silently back. Dead sea horses lay on the shingle.

The summits of Chatyr-Dag and Bobugan-Aïla were muffled in clouds. Flocks of sheep came down the hills with half-wild dogs running after them, glancing distrustfully from side to side.

The autumn and the fog made everything so still that voices carried to my balcony from the little town below. Hot braziers glowed in the market-place where it smelt of roast millet and burned chestnuts.

We were leaving on Monday and Lisa had already ordered the horses to take us to Simferopol.

I thought Lena would come on Saturday but she didn't. I passed the vineyard several times but could see no one. Sunday morning there was still no sign of her. I went to the coach station but found it deserted.

Very worried by now, I walked home and was met by Lisa who handed me a letter.

'A boy brought it round. It must be from Anna Petrovna. I

expect they want to see you to say goodbye. Why don't you go? They're such nice people.'

I went into the garden, opened the envelope and found a narrow strip of paper: 'Come to the three plane trees at six. Lena.'

I was there at five. It was a wilderness with only the three plane trees growing by the dry bed of a torrent and everything around them withered except a few crocuses. There must have been a garden there at some time. The river-bed was spanned by a small wooden bridge and a garden bench with rusty legs stood at the foot of one of the trees.

Early as I had come, Lena was already there. She sat on the bench, her hands clasped between her knees; her scarf had slipped to her shoulders and her hair was ruffled by the wind.

She only turned when I came right up to her.

'You won't understand,' she said, taking my hand. 'No, don't take any notice of me. I'm always talking a lot of silly nonsense.'

She rose to her feet and gave me an apologetic smile. Dropping her head she looked up at me distrustfully:

'My mother says I'm mad. But there, I can't help it. Goodbye.'

She took me by the shoulders, kissed me on the lips and gently pushed me away.

'And now go. And don't look back. Please. Go now.'

Her eyes filled and a tear ran down her cheek, leaving a wet streak.

I went as I was told. But I couldn't prevent myself from looking back. She was leaning against the tree, her head thrown back as though pulled by the weight of her hair.

'Go on,' she called in a changed voice. 'It's nothing, it's all nonsense.'

I walked on. The sky was fading; the sun had set behind the crest of the Kastel. The wind from the Yaïla rustled the dry leaves.

I didn't realise at the time that it was all over—quite finished. Only much later did I understand that life had for some reason taken away from me something that might have been happiness.

We left next morning. It was pouring with rain in the woods on the Chatyr-Dag, and all the way to Kiev the rain lashed the windows of our carriage.

At home my arrival passed, as it were, unnoticed. There was

something wrong with the household; I didn't know yet what it was.

I was, if anything, glad that no one took any interest in me. It left me free to think unceasingly about Lena, though I couldn't make up my mind to write to her.

It was not until 1921 that I revisited the Crimea. By then, whatever there had been between us had become a memory to dwell on but no longer with pain—one of those memories that exist in everyone's life and are perhaps hardly worth talking about.

20
Shipwreck

It was soon after this Crimean holiday that everything in our lives changed at the same time. My father had a quarrel with the Head of the South-West Railway; he threw up his job and our prosperity came suddenly to an end.

We moved from Nikolsk-Botanical Street to Cellar Street where, ironically, we took a flat in a basement.

All we had to live on was whatever Mama made by selling our belongings. Silent men in sheepskin hats took to appearing increasingly often in our dark, cool rooms. They darted their sharp little eyes over the furniture, the pictures and the china set out on a table, had a quiet and persuasive talk with Mama and went off. A couple of hours later a cart would draw up in the yard and remove a table or a carpet, a cheval glass or a chest of drawers.

In the mornings we used to find a Tartar in a black silk skull-cap squatting on his heels in the kitchen, holding up a sheet against the light or examining a suit of my father's. We nicknamed him Shurum Burum.

Shurum Burum would bargain for a long time and go and come back, driving Mama frantic, before he finally shook hands over the deal, and pulling out a pocket book stuffed with tattered notes, spat delicately on his fingers and counted out the money.

My father was hardly ever there. He went out early and didn't come back until after we were asleep. Where he spent his time, we none of us knew. We assumed that he was looking for a job.

Mama had suddenly aged. She neglected her hair and went about with grey strands falling over her face.

Borya moved to a room at the Progress Boarding House, near the railway station, allegedly because it was near the Polytechnical

Institute, but really because he didn't get on with my father whom he blamed for our misfortunes, and because he wanted to escape from the gloomy atmosphere in Cellar Street. He kept himself by giving lessons but was not earning enough to help Mama.

Dyma had also become a 'tutor' as it was called. I alone was too young to teach anyone else, while Galya was too short-sighted to do any work other than helping Mama about the house. We had had to send Lisa away.

One morning the porter brought in a wheezing old man who turned out to be a bailiff and who impounded what was left of our furniture because Father was in debt and couldn't pay. My father had concealed these debts from Mama and it was only now that it all came out. He then took the first job he could find, a very badly paid one at a sugar factory outside the town, and left the flat.

We remained on our own. Misfortune had settled upon us. I realised that we were ceasing to exist as a family, and my memories of the Crimea, of my short, sad love-affair, and of my easy childhood, made it all the more difficult for me to bear.

Uncle Kolya was making an allowance to Mama, and every month when she received the money, Mama wept with shame.

One day at school I saw her waiting to see the Director. I was about to go up to her when she turned away and I realised that she didn't want me to see her.

I could not imagine why she had been to him, but I didn't like to question her. A few days later I was stopped in the corridor by our new Director, Tereshchenko, who had replaced Bessmertny; he was a short, round man with a completely bald head which shone as if it had been buttered (he was known as Butterpate).

'Will you tell your mother,' he said, 'that the School Board has granted her request and exempted you and your brother from paying the school fees. But remember that this is only done for boys who work really well. So I advise you to pull up your socks.'

It was the first time in my life I felt humiliated. When I got home, I said to Mama:

'They've exempted Dyma and me. But why did you do this?'

'What did you want me to do?' she asked quietly. 'Take you away from school?'

'I could work and earn the money for the fee.'

Then for the first time in my life I saw Mama look frightened; it was as though I had struck her.

'Don't be angry,' she said, bowing her head. She was sitting beside the table, sewing. 'How could I let you go out and work?'

Tears poured down her face.

'If you only knew how much it hurts me for all of us, for you especially. How could your father be so thoughtless, so inconsiderate! How did he dare to do it?'

She had taken to speaking of my father as 'he' or 'your father'. She was weeping, bowed over the worn dress she was altering, snippets of cloth and thread scattered at her feet.

Nearly all our furniture was gone and the flat had become dank and empty. A cold bleary light came from the windows, through which nothing could be seen except an endless procession of boots and snow shoes. This perpetual shuffling of muddy feet through the winter slush was distracting and irritating; it was as if all these strangers had invaded our very rooms, bringing in the cold from the street, without so much as a glance or a by-your-leave.

In mid-winter Mama got a letter from Uncle Kolya, which greatly upset her.

That evening as we sat at the round table, pursuing our various occupations by the light of our only lamp, she told us that Uncle Kolya wanted me to go and stay with him in Bryansk, where I could go to the local school, and that he believed this to be essential until my father had found a better job and came back to us.

Galya looked at her in alarm. Dyma was silent.

'Your father is not coming back,' Mama said firmly. 'He has other attachments. It was for their sake that he got into debt and left us destitute. I don't want him back. I won't hear of it—not a word.'

For a long time she sat in silence, her lips pressed tightly together.

'That's that,' she said at last. 'Now what are we going to do about Kostik?'

'It's very simple,' said Dyma without looking at her—he always thought everything was simple. 'This is my last year at school, after that I go to the Moscow Technological Institute. We'll sell everything. You, Mama, and Galya will come and live with me in

Moscow. We'll manage. And for the time being Kostik will go to Uncle Kolya.'

'But why?' Galya said anxiously. 'What sort of a life will he have there? And why should we be parted?'

I was sitting bent over the table, feverishly drawing flowers and scrolls on a page out of my note book. I had recently taken to drawing these elaborate doodles whenever I felt miserable.

'Stop scribbling,' said Mama. 'And I can't imagine what you are smiling at. What do you feel about it?'

'I'm not smiling,' I muttered, though I could feel the stiff smile frozen on my face. 'It's nothing, I'm just . . .'

I fell silent and went on compulsively scribbling.

'Kostik, darling,' Mama said suddenly in a muffled voice. 'Won't you say something?'

'Very well . . .' I said . . . 'Of course, I'll go . . . If it's necessary . . .'

'It's certainly best,' said Dyma.

'Yes . . . I'll be all right . . . Of course . . .' I agreed for something to say.

The whole of my life fell to pieces in that moment. All I could see was scalding loneliness ahead, and that I was utterly unwanted.

I wished I could tell Mama that she didn't have to send me off to Bryansk, that I was no less capable than Dyma of earning my living and even of helping her as well, and that I was terribly unhappy because I couldn't help feeling I was being thrown out of my home, but my throat was so sore and my jaws were so tightly clenched that I could say nothing at all.

The idea passed briefly through my mind of going next day to my father; then all that remained was the thought that I was already, now, completely alone.

At last I managed with difficulty to pull myself together and to say once again that I was willing, even happy to go to Bryansk, but that now I had a headache and would like to lie down.

Going to the cold room I shared with Dyma, I undressed, got into bed, put my face under the bed clothes and lay stiff and wide awake almost through the night. Mama came in and spoke to me but I pretended to be asleep. She covered me with my school great-coat on top of the blankets and went away.

The preparations for my move to Bryansk dragged on into

December. It was hard for me to leave my school and my friends and to begin what I saw as my new and comfortless life.

I wrote to my father, but heard nothing in return for a long time; the reply only came a couple of days before I was leaving.

I usually walked home from school by way of an empty square at the back of the Opera House, nearly always with my friends Stanishevsky and Matushevich who lived in the same direction.

One day as we were crossing the square we passed a slightly built young woman with a thick veil over her face. After walking on a few steps she stopped and looked back.

On the following day we met her again in the same place. This time she came straight up to me and asked:

'Are you the son of Georgy Maximovich?'

'Yes.'

'Can I have a word with you?'

'Certainly,' I said, blushing.

My two friends walked on pretending to be uninterested and not even looking back.

'Georgy Maximovich asked me to give you this letter,' she said hurriedly, digging in her small handbag. 'You see he wanted it to reach you directly . . . Forgive me for telling you this . . . I couldn't refuse to do it for him. I recognised you immediately. You are very like your father. Here it is.'

She handed me the letter.

'You are leaving Kiev?' she asked.

'Yes, in a few days.'

'Oh well . . . What a pity, it could all have been so different.'

'You'll be seeing my father?'

She nodded silently.

'Will you kiss him for me?' I surprised myself by saying. 'He's terribly nice.'

I meant to tell her to love him a lot, and to be very kind to him, but all I could manage to say was 'he's terribly nice'.

'Yes.' She suddenly laughed, showing a row of small and very white glistening teeth. 'Thank you.'

A bracelet tinkled on her wrist as we shook hands and she quickly walked away.

To this day I don't know her name, I never managed to discover it. Only Mama knew it and she took the secret with her to her grave.

The young woman reminded me, by her voice, her laughter, her tinkling bracelet, of the girl I had once seen at Cherpunov's. Had she lifted her thick veil, would I indeed have recognised that same girl, the 'Butterfly from the Isle of Borneo'? I still occasionally have the feeling that it must have been that very same young woman; the one I had had cocoa with at Kircheim's.

Father's letter was short. He told me to endure my troubles with courage and dignity.

'Perhaps some day,' he went on, 'our luck will turn and I'll be in a position to help you. I still believe that you'll grow up to be a real person and succeed where I have failed. Remember the advice I gave you (I have never bored you with too much of it) never to pass a hasty judgment on anyone—this includes myself. Wait till you know all the circumstances and have enough experience to understand a lot of things you can't possibly understand now. Keep well, write to me, and don't worry.'

Only Mama and Galya came to see me off. The train was leaving in the middle of the morning and Borya was at school. As he was going out, he kissed me without saying anything. Mama and Galya were equally silent at the station.

Mama was cold and kept her hands hidden in her muff. Galya clung to her arm; her eyes had got much worse in the past year; she was confused by the crowd and frightened by the hooting of the trains. At the last moment, Mama kissed me, made the sign of the cross over me and, pulling me by the sleeve, took me aside.

'I know it's hard for you and you are angry,' she said. 'But do try to understand that I wanted you at least of all of us, to be spared our poverty and our troubles. This was my only reason for insisting on sending you to Uncle Kolya's.'

I said that of course I understood perfectly and wasn't angry in the least. But in spite of my affectionate words, I was chilled to the heart and only longed for the train to move and put an end to this wretched leave-taking.

It must be that I had taken leave of Mama much earlier, perhaps on the night when she came for the last time to cover me with my greatcoat. When the train finally moved, I saw neither Mama nor

Galya through the window, because a dense cloud of steam from the engine enveloped the platform and concealed everyone.

My heart was as chilly as the carriage, filled with the dingy winter daylight and with piercing draughts. The snow-covered plains were depressing to look at. A ground wind rustled all night, keeping me awake. I watched the flame of the candle in the ceiling-lamp as it bent and flickered, attacked by the wind; I made a bet with myself—if it remained alight, this meant that I could still expect some happiness in my life. It was still burning at dawn and I felt better.

In the morning, when I got off at Bryansk, the frost was such that the air rang with the creaking of boots on the hard snow. The cold clung to the earth like a cloud of smoke. The frozen sun blazed with a crimson glow.

A sleigh had been sent to meet me. There was a sheepskin coat in it with a hood and a pair of gauntlets. I wrapped myself up, and the horses went off at a gallop. We swept through the glittering snow dust and to the frantic jingling of bells, first along a causeway, then on the ice of the Desna. The old town, shaggy with rime and ice, shone like tinsel on its far away hill.

The sleigh stopped at a timber house built on a slope. I climbed up the steps. The door flew open and Aunt Maroossya, grabbing my coat-sleeve, pulled me into the dining-room where patches of sunlight danced on the ceiling, and poured half a glass of red wine down my throat. My lips were so numb with cold that I couldn't speak.

Everything in Uncle Kolya's house was loud and cheerful. The samovar roared, Mordan barked, Aunt Maroossya laughed and the logs in the stoves crackled and shot sparks.

Soon, Uncle Kolya came home from the Arsenal. He kissed me, took me by the shoulders and gave me a shake.

'You're not to let it get you down,' he said. 'You'll see, we'll have a wonderful time.'

At Uncle Kolya's I began gradually to thaw out. As usually happens, my memory pushed what was unpleasant aside. It was as if it were cutting damaged bits out of a cloth and joining the rest together—the autumn in the Crimea and this rowdy echoing Russian winter began to make a continuous whole.

I tried not to think of what had happened in Kiev in between.

Shipwreck

I preferred to think about Alushta, the three plane trees and Lena. I even wrote her a letter, but I didn't have the courage to post it. It seemed to me very stupid and, however hard I tried, I couldn't write a clever one.

21
Artillerymen

The artillery officers at the Bryansk Arsenal had nicknamed Uncle Kolya 'Colonel Vershinin'. He did indeed—with his lively dark eyes and his small black beard—even outwardly recall Chekhov's Vershinin, or at any rate the image we had of him.

Like Vershinin, Uncle Kolya believed in, and was fond of talking about, a brighter future and was gentle and ebullient. But unlike him, he was an excellent metallurgist and the author of many learned articles on the properties of various metals. These he translated into French, which he possessed to perfection, and published in the Paris *Revue de Metallurgie*. They appeared in Russia as well, but much later than in France. At the time when I came to Bryansk, he was enthusiastically absorbed in the production of Damascus steel.

His zest for life was remarkable. He was interested in everything. He subscribed to almost all the literary journals, played the piano beautifully, knew a lot about astronomy and philosophy and was a witty and indefatigable conversationalist.

The most devoted of Uncle Kolya's friends was Rumyantsev, a bearded captain, who looked like Fet, except that he had bright red hair, weak eyes and a kindly disposition. No part of his army uniform ever sat on him properly, and even the schoolboys in Bryansk teased him about his sloppy appearance.

It was hard to get a quick impression of him. Wreathed in tobacco smoke and shyly hidden in the darkest corner of the room, he was even hard to see as he sat huddled over a chess board, absorbed in a problem. If he succeeded in solving it he rubbed his hands and burst into a peal of laughter.

He seldom took part in a general conversation, only clearing his throat and screwing up his eyes as he listened to other people talking. But if the subject were politics—say, the Duma, or the strikes—he came to life at once and voiced highly subversive opinions.

He was unmarried and his three sisters lived with him. All were short, had cropped hair and wore pince-nez. All smoked and wore stiff black skirts and grey blouses on which, as though by agreement, a watch was fixed at exactly the same spot by a safety-pin.

The sisters were always hiding someone in Rumyantsev's flat— a student, or a man in a black cloak, or a woman as austere-looking as themselves. Uncle Kolya warned me never to breathe a word about anyone who might be staying at the Rumyantsevs'.

Apart from Rumyantsev and his sisters, a frequent visitor at Uncle Kolya's was Staff-Captain Ivanov, a meticulously clean little man with a neat blond beard and a high thin voice.

Like most bachelors, Ivanov was in need of a home, and scarcely an evening passed without his coming in for a chat. Each time, as he removed his coat and his sword-belt in the hall, he explained, blushingly, that he had just happened to be passing by, or that he needed to consult my uncle about something to do with the service —after which he stayed until midnight.

I was grateful to Ivanov for breaking me of my habit of being ashamed of doing simple things for myself.

One day I met him in the market; he was buying potatoes and cabbages.

'Could you help me to get these into the cab?' he asked me. 'Peter is ill, so I have to do everything myself.' (Peter was his batman.)

As we were carrying a heavy sack full of cabbages over to the cab, we met a pretty girl who was my German teacher at school. In reply to my bow, she stared, giggled and turned away. I blushed.

'You shouldn't let it worry you,' said Ivanov. 'It's not as if you were doing something wrong. My recipe for dealing with people who stare at me is to stare straight back. It's most effective.'

We got into the cab, by now piled high with vegetables, and drove along the main thoroughfare, Moscow Street. We came across a lot of people we knew including General Sarandinaki, the head of the Arsenal, driving past in his carriage and pair.

Every one of them grinned when they saw us, but Ivanov

looked them straight in the eye, embarrassing them so much that they stopped laughing and actually ended by giving us a friendly nod of greeting. The General even stopped his carriage and offered to lend Ivanov his batman. But Ivanov politely refused, saying that he could manage his simple chores quite well by himself. The General raised his eyebrows, gave his coachman's back a slight prod with his black scabbard, and the grey horses set off at a trot.

'You see how simple it is,' said Ivanov. 'I never believe in being defeated by prejudice.'

I knew he was right, of course, but I hated being stared at, all the same. The habit was too ingrained.

I used to catch myself out in a terror of behaving differently from others, and in being ashamed of my poverty and trying to hide it from my classmates.

Mama regarded the change in our fortunes as the greatest of tragedies and did everything in her power to conceal it from her friends. Everyone knew that my father had deserted his family, but if anyone asked her about it, she invariably replied that he was only away on a short trip and that everything was going well with us. She sat up for nights on end, mending and altering our clothes for fear that 'people might notice' the signs of our destitution. Her courage had forsaken her and her timidity had communicated itself to us.

As we were driving uphill to Ivanov's house, the cabbage sack fell over on its side, spilling the cabbages. To the delighted shouts of the street-boys, they went rolling and bouncing down the road. The driver pulled up and we started picking them up.

I suppose I must have gone scarlet, because Ivanov gave me a glance and said:

'I'll do it. Why don't you go home now?'

If before, I had felt ashamed of picking up cabbages in front of the passers-by, now I felt so ashamed of myself that tears came to my eyes. I threw myself on the remaining cabbages in a frenzy and, in passing, cuffed the ears of a small boy, the son of Samokhin, the local merchant, who had been dancing about on the pavement, shouting:

> '*A highschool boy has come to grief,*
> *Look, he's lost a cabbage leaf.*'

Young Samokhin ran away home, rubbing his eyes and howling.

Judging by the sly expression on Ivanov's face, I felt sure that he had spilled the cabbages on purpose.

After this incident, I went to the other extreme and began positively to show off. Every morning I went out with a wooden shovel to clear the snow in front of the house, I split firewood, carried the logs, made up the fires and in general, so far from avoiding them, begged to do the chores. For a long time young Samokhin hid in a gateway and yelled 'Blue Steak' whenever he saw me (we were called 'blue steak' on account of the colour and shape of our school caps), but it no longer affected me in the least.

The impression made on me by Ivanov's practical sermon on the art of living was reinforced by those of Karavayev, a narrow-chested Lieutenant-Colonel who had founded the first consumers' co-operative in Bryansk and ran a grocery shop in Bolkhov Street. He worked in it himself, fetching the goods and trading over the counter in the narrow hut which served as the premises.

His undertaking produced a commotion among the merchants of Bryansk and the head of the Association of Traders sent letters denouncing him to the Artillery Staff-Headquarters in Petersburg. But the Bryansk intellectuals as well as the workers at the Arsenal stood firmly behind him. The denunciations did no good and the shop flourished and grew more prosperous day by day.

We all helped Karavayev in turn and he took me on as his regular assistant.

I spent almost all the leisure I had in the shop, breaking open the smelly cases of groceries and weighing out flour, sugar and salt, while Karavayev, wearing a coarse apron, like a blacksmith's, on top of his elegant uniform, worked with despatch, cracked jokes with the customers and told me interesting stories about where the different groceries came from.

The shop handled goods from every part of the country— tobacco from Theodosia, wines from Georgia, caviar from Astrakhan, lace from Vologodsk, glassware from Malsk, mustard from Sarepta and chintz from Ivanovo-Voznesensk. It had a smell of herring brine and soap, and, more powerful than any other, a wonderful smell coming from the fresh sacking kept in the storeroom at the back.

At the end of the day, Karavayev locked and bolted the door and we had tea. The kettle jiggled on the iron stove and I fetched honey cakes called *zhamki* from the wooden locker while Karavayev split a sugar loaf with a flat Japanese bayonet, sending blue sparks flying from the sugar.

There was always someone who dropped in to tea—Ivanov or Rumyantsev's sisters, or Aunt Maroossya.

Ivanov would sit down on an empty case and, without taking off his coat or even his gloves, start proving to Karavayev that Russia hadn't reached the stage of co-operatives. Karavayev coughed, choked, flapped his arms and shrugged his shoulders at Ivanov's arguments.

Aunt Maroossya always bought home-made biscuits and cakes.

The Rumyantsev sisters sipped their tea from their saucers and flashed their pince-nez. They called Karavayev a Don Quixote and said that groceries were a triviality and co-operatives did no good because what the country needed was a great upheaval.

At this Karavayev started to jingle his spurs and to sing *Malbrouk s'en vat-en-guerre*, and the sisters called him a reactionary and went away.

In the early spring, the shop burned down. It was a case of bare-faced arson—the door had been broken in and paraffin poured over the shelves. The entire town knew it to be the work of the rival shopkeepers, but the investigation dragged on and led nowhere. Karavayev lost weight and his cough got worse. Waving his arms and shrugging his shoulders at the cough he said:

'*Finita la comedia*—only an upheaval will do Russia any good. Let the whole country get up on its hind legs, then we'll get somewhere.'

The losses caused by the fire were enormous. They were covered with difficulty by the members of the co-operative, mostly workers from the Arsenal or Karavayev's fellow officers. The astonishing thing was that the largest share of the debt was assumed by Staff-Captain Ivanov. A thrifty man, he had put aside several thousand roubles over his years of service and he now gave almost the whole of this money to Karavayev.

I spent the spring and summer in this artillerymen's united family. But the pain and bitterness of my experience in Kiev remained with me. My parents were always in my mind and I sometimes felt ashamed of living in my uncle's hospitable house where the mood was always happy and equable. The basement in

Cellar Street seemed even drearier by contrast. I pictured to myself the cold rooms, the empty table, its cloth littered with breadcrumbs. Mama's troubled face and Dyma pale and exhausted by tutoring.

I seldom heard from Mama and never from Dyma or Galya. Sometimes I wondered if Mama could perhaps no longer afford the postage stamps. I ought to do something to help her, but I couldn't think of anything to do.

I could not get used to the school in Bryansk where I was very much younger than any of my classmates. More and more, I felt homesick for my old high school in Kiev and in the end I wrote to the Latin teacher, Suboch, who had been my form master. I told him frankly all that had happened to me and asked him if he could arrange for me to go back. The reply came almost by return.

'As from the beginning of the school year in September,' he wrote, 'there is a vacancy for you at the school. You will be in my form. You won't have to pay anything and you can keep yourself by teaching. I can put you on to several coaching jobs, so that you will be independent: it means living modestly, of course, but at least you won't be a burden to anyone. Try not to worry too much about what you have been through—*tempora mutantur et nos mutamur cum illis*—let's hope we change for the better.'

I read this briskly efficient note and was terribly moved. I realised how deeply affectionate it was but I also realised that from now on I must make my life by my own efforts and without relying on anyone.

The realisation alarmed me, even though I was almost sixteen.

22
Kean

Posters had been put up on the hoardings, announcing the arrival of Orlenov, a Moscow actor who was on tour in the provinces.

The announcements were printed on very thin paper with a rough surface. The paste soaked through them and the goats tore them off the boards and ate them, going about with yellow strips hanging from their mouths, on which could be read in bold print the words 'Genius' and 'Dissipation'.

From such of the posters as had escaped destruction, we learned that Orlenov was appearing in the character of the English actor Kean, in a play entitled *Kean, Genius and Dissipation*.[25] My uncle took seats for us well in advance, and for days we could talk of nothing but Orlenov.

The play was being put on at the Summer Theatre. This was a wooden building which stood in the Municipal Gardens, its pink paint was peeling off its walls. For years layer upon layer of advertisements had been pasted on them; now they hung in thick, faded, rain-washed tatters.

For a long time the theatre had been boarded up. Bats flew out from under its eaves at dusk; girls who were dressed in white, shrieked at sight of them—there was a superstition that bats will fasten on to any white surface and can never be prised loose.

The abandoned theatre looked mysterious and romantic. I was sure that in its empty hall and dressing rooms, ribbons and tubes of grease paint, withered bouquets and yellowing sheets of music lay scattered about to this day—mementoes of the time when, according to local tradition, a touring company had put on a season of light opera.

I liked imagining those far off days, when young women with

rouged cheeks and blackened eyelids had tripped along the creaking boards from their dressing rooms to the stage, holding up their velvet trains, and impudent lovers had strummed seductively on their guitars, wrenching the hearts of the simple townsfolk with their cruel love songs:

I dreamed about a day which never came
I dreamed of someone who will never come . . .

The old theatre had seen it all—the gypsy girls with lovely voices and the bankrupt country gentlemen who used to gallop sixty miles to hear them sing, the ensigns with black side-whiskers, the merchants in brown bowlers, and their shy brides trembling in pink tulle as fluffy as foam.

For me, the theatre conjured up the thought of July nights gleaming with summer lightning above the tops of the lime-trees, nights which made the blood sing and every hesitation and regret vanish in the flame of a passing love. They were nights when the world could be flung away for a single glance, to the jingling of horse-bells and the shouts of the tipsy coachman—a glance like lightning, flashing black across the sultry night filled with the scent of the lime blossom and the distant rustling of the forest of Bryansk, a dark, impenetrable forest, healing the heart of melancholy and betrayal.

The walls of the theatre held the echoes of long silenced voices and the memories of reckless living, seductions, duels, muffled sobs and fervent passions.

The theatre seemed long dead and shrouded in cobwebs and never destined to be used again.

But it was opened up, swept, dusted and aired; the aisles were carpeted and the velvet upholstery of the boxes was brushed, after which it turned from grey to cherry-red.

Finally the chandelier was lit high up under the roof. Its pendants twinkled, dim and uncertain, but at the first chords of the overture they shuddered, came to life and boldly shone with hundreds of rainbows and tinkling stars.

Elderly ushers in white cotton gloves appeared at the doors. A smell of scent and sweets mingled with a gust of freshness from the garden. A murmur arose, of muffled voices, creaking chairs, jingling spurs, laughter, and the rustling of the programmes decorated with vignettes of lyres and oak leaves.

'Orlenov, Orlenov,' could be heard from every corner of the hall.

Uncle Kolya and Aunt Maroossya took their seats in the box, my uncle in his natty uniform frock coat with its black velvet lapels, my aunt radiating the ashy brilliance of her new grey dress, her hair and her shining grey eyes—it was a long time since she had been to the theatre.

Staff-Captain Ivanov walked calmly down the aisle, small spurs clinking softly on his boots which had pointed toes.

Even Captain Rumyantsev had combed his square red beard and put on a frock coat. His face was hot and he kept reaching into his back pocket for his handkerchief. His three sisters sat in a tight row, their cheeks blazing.

My two friends from Ryovna were there, Volodya Rumyantsev and Pavlya Tennov. Volodya was tucked away in the gallery— there was a seat for him in his brother's box but he had quarrelled with his sisters. Pavlya lounged negligently with a supercilious smile—it was hardly for him, an old Petersburg student, to get excited about provincial theatricals!

My aunt picked a piece of fluff off my collar, smoothed my hair and said:

'Very nice!'

I glanced at myself in the tarnished mirror at the back of the box—I was very pale and so thin that I looked as if I might break in two.

The curtain went up.

I had seen a lot of good acting in Kiev, but the acting of the slight, sad, hatchet-faced man on the stage was miraculous. With every intonation and gesture he revealed more and more of the greatness of Kean, of his sickness and of his nobility. When he exclaimed in his ringing voice, 'the arrow has struck, the deer is wounded', the whole of his despair and need for mercy rang out in that passionate cry.

I was trembling by the time the stage quarrel began between the actors in the audience. I wept when the curtain was lowered and the old English stage-manager came out and announced brokenly, 'The sun which shone over England has set. The great actor Kean has become insane.'

Aunt Maroossya turned to me, tapped me on the hand and was

beginning to say something jokingly, when she gave an exclamation of astonishment and rose to her feet. Uncle Kolya looked round and also got up.

The whole auditorium was rocking with applause.

I turned. Behind me stood my father, as tired as ever and with the same affectionate, sad smile on his face, but with his hair gone completely white. Everything spun round before my eyes and turned black. My father caught me in his arms.

When I came to my senses, I was lying on the small divan at the back of the box. Someone had undone my collar, water was running down my chin and my aunt was bathing my temples with eau-de-Cologne. My father raised me by the shoulders, made me sit up and kissed me.

'Sit still for a bit, you'll be all right in a moment,' he said. 'Didn't you get my telegram?'

While Orlenov, exhausted, was taking his calls and being showered with flowers, my father told us briefly that he had found a job at the railway works in Bezhitsa, only six miles from Bryansk. He had just arrived, called at Uncle Kolya's and, finding no one in, had followed us to the theatre.

'How is Mama?' I asked him.

'Mama?' he repeated vaguely. 'Oh, by the way, I must give you a letter from her. Mama doesn't want to come to Bezhitsa. She's going to Moscow with Dyma, perhaps for good. She's taking Galya with her, of course.'

'And me? Did she say anything?'

He thought for a moment.

'I don't think so. But then I saw very little of her. I expect it's all in her letter. Here you are, read it.'

I quickly read the letter. The applause was still continuing. The letter was short and dry.

Mama wrote that I must stay at Uncle Kolya's for the time being, until her own life had taken more shape. There was nothing very cheerful she could tell me at the moment. She was moving to Moscow next month, in July, and she wanted me to spend the rest of the summer in Bryansk, though I could go to my father in Bezhitsa if I preferred—but on the whole, she would feel happier and easier in her mind if I remained at Uncle Kolya's. 'We'll be passing through Bryansk on our way to Moscow—unfortunately we can't stop, but I'll send you a telegram and you'll come and see us at the station, then we can talk things over.'

After I had finished reading, I heard Aunt Maroossya laughing and saying to my father:

'We won't give him up to anyone, you know—not even to you, Georgy Maximovich.'

'Not for anything,' said Uncle Kolya. 'But we'll have a talk about it afterwards, shall we, Georgy?'

'Yes, let's,' agreed my father.

We went out through the Municipal Gardens where the incandescent lights were hissing among the trees and the brass band was playing a dashing military march—blaring and thumping for all it was worth, as though delighted that the play was over and it could make as much noise as it liked.

We got into the carriage and started downhill, the horses picking their steps.

I was feeling discouraged by Mama's letter. Evidently my parents hadn't made it up, but why did she have to write to me so coldly? Was she beginning to forget me? Did anybody want me?

My father was busy talking to Uncle Kolya. Why hadn't he asked me anything about myself? I had plenty of troubles I wanted to talk to him about. Perhaps if I could get them off my chest, I could cope with them better.

Everybody liked me and was nice to me at Uncle Kolya's—not only my uncle and aunt but their friends as well—yet I never ceased to feel a weight on my mind; I couldn't tell them about for it fear of hurting their feelings, and I did my best to conceal it.

The words of Suboch's letter came back to me—that it was in my power to stop being a burden to others. Everything became crushingly clear to me. He meant that I was a burden to all of them. My father had his own life. Did I even know if he was going to live in Bezhitsa by himself?

As for Mama—no doubt it was because of Galya that she had become so easily reconciled to the idea of giving me up. Galya was going blind and the doctors could do nothing to help her. It was driving my mother desperate. She was completely engulfed in Galya's misfortune. Perhaps there was simply no room in her for anything except her raging pity for Galya.

A dusty moon hung over the city. The iron roofs, flooded by

its light, looked as if they were wet with rain. Aunt Maroossya leaned over to me and asked:

'May I see the letter?'

I gave it to her. She folded it up very small and tucked it inside her glove, fastening the mother-of-pearl button over it.

My head had started to ache. The pain was so bad that it brought tears to my eyes.

'What's the matter?' asked Aunt Maroossya.

'I've got a bad headache.'

'I'm sorry. I expect it's all been too much for you.'

When we got home I was sent to bed. I lay listening to my father talking to my uncle and aunt in the dining-room and kept wondering when he would come in at last, to say goodnight.

The night air from the window was making me drowsy. As I was falling asleep, I heard Orlenov cry out in a tormented voice in the dining-room, 'The arrow has struck, the deer is wounded,' and immediately after that, very gentle music somewhere far off, on the very edge of the night, slowly dying away in the distance, as though leaving me regretfully, with a last lingering, caressing look.

Then Aunt Maroossya said: 'You've got a boy who isn't strong, it's been too much for him.'—'Who has?' I asked. 'You?'—'Go to sleep, I'll stay with you,' said my aunt's voice. 'Will you pour out the tea, Kolya?' Teaspoons went round and round, tinkling against the glasses, spinning faster and faster. They made me giddy and I felt myself falling. I fell a very long way down and I forgot everything on the way.

For several days I was ill in bed, with a fever and a headache. Meanwhile, my father left for Bezhitsa.

As soon as I was well again, Uncle Kolya took me to see him.

Bezhitsa was a dreary, rain-soaked factory settlement, with crooked birch trees growing in the back yards. The soil was mixed with porous slag from the furnace. The factory chimney smoked.

The house and the flat smelled of coal dust. The furniture was dingy. No one shared the flat with my father.

We found him reading an encyclopædia. He was delighted to see us.

'I realise it's no place for Kostik,' he said to my uncle. 'It's boring and lonely and uncomfortable. I won't stick it out myself for very long.'

'Then what will you do?' asked my uncle sternly.

'Go somewhere else. I don't much care. Life is a bit of a mess. It's my own fault, of course.'

I sat looking at him. He was a different person from the one I remembered in 1905, or still further back, in Gorodishche, or Gelendzhik, or in Vrubel's hotel room. It was as though the one I remembered had been himself and this one were his twin brother who hadn't made a success of his life.

23
The Highway

Here it was at last, the first touch of autumn.

At the back of my uncle's house there was an old apple orchard on a steep hill-slope. Its hollow trees and toppling fences were covered in lichen. Hardly anyone ever went into it except myself.

I used to take a note book with me and go and lie under the trees and write poetry. Very bad poetry it was, as I remember, for in it everything was dissolved in a vague melancholy blur. Busy ants scuttled about on the page, and dead twigs dropped down on it. The sky, deep and transparent, sparkled above the orchard. The wind swept the sky clean and piled up the clouds on the farther bank of the river. I once tried to count them but stopped, dazzled and giddy, when I got to two hundred. The autumn was as yet only giving the first warning signs of its approach—a dry leaf on a bench or a small green caterpillar letting itself down on a cobweb just above my head.

I had spent the whole of the summer in Bryansk, at Uncle Kolya's. During the holidays I used often to go and see him at the Arsenal, either at his laboratory or at the foundry workshops.

I enjoyed watching the steam hammer at work. Captain Ivanov told me he had known a foundry worker at the Obukhov works, who could stand a tumbler upside down, put a walnut on it and crack the nut with a two-ton hammer without breaking the glass.

I liked everything about the Arsenal—the low buildings dating back to Catherine the Great, the yards overgrown with weeds and cluttered up with iron castings, the lilac bushes outside the walls of the workshops; the shiny, greasy copper cylinders of the old steam engines, and the smell of alcohol in the laboratory, the bearded foundry workers and the clear fountain of bluish artesian water from a well in front of the entrance.

I was soon to say goodbye to all this—the foundry and Bryansk and Uncle Kolya's friendly and comfortable house—perhaps for a very long time.

I was going to Kiev in the autumn. This had been finally settled at the family council held in Mama's compartment at Bryansk station, when she was on her way to Moscow with Dyma and Galya. I went to the station with my uncle and aunt.

Mama looked much older, and her voice sounded apologetic when she spoke to my uncle, as if she were trying to justify herself in his eyes.

Galya was by now almost completely blind, and she was getting hard of hearing as well. When anyone spoke to her, she peered through the thick lenses of her spectacles, trying to make out who it was, and then answered off the point. Dyma was gloomy and self-possessed.

Mama hugged me, looked me over from head to foot and said I was looking much better; she sounded disappointed.

Galya kept repeating: 'Kostik, where are you? Oh, you're here. I can't see you.'

Aunt Maroossya, talking very fast, said it was madness for me to go to Kiev, though of course she didn't know and it was not her business to meddle in our affairs, but . . .

Uncle Kolya stopped her with a warning glance.

Mama made no reply. She was watching the platform through the window, her eyes black with anger.

'At last!' she said. 'Better late than never!'

My father came hurrying along. He had just arrived, by the workers' train from Bezhitsa. He was wearing a black suit, shiny with age.

The second bell went as soon as he had got into the train. We began to say goodbye. Father kissed Mama's hand and said:

'I'll make myself responsible for Kostik, Manya. I'll send him enough for his living expenses every month.'

'I hope you do,' said Mama. 'Try to remember this at least—it isn't much—I beg of you.'

Dyma coldly took his leave of him. Galya fumbled for his face with her hands. Father turned so white that even his eyes seemed to grow pale.

The third bell rang and we got out. Mama said to me through the window that I could be sure she would come to see me in Kiev next winter.

The train started. My father stood with his head bared, watching the wheels. He didn't want to come to Uncle Kolya's with us and refused on the pretext that he had some pressing work and was obliged to take the first train back.

My uncle and aunt were silent during the drive home. My aunt was biting the edge of her handkerchief; finally she looked up at Uncle Kolya and said:

'Honestly, I can't understand it. How can they possibly . . .'

My uncle stopped her with a frown and a glance in my direction.

I sat feeling ashamed of our family troubles and of the nuisance they were being to others besides ourselves. My one longing was to get quickly away to Kiev and forget all about it. It was better to be alone than to live in this fatiguing and bewildering tangle of mutual hurts and resentments. I wished August would come soon.

At last it came, with falling leaves and sullen rains. The morning I was leaving, there was a blustering wind scattering the drizzle. The wet coaches of the Moscow-Kiev train were already at the station when we arrived. My father had promised to see me off but he didn't come.

Uncle Kolya stood about, making simple little jokes. Aunt Maroossya slipped an envelope into my pocket, saying: 'Read it on the way.'

When the train moved, she turned aside. Uncle Kolya took her by the shoulders and turned her round. She gave me a smile and again turned away her face.

The raindrops sliding down the window prevented me from seeing anything. I pulled the window down and leaned out. Uncle Kolya and Aunt Maroossya were still on the platform, waving to me. Steam was drifting to the ground. Very far away, at the back of the train, I could see a clear strip of sky. Over there the sun had come out. I took it as a good omen.

I got the envelope out of my pocket. There was some money in it and a note:

'Look after yourself. You are now by yourself on the highway of life, so don't forget your provincial relations—they love you very dearly and are always there to help you.'

24
Wild Alley

Borya was still living at the Progress Boarding House near the station. He gave me a friendly though patronising welcome.

'Full marks to you for deciding to stand on your own feet. You'd better stay with me for a while. Then we'll find you something better. You certainly won't want to live here.'

'Why?'

'You'll see.'

I soon saw. The moment Borya had gone to the Polytechnic, a puffy-looking young man with a face like sour cabbage appeared in the room; hanging on him were a dusty student's jacket and green trousers baggy at the knees; his bulging expressionless eyes slowly took in the room, the food-shelf and myself.

'Count Potocki,' he introduced himself. 'Your brother's closest friend. Former student at the Polytechnical Institute—left it on grounds of ill health.'

'Oh, what's wrong with you?' I asked with sympathy.

'Everything,' said Count Potocki, scooping a handful of Borya's cigarettes from the box on the table. 'I suffer unutterably. As a result I failed in my examinations three years running. The examiner was Professor Paton. Do you know Paton?'

'No.'

'A savage beast!' Potocki swiped the salami off the table and slipped it into his pocket. 'No sympathy whatsoever with anyone who has ambition. There's only one thing that does me any good —ordinary creosote—but my people have held up my allowance so naturally I've run out of cash and I can't go to the chemist's. Would you consider it?'

'Consider what?' I asked, puzzled.

173

'All right, all right,' Potocki said with a good-natured smile. 'I'll stop fooling. What I dropped in for was to ask Borya to lend me three roubles, but I've missed him. You wouldn't have it?'

'Of course!' I dived into my pocket. 'Three roubles, you said?'

'Ah, my dear young man,' exclaimed Potocki in distress. 'If it's a lout who wants to borrow money from you, he'll always ask for more than he needs, but if it's an honest man, he'll ask for too little. If I were a lout, God forbid, I'd have said twenty roubles; as it is, I told you three. You'll ask me which is the correct figure. As usual the truth lies in-between. Twenty minus three makes seventeen, divide by two—eight and a half, say nine to round it off. So shall we say nine?'

I gave him ten. He took them very strangely. I didn't actually see him handle the notes—they dissolved in the air.

All this time the door had been creaking on its hinges; it now flew open and a little woman in a pink dressing gown whirled into the room, her heels clicking loudly. Her slippers were too large for her.

'Why?' she cried out passionately. 'Why give money to this monster? Give!' She turned on Potocki, clutching his sleeve.

The seam cracked and split. Potocki tore himself free and raced for the landing; the woman dashed after him, her heels going off like pistol shots.

'Give!' she screamed. 'Give me five roubles! Three at least! Two!'

But the Count was down the stairs and out into the street in a flash. The woman leaned against the wall and sobbed, her voice unpleasantly artificial.

Lodgers poked their heads out of every door. This had the advantage of letting me see them all at the same time. A youth in a lilac shirt came out of his room, doing up his pink celluloid collar.

'Madame Gemenük,' he shouted imperiously. 'Kindly take steps!'

The landlady, a stout woman with dark, languid eyes, went up to the woman in the dressing gown and said in an unexpectedly clear and vicious voice:

'Back to your room. And stop this noise. Or you'll end up in the police station, my word of honour as a woman.'

Wild Alley

The other went quietly back to her room, while the corridor continued to buzz with gossip about the Count.

When Borya came in and I told him about the incident, he commented that I had got off cheaply and advised me to be less gullible in future. Count Potocki had never been a count, a Potocki or a student—he was a clerk at the law court who had been dismissed for drunkenness.

'I've put the fear of God into them,' he added, 'so they leave me alone. But they'll try every possible trick on you. You'd better just avoid them. The house is full of riff-raff.'

'Why do you stay?'

'I'm used to it,' he said. 'They don't worry me.'

A month later, Borya found me a room 'with board' in Wild Alley, at the flat of a Panna Koslovskaya, an old lady who knew Mama.

My father had sent me one instalment of my monthly allowance, and I reckoned that, even if he never sent me another I could live on what I had for three months before I started giving lessons.

The only other people in the flat were Panna Koslovskaya herself and her son Romuald, a lieutenant in the Infantry. The rooms were small, the floors tacky with cheap paint; the windows looked out on a garden in which all but a couple of trees had been cut down—in winter it served as a skating rink. Fir saplings were then stuck into the snow drifts along the edges of the garden to protect it from the wind. They soon went yellow. It was only a cheap rink used by the children in the neighbourhood. It didn't even have a band—only a gramophone with an enormous purple horn.

Wild Alley was indeed wild. It was a cul de sac ending in a waste lot buried under snow drifts and mounds of cinders. The cinders gave off greyish wisps of smoke. There was always a smell of burning.

I decorated the walls of my tiny room with portraits of Byron, Lermontov and Victor Hugo. At night I read by the light of a kitchen lamp which only fell on the desk and the portrait of Hugo. The old man gazed at me sadly, his head supported on his hand, his wrist emerging from a round, starched cuff. He seemed to be saying: 'Well, young man, what next?'

I was reading his *Les Misérables* and enjoying his furious excursions into history almost as much as the plot of the novel.

I got through a lot of books that winter. Reading was an escape from a loneliness I found it hard to get used to. I remembered our life in Nikolsk-Botanical Street, Lena, the artillerymen, the fireworks in the old Ryovna park—I had always had a lot of people in my life, now I was living in a void. The lamp hissed softly on the table, and for some reason the sound intensified my feeling of solitude.

But after a few months I got over the hump. I noticed that the worse the appearance of reality, the more conscious I became of such good as there was underneath it.

I was beginning to realise that the good and evil in life lie side by side and that the good can shine through a fog of lies, destitution and misery, like a sunset at the end of a rainy day shining behind clouds and lighting them up.

I was trying hard to find signs of good and naturally I often found them. Sometimes they caught my attention unexpectedly, like the gleam of Cinderella's glass slipper below the ragged edge of her drab grey skirt, or her gentle, attentive regard meeting mine in a crowded street. 'Don't you recognise me?' it said. 'These rags are only a disguise. When I take them off, I'll be a princess. Life is full of the unexpected, I assure you. You mustn't be afraid.'

That winter, my head was full of such muddled ideas.

I was at the start of my way but I felt I knew it all to the end. I had read a poem by Fet and I took it as a prediction:

> *Out of the realm of blizzards, ice and snow,*
> *How fresh and pure your month of May leaps forth.*

I read this poem out loud to myself, and Panna Koslovskaya listened from behind her partition wall. Lieutenant Romuald always came in late and sometimes not at all, so she was glad of the sound of a human voice.

25
Autumn Battles

Both teachers and school friends gave me as warm a welcome as I had received from Borya. Even Father Tregubov referred to the Prodigal Son in a manner befitting the occasion.

Suboch cross-examined me about my living arrangements and promised to find me a teaching job within a month. Inspector Bodyansky emitted the loud snort which he used as a terror weapon against the new boys and said:

'Found guilty but with extenuating circumstances. Go to your classroom and keep out of trouble.'

But I was destined to get into trouble again.

Every form in the school was divided in two sections, an aristocratic and a democratic one. The boys in Section One were mainly blockheads who were sons of generals, landowners, important officials and financiers; those in section two were mostly plebeians, Jews and Poles. The division was clearly deliberate and ordained from above.

Between the two sides there was a ceaseless enmity which usually only expressed itself in sarcasm and recrimination. But, traditionally, a pitched battle was fought once a year, during the autumn term. The whole school took part in it except the bottom and the top forms (the seniors were so grown-up that they would have lost face by fighting). Only very occasionally was there a Sabbatical year.

In order to evade the vigilance of the authorities, the date was changed year by year, but the supervisors always knew by some warning signs of the approach of D-Day. They became increasingly nervous and used every form of cunning to prevent the engagement. A whole class, suspected of instigating it, was dismissed immediately after the first period of study, or two or three classes at a time were sent on a picnic, or all the exits to the garden were suddenly blocked. But none of these devices worked: the battle took place on the appointed day, always during the midday break.

Individual boys were 'exempted' from fighting by their class. They were those who either were not strong enough or, like myself, had a genuine aversion even for the spontaneous, daily outbreaks of fisticuffs, and still more for organised warfare. There was no point in conscripting them—they would in any case have been useless.

To distinguish them from the rest, they were required to remove their belts for the duration of the battle. It was an iron rule that, on this condition, they were left unmolested. All the same, they preferred to keep out of the way and usually watched from the classroom window.

The battle was heralded by a sudden dead silence throughout the building. In a few seconds the corridors were deserted; everyone was in the grounds.

Then came a menacing, muffled roar (Inspector Bodyansky blenched and crossed himself) and, through the clouds of dust raised by the advancing formations, a hail of conkers whistled like grape-shot.

Kazimir, Maxim, Coldwater—all the proctors—sprinted into the grounds, followed by a jostling crowd of supervisors. The corridors echoed to the banging of doors and the excited voices of teachers. Inspector Bodyansky ran down the stairs, pulling on his coat and slamming on his hat as he hastened to the battlefield.

On one occasion Father Olendsky, the Catholic chaplain, came racing after him. We climbed on the windowsill, quite expecting him to raise his crucifix aloft and appeal for an armistice. But instead of this, the good father rolled up the sleeves of his cassock and went to work with remarkable force and dexterity, separating the combatants and flinging them to right and left. The boys bounced off him like tennis balls. He must have had an excellent training as a child. We saw him later, on his way back to the teachers' common room; judging from his happy, flushed face, his part in the battle, even though only as a peacemaker, had given him enormous satisfaction.

As soon as the fighting began, all the doors into the garden were thrown open, to enable the proctors and supervisors to drive the boys back into the house in batches, as they caught them.

'It's begun!' squealed the street boys outside.

Just what had begun, it was difficult for the onlookers in the classroom to make out. Dust flew, branches cracked on the trees, the air filled with yells and the sound of trampling, as though two herds of elephants were stampeding each other.

Then at last—obliterating all else, echoing through the corridors and swelling to the volume of thunder—there arose a shout of triumph. This meant that the second section had won. I don't remember a single case of the first section coming out on top.

Nearly always in the front rank of the victorious army was to be found a boy with a snub nose and a challenging expression—the future writer Mikhail Bulgakov[26]. He cut into the battle wherever the danger was at its height, and victory followed him, crowning him with a shining wreath of his own dishevelled locks.

The vanquished hated him and once tried to discredit him after a battle by pretending that he had used his steel belt buckle as a knuckle-duster, but no one believed this wicked slander—not even Inspector Bodyansky.

For the first and last time, I was myself on this occasion a combatant. I had a score to settle with Khavin, the son of a broker on the Kiev stock exchange. The unconscious cause was Panna Koslovskaya.

Khavin was a detestable, overgrown youth who, when he sat in his parents' box at the Opera, languidly blew kisses to girls in the audience. He drove to school in a carriage and pair, and had nothing but contempt for the plebeians in section two.

Almost every Sunday I used to take Panna Koslovskaya to her Catholic Church. The old lady could barely see and was afraid to go out by herself, so she accepted my company and the arm I offered her to keep her from stumbling, although it worried her dreadfully to give me so much trouble and, blushing like a girl, she apologised unceasingly. Lieutenant Romuald rarely accompanied her; I suspected him of being ashamed of his mother with her clumsiness and her old-fashioned clothes; at any rate, most Sundays he was 'devilishly busy'.

One Sunday we came face to face with Khavin in the street. He raised one eyebrow in an expression of scornful amazement, looked Panna Koslovskaya up and down, grinned, whistled, snapped his fingers and walked on.

As it happened, the battle took place the following day. As soon as it started, I went into the grounds where Khavin was watching from the side. He was not wearing his belt, neither was I. We had both been exempted. Nevertheless I walked straight up to him and slapped his face. He gave an odd little squeak, and Twerp the supervisor grabbed my arm.

Next day I was summoned by Inspector Bodyansky.

'What is all this?' he asked. 'I could just have understood it if you had been a "conscript" like the rest of your Hottentots. But to go up to a man and strike him on the face out of the blue!— Why?'

'I had my reasons, Pavel Petrovich. I've never fought before in my life, you know that.'

'I see. All the same, you are in danger of losing your scholarship for the rest of the year, so you'd better tell me.'

I refused stubbornly to say anything except that I had felt justified in striking Khavin.

'All right,' said Bodyansky. 'I believe you. We'll consign the incident to oblivion.'

It was the more generous because after each battle he and the Director had to face the School Board and the parents of the battered victims.

'It all comes of your having no respect for authority,' he told us bitterly. 'You with your Ibsens and your Leonid Andreyevs. A nice lot of enlightened young people I've got in my charge! Future pillars of society indeed! Zulus and troglodytes, that's what you are.'

26
Living Languages

The only 'dead' language we learned at school was Latin. This was our main subject. It was taught by our form master Suboch. He looked like a tall thin tom-cat but he was a kind man and we were fond of him in spite of the devastating Latin tests he sprang on us.

Our progress was closely followed by Inspector Bodyansky who repeatedly told us that 'Latin was the greatest achievement in the whole history of language'.

Greek was optional and few people took it. The master was an old Czech who went about covered in a layer of cigarette ash and advanced so slowly down the corridors on his pitifully rheumatic legs that he never arrived for his class on time; he was consequently known as 'Late' instead of by his own name which in Russian meant 'Early'.

Our only 'living' languages were French and German. Both were very badly taught.

The Frenchman, Serremout, had a withered arm and a red imperial. He always brought a batch of oleographs to school with him and hung them on the walls. Most of them illustrated the life of a rural community in an unidentified country: in spring the men ploughed and wore straw hats with fluttering ribbons, while their wives, in tight laced bodices, fed yellow chickens; in summer they mowed and danced round their haystacks, waving branches of dog-rose; in the autumn they threshed in front of toy cottages, and in winter, for want of anything else to do, they skated on a frozen stream. But even these pictures were full of interest compared to others, which were of kittens playing with balls of wool in sparsely furnished, geometrical rooms.

Having hung them up and drawn our attention to them with a

pointer, Serremout asked us in French: 'What do we see in this interesting picture?' We chorused in French that in this interesting picture we could clearly see some *braves paysans*, or a pretty kitten playing with a nice old lady's ball of wool.

This went on for two years until one day the Inspector brought a new French teacher to our classroom—Monsieur Hauvas.

Hauvas had arrived straight from Brittany without knowing a word of Russian, and ours was the first lesson he was giving in this enigmatic country. He was short, fat and so indifferent to what we did that he never took the trouble to lose his temper.

As soon as Bodyansky left him to our mercy, Régamé, a French boy, stood up and told him respectfully in faultless Parisian that it was customary to start every lesson with prayers. Hauvas smiled politely, evidently accepting this as a local eccentricity.

Littauer, who was a Jew but had an excellent knowledge of the Liturgy, then got up and intoned the Prayer before Studies, recited it five times and went on to the Ekthenia, the Creed, the Lord's Prayer and the prayer of St. Ephraim Sirin. Hauvas stood with his head bowed but looking puzzled. 'O Lord,' chanted Littauer, 'deliver us from sloth, despondency, idle chatter and vain ambition.' We repeated the words after him, keeping an eye on the clock. We were afraid that he would run out of prayers, but he went through the Creed once more and concluded by singing 'O Lord, save thy people'.

The bell rang. Hauvas faintly shrugged his shoulders and made for the teachers' common room; his black frock coat glinted in the sun and sailed glossily down the passage.

We were giggling under the cover of our raised desk lids when Inspector Bodyansky rushed in, panting:

'So it's blasphemy now, you louts! Who organised this? You, Littauer!'

'Why me, Pavel Petrovich?' Littauer rose to his feet. 'You know I am a Jew.'

'Oi-oi-oi! Am I to believe your arm would drop off if you made the sign of the cross? Take your books and go home. And ponder the fact that this is the second conduct mark you've lost.'

With Hauvas we plunged into the jungle of irregular verbs. The noble French tongue became a system of dusty rules. We floundered in the mysteries of *accent aigu*, *accent grave* and *accent circonflexe*. In time we came to think of the living language of Flaubert and Hugo as something utterly divorced from what Monsieur Hauvas was teaching us.

The older we grew the more interested we became in French writers and the more anxious to read them in the original. Giving up all hope of ever doing this with our phlegmatic Breton, we learned French on our own or with private tutors, while Hauvas continued to conjugate and to decline, his eyes fixed on the cold Russian snow outside and empty of all expression except nostalgia for an open fire.

We asked him about Balzac and Dumas, Hugo and Daudet, but he told us that such authors were not for schoolboys who were still capable of confusing the future tense with the conditional.

In time we learned that he had a small house in a little Breton town and an old mother who lived in it and bred rabbits, and that Hauvas himself had only come to Russia in the hope of making enough money within a few years to retire, go home and engage in the cultivation of mushrooms which could be sold profitably in Paris. This explained his total lack of interest in both Russian and literature.

Only once did he have a talk with us from the heart. It was a spring day. He was looking forward to his summer holiday in Brittany and feeling relaxed.

Joking gloomily, he told us that man was made for a quiet life and ought therefore to stick to the rules and be content with little.

He then told us of how, as a child, he used to go out with his grandfather and catch lobsters. He sighed thoughtfully and fell silent. The chestnuts outside the window were in full bloom. Spring blew in our faces, with its warm, fresh breath. He gave it a discouraged look and shook his head. He had been flung into an alien world like a plump maybug shaken off its leaf—all because he was poor and could only build the peaceful shelter he wanted for his old age out of the proceeds of his dreary labour. 'Oh well,' he said. 'That's life. We mustn't grumble. Patience is rewarded in the end.'

We said nothing because at that time we were firmly convinced that patience was a form of imbecility.

Many years later, I told the story of Serremout and his oleographs to my friend, the writer, Arcady Gaidar.

Gaidar was overjoyed—he had been taught French by the same system; we could talk of nothing else for days.

We were staying near Ryazan, fishing and taking long walks in the country. 'What do we see in this picture?' Gaidar would suddenly ask me in French, and at once reply: 'We see an inhospitable village and two frustrated travellers shaking its dust from their shoes. We see villagers who have refused to give the travellers three eggs in exchange for a handful of tobacco.'

On our way back to Moscow, by train along the unfrequented line between Tuma and Vladimir, he woke me up in the middle of the night to ask me:

'What do we see in this interesting picture?'

I couldn't see much because the candle flickered in the ceiling-light and sent long shadows scurrying down the carriage.

'We see,' Gaidar explained, 'a railway thief abstracting a pair of felt boots from the basket of a nice old lady.'

With these words, Gaidar—a good-natured giant of a man—leapt from his upper bunk, grabbed a nimble fellow in a check cloth cap by the collar, removed the boots, and told him:

'Go—and never let me set eyes on you again.'

The thief raced down the corridor and jumped out of the moving train.

Our German lessons were more interesting—not because Oskar Theodorovich Johanson was a good teacher but because he sometimes provided us with occupations other than German, such as making copies of his operatic score, 'The Spirit of Tokay'.

Johanson was an elderly and nervous Viennese. He came to school carrying a chair leg—when the noise in class became unbearable, he banged with it on the table and we quietened down.

Johanson's passion was music. He had intended to become a composer but some obscure chapter in his life had made this impossible and he had turned to teaching in disgust. His demands upon our German were minimal. If we hadn't done our homework, he looked at us sadly through his pince-nez and gave us one mark less than if we had.

When I was in the sixth form, Johanson one day left his score in the tram. It was his only copy. He put an advertisement in the newspaper but heard nothing in reply. He stayed away from school for a whole week and when he returned we could hardly recognise him—he was grey in the face and had a torn muffler tied round and round his yellow neck. That day, the silence in the classroom was deathly.

'So, my dear young people,' Johanson began, 'it's all over. My opera was my life's work. It kept me young. It was the music of happiness. You'll ask me where happiness is—it's all around us. In the rustling of trees, in wine, in the voices of birds and women. Everywhere. I once dreamed of becoming a wandering musician. I envied the gypsies. I wished to play at village weddings and in woodmen's cottages. For lovers and for poets, for heroes and for hermits—for those who, though betrayed, have kept their faith in human goodness. It was all there in my music—everything. I hoped that I would die in peace once my opera had been produced in Vienna. I thought: perhaps my old friend, the poet Altenberg will come and sit in his box, looking like a teddy-bear, and listen to it, and tears will come to his eyes. This will be my best reward. And perhaps my opera will be heard by one who has never believed in me.'

Johanson talked and talked, examining his long, thin fingers. He seemed to be intoxicated with grief. His style was always a little inflated and theatrical, but at the moment we were unaware of this. We sat listening, our eyes downcast.

Afterwards Suboch came up to us during the break and said:

'I wanted to warn you to be very considerate to Oskar Theodoro-vich today, he's terribly upset. But I expect you've thought of it yourselves.'

That day the call went out to every form: 'Find Johanson's score at whatever cost.' Who first thought of it, I don't know: but the message was passed from mouth to mouth, and the afternoon found us huddled in knots like conspirators, planning the operation and seething with impatience to begin the search.

The hunt started that night and went on for several days. We questioned tram conductors, we did the round of the markets, we went through the stacks of wrapping paper in the shops. And finally, in the Lukyanovka Market, the opera score turned up.

It was found by an eighth form boy who overheard a market woman complaining that the sheets were no good for wrapping up lard: the ink ran and the customers were annoyed. Thanks to this, only two pages of the score had been torn out.

It was the eighth form that returned it to Johanson. We did not witness the ceremony—we only saw Johanson coming away from the classroom surrounded by the seniors. His face looked bare without its pince-nez, his steps were tottering and two boys were holding him up on either side. Inspector Bodyansky stood at the door of the teachers' common room, smiling and nodding. Johanson fell into his arms and they kissed.

This was in March. Later that spring I received a formal invitation requesting the honour of my presence at the performance of a part of Johanson's opera at the house of one of my friends.

When I arrived on the appointed evening at the house in Bibikov Street, I found the wide staircase brilliantly lit and two large drawing rooms crowded with guests. Most of them were boys from the High School but there were also some schoolgirls and a few grey-headed musicians and actors.

Johanson was not yet there. I waited on the landing to see him arrive. Finally he appeared; slim and youthful in his elegant frock coat, he ran lightly up the stairs and strode into the room. Everyone clapped.

The orchestra, composed of a string quartet and a piano, struck up. I was amazed at Johanson's achievement. It really was the music of happiness or rather of the joy and sorrow of lovers—a sorrow as anguished as that of Tristan and Iseult. It would be hard to convey its qualities of melody and strength.

At the end of the concert, when most of the guests had paid their respects to Johanson and gone, the rest of us stayed to supper and later at night, saw Johanson home. He stopped at a telegraph office on the way, to send a telegram to Vienna. He came out looking a little sad, and told us that he had waited for this joy too long. When happiness is too long awaited, it partly turns to sorrow.

27
'Gentlemen Schoolboys'

No one could yet have predicted what we, 'gentlemen schoolboys' as Bodyansky addressed us, would make of our lives—what, for instance, was in store for Bulgakov.

He was older and left school before me, but I very well remember his extraordinary vitality, the ruthless tongue which made people afraid of him, and the sense he gave us of determination and strength—we felt it in everything he said, however trifling.

He was full of imagined experiences and mystifying hoaxes and jokes. By the time he finished with it, the school in which we led our so familiar, prosy lives, became a world of incredible personages and events.

Any colourless character, such as Twerp the Supervisor, once caught up in the circle of Bulgakov's inventiveness, developed a mysterious double life and grew to the stature of a Sobakevich or a Tartarin—no longer just the Twerp we knew with his puffy alcoholic nose but the hero of ludicrous or monstrous happenings.

Whatever part his imagination touched, it shifted for us just over the edge of the real, actual world around us into the realm of phantasmagoria.

After he left school, we didn't meet again until 1924. By then he was an established writer, but he had remained faithful to Kiev. When I saw his play *The Day of the Turbins*, I immediately recognised the decor of our school and that honest fellow but unspeakable bore, our old proctor Maxim. I could almost hear our Kiev chestnut trees rustling in the wings.

Several of the men who were at school with me have since become well-known writers of fiction, playrights or actors (Kiev has always had a passion for the theatre).

Story of a Life

Could it have been by accident that, in so few years, the school produced so many people who are prominent in literature or art? I don't believe it. Suboch used to tell us that 'nothing in life is an accident except death'. We call a thing an accident when we forget or are too lazy to discover what caused it.

In the case of our generation in Kiev we forget how much our masters taught us, and how good the Kiev theatres were; we forget that, already then, we were all, to a boy, in love with poetry and philosophy; we forget that, in our schooldays, Chekhov and Tolstoy, Serov and Levitan, Skryabin and Kommissarzhevskaya,[27] were still alive.

We forget the revolution of 1905, the student meetings we schoolboys managed to attend, the conversations we overheard, and that Kiev had an old and strong revolutionary tradition of its own. We forget how we sat up reading Plekhanov and Chernyshevsky, and the pamphlets on soggy grey paper bearing the slogans 'Workers of the World Unite' or 'Land and Freedom',[28] how we read Herzen and Kropotkin, the *Communist Manifesto* and the novels of Kravchinsky.

We forget Idzikovsky's famous bookshop, the symphony concerts, the parks, the crisp and radiant Kiev autumn, and the noble solemnity of Latin which accompanied us throughout our school years. We forget the Dnieper, the soft foggy winters, and the rich and gentle Ukraine which encircled the city with its fields of buckwheat, its thatch and its beehives.

To define what exactly was the influence upon us of the sum of all these varied, unrelated things would be impossible, but the influence certainly existed, and it imposed its own poetic structure upon our thoughts and emotions.

We read insatiably. Our understanding of the Russian literary tradition in all its classical simplicity and depth came to us later than our taste for some of the writers of the West, whom we found easier, and who attracted us by their elegance, their tranquillity and their perfection of design. It was easier for us in those days to love the cool transparency of Merimée than the torments of Dostoevsky; Merimée, like Flaubert, was as serene as a summer sky (Dostoevsky was like a thunderstorm which makes you run for cover). And we found the same freedom from doubt in Dickens; and in Hugo; and in Balzac.

'Gentlemen Schoolboys'

Perhaps it was the 'Universal Library' which was partly responsible for our choice of reading. Its yellow paper-backs flooded
the bookshops; for twenty kopecks, you could get anything from
Mont Oriol and *Eugénie Grandet* to *The Wild Duck* and *La Chartreuse
de Parme*, and we bought and read everything with intoxication.

At one time we were utterly carried away by Verlaine, Leconte
de Lille and Théophile Gauthier. We read them both in Russian
and in the original. Their French, at times as elusive as a breath
of scent, at others as hard as steel, acted upon us like witchcraft.

We loved their poetry partly for its music as well as for its
mistiness—as light as a haze on a spring day—and partly because it
created for us an image of the poets themselves—and of Paris.
This poetry was one among the many enchanting associations which
the idea of Paris held for us. Slate roofs, boulevards, rain, street
lights, the sky pink over the Seine at night, and poetry—this was
the Paris of our simple imagination. It was as inconceivable without
poetry as without kisses or barricades.

Later, this poetry paled for me beside the living gold of the
Russian poetic tradition. As we grew older, the hold which Russian
literature—perhaps the most powerful in the world—established
over our minds, made us relegate the literature of the West to a less
prominent though still honoured place.

We were also interested in painting. The painter Gué[29] was an old
pupil of the High School and his name was engraved in gold on the
white marble panel of honour in the Assembly Hall, among those
of others who had passed out with distinction or become famous
later in life; but we disliked his gloomy style and moralising tone.
The delayed vogue of the Impressionists was just coming into its
own.

My friend Shmukler was studying painting with the Kiev
Impressionist Manevich. I loved his pictures of small suburban
houses and gardens, painted in bold thick strokes as though put
on with a palette knife.

I often went to Shmukler's house. His father was a well-known
doctor who treated many poor patients for nothing. As a young
man he had wanted to be an opera singer. For some reason he
failed, but the opera remained the dominating passion of his life.
Everything about the Shmukler home spoke of the opera, not

only the host who was a vast, clean-shaven man with a resounding voice, but the open grand piano, the scattered sheets of hand-written music, the jardinières awaiting floral tributes, the collection of posters and portraits of singers, and the opera glasses with mother-of-pearl handles. Even the incessant noise in the flat was operatic. The shouting at the children and the impassioned arguments, swelling from *moderato* to *allegro* to *forte*, sounded like roulades and recitatives, duets, trios and arias for male, female and child voices; all had their hidden *leitmotif*. Ringing out uninhibitedly like *bel canto*, the Shmukler voices carried from the flat, all the way down the stairs and into the street.

Much as I liked this rumbustious household, I enjoyed still more my visits to my other school friend, a Pole called Fitsovsky, who lived by himself in a small rented room.

A stocky boy with a strand of chestnut hair falling over his forehead, Fitsovsky had an unshakable equanimity and regarded almost everything as an unnecessary fuss.

He had various eccentricities which annoyed the teachers. Thus he evolved a private language with Stanishevsky, another Pole who was his neighbour in the classroom. They commmunicated in pure Russian but, by speaking it very fast and accenting the wrong syllable in each word, made it incomprehensible to everyone else.

Fitsovsky made me learn Esperanto. Invented by the Warsaw oculist Zamenhof, it had the merit of being easy. Newspapers in Esperanto were published in various countries; what interested us in them were the lists of addresses of those who wished to correspond with people abroad.

In time I acquired pen-pals in England, France, Canada and even Uruguay. At first we exchanged picture postcards—views of Kiev in exchange for views of Glasgow, Edinburgh, Paris, Montevideo and Quebec. Then, at my suggestion we widened our scope to portraits of writers and illustrated magazines. The splendid head of Byron which hung on my wall had been sent me by a young English doctor from Manchester. The portrait of Hugo came from a French girl who lived in Orleans. She was full of curiosity and asked me many questions, such as whether it was true that Russian priests wore vestments made of pure gold and that all Russian officers spoke French.

We gathered at Fitsovsky's one evening a week. Very little

was drunk at these parties (all we could afford was a bottle of cheap brandy between us). What we principally did was to play at being Lermontov's hussars, read poetry, argue, make speeches and sing. The party went on into the early hours, and when the dawn came filtering through the cigarette smoke, it seemed to us the dawn of a new life—the remarkable new life which awaited us just outside the door. The best dawns were in spring, when we came out, our heads filled with romantic tales, to find the clean morning air ringing with birds.

The remarkable life awaiting us on the doorstep was elusively connected in our minds with the theatre. We were fascinated by Russian drama and by Polevitskaya who acted Liza in *The Nest of Gentlefolk* and Nastasia in *The Idiot*.

To go to the theatre we needed a signed chit from Bodyansky. He only gave us one a week, but I developed a talent for forging chits and became so good at it that Bodyansky himself could not distinguish his signature from my forgeries.

'You should be sweating at your Latin, not hanging about in the gallery,' he roared at us. 'A nice lot of respectable boys!— Forgers, every one of you!'

After the play we waited for Polevitskaya outside the stage door. She came out, tall and with shining eyes. She smiled at us and got into her sleigh. The horses shook their harness. The bells jingled along Nikolayev Street and died away in its snowy distance.

We scattered and went home through the gathering snow. Our cheeks blazed. We carried our effervescent happiness back with us, along the slippery pavements, and it kept us awake for a long time.

It was in the light of the street lamp flickering on my wall. It was in the armfuls of snow falling and covering the earth. Dimly heard through warm layers of sleep, it sang to me all night, its everlasting song of love and sorrow.

Horses galloped and a sleigh whistled past the house. Who was hurrying where so late at night?

In Lieutenant Romuald's room a guitar string twanged of itself, its vibrations slowly dying away—a silver hair, then a silver cobweb, then nothing.

Thus I lived through that winter, in a state of joyful excitement, in a bustle of days in which the strands of reality and of poetry were inextricably mingled.

By then I was living quite independently. I kept myself by giving lessons and earned enough for my rent, my food and my books. No doubt because I was young, I had not a trouble or a worry on my mind.

28
Royal Visit

Any important visitor to Kiev was invariably shown over our school. It was one of the oldest in Russia. The authorities were proud of its history and of its grand, uncomfortable building, the most notable feature of which was its white marble Assembly Hall with windows at both ends; it remained almost as grandly cold in summer as in winter.

We liked high dignatories to visit us because they nearly always asked the Director to give us two or three days' holiday for the occasion, and the Director always agreed.

But sometimes there was trouble. We believed King Peter Karageorgy of Serbia to be a wicked tyrant who had usurped the Serbian throne after a bloody palace revolution.

The preparations for his visit began a week in advance. We were taught the Serbian national anthem and instructed to shout 'zhivyo' in Serbian instead of the usual Hurrah.

Monsieur Hauvas wrote the text of the welcoming speech which the Director was to make in French. He was very proud of it—he had never written an address to a King before.

The Director—'Butterpate' Tereshchenko—learnt the speech by heart, as any one of us would have done in his place. But Butterpate had a very bad memory and was feeling nervous. He asked our new Inspector Ivanov (Bodyansky had been appointed Director of another high school) to provide him with the services of the best prompter in the school.

We disliked Tereshchenko and refused to tell Ivanov who our best prompter was—let Butterpate get out of his own mess.

In the end we gave in, but only on condition that Borimovich who had been given an unjustly low mark should get a better one. An agreement was reached.

The best prompter was Régamé. He was shown the text and prepared a crib. It opened with the usual '*Sire, permettez nous . . .*' Translated into Russian, the first sentence read curiously as 'Sir, permit us to welcome you within our grey-haired walls.' We were delighted, learned it by heart and recited it in an imitation of Butterpate's voice every time we heard him pass our door.

The school was scrubbed and polished to a festive sheen. On the morning of the royal visit a red carpet was put down on the wide staircase and the chandeliers were lit in the hall although it was a bright day.

We came in our parade dress and were lined up in two rows in the vestibule. Suboch stood beside us with a parade sword buttoned into the pocket of his uniform so that only the gold hilt showed; he smelled of eau-de-Cologne and his pince-nez flashed like a pair of diamonds.

Against one of the marble pillars stood Butterpate, his face white as a sheet and his medals clinking on his tightly buttoned coat.

Cheering broke out in the street where the guard of honour was lined up. It grew louder as the royal carriage approached. The band struck up. The doors flew open. Suboch cast a despairing glance at Régamé and advanced to welcome the King.

The King, a short man with a hooked nose and a grey moustache, wearing a pale-blue coat with silver braiding, came briskly forward. The space between the doors behind him was blue with uniforms and glossy with top hats.

The porter Vassily, a former all-in wrestler, lost his head and, instead of relieving the King of his coat, tried to help him on with it. The King struggled and broke free, his face flushing. An adjutant sprang to his side and took the coat, moving Vassily out of the way with a white gloved hand. Vassily stood at attention, panting, his eyes glazed as though he were drunk.

'*Sire*,' said Butterpate, bowing and signalling urgently with his left hand behind his back—he had forgotten his words. Régamé prompted him with professional smoothness.

The King looked severely at the flushed top of the Director's

194

bald head; he was still breathing heavily after his struggle with Vassily. Then he overheard the prompting and grinned.

The Director somehow stumbled through to the end and, pointing to the narrow aisle between the dark blue rows of school-boy uniforms, invited the King to proceed to the Assembly Hall.

The King moved forward, his suite pouring after him with a clatter of swords on the metal floor and a glitter of epaulettes.

A step behind the King came the martial figure of General Ivanov, Commander of the Kiev area.

Following the suite came the King's ministers bearing their top hats in their hands.

We had plotted a demonstration. As soon as the King stepped into the aisle, we all shouted loudly and in unison—not *zhivyo* but *zhulyo*, which sounded very much the same but meant 'scoundrel' in Russian. The acclamation echoed against 'our grey-haired walls'.

The King walked on unsuspectingly, smiling and nodding.

Suboch paled. General Ivanov clenched his hand behind his back, the white kid glove he held in it shaking with fury. Butterpate stumbled and hurried on.

As the royal party mounted the steps, the school choir on the landing above intoned the Serbian national anthem.

Suboch fixed us with a hard stare; but we were standing at attention with nothing on our faces but the respectful emotions appropriate to the hour. He shrugged his shoulders and turned away.

This was not the end of it. As the procession passed us on the way out, we repeated our performance with the same deafening unanimity. Matushevich, a future opera singer with a deep and powerful voice, gave such a roar that the King swerved away from the blast. But again he noticed nothing wrong and, quickly recovering himself, nodded a polite acknowledgment.

Only when the Serbian Prime Minister who was believed to be a liberal came past, did we change the greeting to a clear and distinct 'Zhivyo Pashich'.

All that happened after the state visit was that twelve of us got a dressing down from the Director and were rusticated for three days. The authorities were clearly afraid of publicity and trying to hush things up. What the purpose of our three day rustication was I never discovered. They were days of undisturbed leisure, reading, walks along the Dnieper and visits to the theatre.

Needless to say, the attempt to hush up the incident proved unsuccessful. We became the envy of the entire school, and indeed of the two other high schools which were never honoured by official visits.

29
A Sad Waste of Time

To this day I am suspicious of people with small round eyes like black olives, such as those of my pupil Maroossya Kazanskaya. Their expression was utterly blank—they lit with curiosity only when a dashing young officer or a lycée student in a coat with a smart beaver collar passed by the window. At sight of either, every piece of knowledge she had painfully acquired—dates, geography, syntax—vanished from her mind.

'They're a decent family but I'm afraid the girl isn't bright,' Suboch had warned me when he found me the job.

The family consisted of Maroossya and her parents—a retired general and his French wife. The General was almost a dwarf, but with a magnificent beard. He was a very clean little officer, with plump hands and watery eyes—but they flashed with anger when he remembered his enemies—the rivals who had outstripped him in the service such as Generals Sukhomlinov, Dragomirov, Kuropatkin and Rennenkampf. Kazansky had retired with the rank of Adjutant General; he had been Commander in various military districts and had given lessons in strategy to Nicholas II before his accession to the thone. 'But at strategy that young man was no good at all,' he used to say. For Kazansky, the last 'real' sovereign had been Alexander III.

He had an excellent library of books on military science, but they were kept under lock and key and I never saw him read any of them. Usually he was either reading *The New Times* or playing patience, a cross little pomeranian curled up on his lap; its eyes were as black as Maroossya's.

When I left the house after my sessions with Maroossya, the General usually accompanied me as far as the Galitsky Market. He enjoyed this daily walk and was much more lively than at home; he joked, laughed, told anecdotes of his army life and stopped to prod the stomach of some junior officer who had sprung to attention to salute him: 'Pull it in, old man. You fellows are all the same, all one ever sees is your stomach.'

His wife addressed him as 'Angel' and the General called her 'Muff'.

Rarely have I seen a more boring woman than Madame Kazanskaya. Blinking tears from her spaniel eyes, she sat endlessly sewing pinafores for Maroossya, or painting purple irises on pink satin ribbons which she gave away as birthday presents to her friends. Some of them hung them on their walls or put them on the little tables in their drawing rooms, or tried to use them as book markers—but for this they were too wide—while the more discriminating kept them out of sight. But still she painted with a compulsive persistence. Her own flat was festooned and swathed in ribbons; they crackled and caught at your fingers whenever you moved. It was enough to make a shy guest come out in a nettle rash.

The flat had lofty ceilings and large windows, but the light in it was always cold and grey, as though the sunshine lost its warmth and sparkle as soon as it came in; it lay on the floor as drab as dusty pieces of paper.

The Kazanskys' outlook on life at first puzzled me. They believed in a deity which had organised the world in a manner beneficial to themselves—a sort of Governor General on a world-wide scale, who kept order in the universe and looked after respectable families.

Their other divinity was Maroossya. They loved her with the morbid love of an elderly couple for an only child. Her whims charmed them, her wishes were sacrosanct; at a frown from her, the General removed his spurs and padded about the flat, sighing, while his wife hastened to the kitchen to prepare the child's favourite soufflé.

Their plans for Maroossya's marriage were their chief subject of conversation. The search for a husband went on unremittingly and became an obsession. Madame Kazanskaya's memory was a bulky ledger filled with the names of all the eligible bachelors in Kiev and the South-West Provinces of Russia.

A Sad Waste of Time

Maroossya went to a private school kept by a Madame Duchinskaya who was highly conscious of the consideration due to the respective social standing of the parents of her pupils. But Maroossya was so backward that even the General's rank was insufficient to keep her from the bottom of her class. Her failed examinations were a recurring family tragedy. Maroossya locked herself in her room and declared a hunger strike. Her mother was convulsed with sobs. Her father hurled himself about the flat, swearing vengeance against 'the Jewish gang' who ran the school. Next morning he dressed in his parade uniform, put on all his decorations and went to see Madame Duchinskaya. Maroossya was upgraded and there was a short interval of peace.

My first coaching session with Maroossya convinced me that it was impossible to make her understand anything. Taking a calculated risk, I made her learn her text books by heart, memorising them page by page like an abracadabra. I could have taught a parrot by the same method. It was exhausting but my efforts were rewarded. Maroossya brought home better marks.

That evening, when I rang the bell, the General himself opened the door. His step was springy and he was rubbing his hands. Maroossya, in a new dress and with bows in her hair, was waltzing with a chair for a partner in the drawing room, while her French teacher, Mademoiselle Martin, played the piano and the dog jumped and barked in a frenzy.

Madame Kazanskaya, in a dress with a long train, led the way to the dining room where a celebration dinner was served. At the end of it, the General neatly drew the cork from a bottle of champagne. He poured it generously and drank it like water. His face flushed and he waved his hands, his cuffs twinkling. After a while he became despondent.

'Every man has his own cross,' he said. 'Women, my dear fellow, don't understand. They have no brains.'

'Angel!' cried his wife in alarm. 'How can you say such a thing!'

'Hell,' said the General. 'Drink up, young man. As the poet said, "O what a fate, dear Lord, to be the father of a grown-up daughter!"'

'Angel!' moaned his wife. 'How can you!'

'My dear Muff,' said the General in a dangerously soft voice.

'Who do you think you're talking to? I have taught an Emperor and I won't be corrected by silly fools. 'Shun!'

In the end he cheered up again, leapt from his chair, waving a napkin, and went into a Russian dance, finally collapsing and having to be revived with spirits of valerian.

Mademoiselle Martin and I left the house together. The street lights were hardly visible. It was a cold, foggy March evening.

'Oh, how tired I am,' sighed Mademoiselle Martin. 'I simply can't go on teaching that idiot of a girl and going to that idiotic house. I'm going to give notice.'

I envied her. But the Kazanskys were paying me the fabulous sum of 30 roubles a month. My father had just thrown up his job at Bezhitsa and gone to his parents' farm in Gorodishche. Knowing that Mama was not in a position to help me either, I had lied to her, saying that I was earning 50 roubles a month, and begged her not to send me any money.

Mademoiselle Martin and I said goodbye at the corner of Bibikov Boulevard. It had started to snow heavily. An incandescent light hissed over the door of a chemist's shop.

I stood watching her as she moved swiftly down the boulevard with a gliding motion as though she were taking very small steps on roller skates, her head bent and her muff raised to her face to shield it from the snow.

The champagne had had a strange effect on me. At moments my mind clouded agreeably and everything seemed to be full of a new and enchanting significance; at others it cleared and I saw myself with my life unchanged: tomorrow I would take the same street as I had taken today—I knew it to the last shop sign—pass the same cab drivers, policemen and kiosks, climb the same staircase with its yellow walls, ring the bell, hear the dog yapping and find the same general's greatcoat, with its red lapels and with its buttons fastened all the way down, hanging on the stand in the hall.

Then the haziness came back, and I thought of the natural kinship between lonely people such as Mademoiselle Martin, Fitsovsky and myself, and of how we ought all to be friends and help each other, and face our difficulties together.—But where had I got the idea that Mademoiselle Martin was lonely? I had hardly spoken to her. All I knew of her was that she came from Grenoble, and that she had dark and rather sullen eyes.

A Sad Waste of Time

After a while I turned and went to Fitsovsky's. He was out, but I found the key in its usual place and walked in.

The room was dark and cold. I lit the kerosene lamp and the small iron stove and, lying down on the worn divan with my greatcoat over me, opened a book of poetry I had picked up from the table.

'Slowly the autumn morning dawns,' I read, my head swimming again and a warm light shining on the page and on my face. 'Slowly a yellow leaf drifts down. The sky is clear as glass—the air is wonderfully fresh. The soul shall not escape invisible decay.'

I put the book aside and thought of my future; it seemed filled with joys and sorrows, all equally fascinating. The darkness which concealed them was like this night with its gleaming snow drifts, the silence of its parks, the glow of its street lights. The night hid in its darkness the people who were some day to become close to me, and the promise of the dawn which was certain to come. The night secreted all the mysteries, all the encounters, all the happiness of the future. How good that was!

The poet was wrong. I and my generation were young, we believed and we loved. We were not in danger of 'invisible decay'. We would see to it that our spirit escaped it. We would struggle to the death for our wonderful future.

So I thought as I lay on Fitsovsky's divan. We were strong, we had what it takes—and to hell with the ant heap of the Kazanskys.

When I got home to Wild Alley, Panna Koslovskaya handed me a telegram. It said that my father was dying at Gorodishche.

I left town the following morning. My father's death broke one of the threads which had bound me to my family. One by one, the rest of them were shortly to break as well.

30

The Inn on the Braginka

The old river steamer was slowly paddling its way up the Dnieper. It was late at night but I couldn't sleep in the airless cabin. I went on deck.

It was pitch dark. The wind, blowing out of the darkness, carried drops of rain. An old peasant in a patched coat stood looking up at the captain's bridge, the light of a dim lantern fell on his face.

'Do an old man a favour, Captain,' he begged. 'From here it's less than a mile to my village. If I have to walk from Teremtsev it will take me all night.'

'Are you joking?' said the Captain. 'I can't see my hand in front of my face. Do you expect me to smash up my boat for you?'

'It's no joking matter. My village is just over that hill,' he pointed into the darkness. 'Please be so kind, Captain.'

The Captain pretended not to hear. 'Terenty,' he asked the helmsman, 'can you see anything?'

'Not a thing. I'm steering by sound.'

'We'll foul the boat,' the Captain sighed.

'Nothing will happen to your old tub!' the peasant muttered angrily. 'What kind of a captain are you anyway? You should be selling apples in the market, not taking boats up the Dnieper. Are you going to put me ashore or not?'

'Just you go on talking.'

'I'll talk to you all right. Who ever heard of a passenger steamer going all the way to Teremtsev non-stop?'

'Can't you understand?' The Captain's voice rose plaintively. 'It's dark. I can't see. Where am I to land you in this? You tell me.'

'Just here! Exactly opposite to where we are now!' He again pointed into the unrelieved blackness. 'You let me stand on the bridge and I'll show the helmsman.'

'Go to hell, will you,' said the Captain.

'Aha!' the peasant cried excitedly. 'You refuse, do you?'

'Yes, I refuse.'

'So you don't care whether I get home in time for my daughter's wedding or not! Bullying an old man, are you?'

'Your daughter isn't my business.'

The peasant lowered his voice menacingly. 'And what about Andrey Gon? Is he your business or not? Well, let me tell you, Andrey Gon himself is coming to the wedding.'

The Captain was silent.

'Lost your tongue, have you?' said the peasant nastily. 'I see you call your old tub *Hope*. A lot of hope you have of getting home safely if you don't put me ashore. Andrey Gon is a relation of mine. He won't forget this.'

'Stop threatening me,' growled the Captain.

'Sidor Petrovich,' said the helmsman. 'You can see what an obstinate old man he is. Why not put him ashore? We don't want to get mixed up with Andrey Gon.'

'All right,' said the Captain. 'Come up and show Terenty the way. Only try not to wreck the boat.'

'Goodness me! Don't I know the Dnieper like the back of my hand! And don't I know the boat is Government property!'

He went up on the bridge and took command.

'Over to the left! Hard over, or you'll miss it. That's right. Still harder.'

Willow branches lashed the side of the boat; it scraped bottom and stopped. The thud woke up the passengers on the covered deck below.

A sailor shone a lantern from the bow and we saw that the boat had stopped in the flooded undergrowth, about thirty yards from the dry land; dark water was swishing among the bushes.

'Well, there you are,' said the Captain. 'We're there. Now get out.'

'How can I get out here?' The old man was surprised. 'It's out of my depth. I could drown.'

'That's not my business. You asked for it. Get out!' he shouted, 'or I'll have you thrown overboard.'

'It's very strange . . .' muttered the old man, walking to the bow. He crossed himself, climbed over the side, and jumped. The water came to his neck. Cursing loudly, he splashed his way to the shore, while the boat backed slowly out of the under-growth.

'You all right?' shouted the Captain. 'Still alive?'

'No thanks to you,' the old man yelled from the bank. 'Andrey Gon will hear all about it, you can be sure of that.'

All that summer bandits had been infesting the Province of Chernigov and the wooded region of the Polessye. They robbed the mails and the trains and they attacked isolated houses and farms. The most daring and elusive of the bands was the one led by Andrey Gon. Again and again, detachments of Dragoons and forest guards had encircled him in the forest, driving him into the dangerous swamps of the Polessye, but each time he broke free and continued to ravage the countryside, the glare of burning houses once again marking his tracks on a dark night.

Legends had already grown up around him. A student from Chernigov according to some, a village blacksmith according to others, he was thought to be a Robin Hood who attacked only the rich and protected the poor and oppressed.

I was on my way to the Polessye to stay with some relations of ours called Sevryuk, whose estate was well within Gon's territory. It was Borya who had arranged for me to spend part of my holiday with the Sevryuks. I had never met them, but Borya said, 'You'll like them. They're a bit eccentric but very nice, and very simple. They'll love having you.'

I accepted because I could think of nowhere else to go. I had passed into the eighth form; my examinations were just over and I had a long and boring summer in front of me. Mama had stayed in Moscow; Uncle Kolya had taken Aunt Maroossya to drink the waters in Kislovodsk; and I didn't feel like going to Gorodishche because, judging from Uncle Ilko's letters his marriage was breaking up. I had seen enough of family quarrels and had no wish to be involved in any more.

It was the evening of the second day of the journey when the boat pulled alongside the flat Polessye bank. Clouds of mosquitoes buzzed overhead. The sun was setting in the whitish mist above the river. The air on the wooded bank felt chilly. A fire had been lit and three lean riding horses were standing beside it; a cart waited a little way off.

The Sevryuks had come to meet me. There was Sevryuk himself, who owned the estate—a tall, thin man in knee boots and a tussore suit, a slightly built young woman, his wife, and her brother, a student.

They settled me into the cart, jumped into their saddles, clicked their tongues and briskly set off at a swinging trot, soon vanishing ahead.

Left alone with the taciturn driver, I got out and walked beside the cart. The grass on either side of the sandy track stood in black puddles of swamp water in which the faint remnant of the sunset seemed to smoulder on and on, inextinguishably. Flights of wild duck passed overhead with a rhythmic swishing of wings. A ground mist seeped out of the undergrowth, leaving grey tatters on the bushes.

We passed through a wood. Then, hundreds of frogs all shouted at once, the cart rumbled over planks, and I saw the Sevryuks' house—a strange octagonal wooden building with many outhouses and verandahs, standing in a clearing in the forest.

That evening we were having a light supper when a stooping old man wearing sandals and a cap with a broken peak walked into the dining room; he slung his gun off his shoulder and leaned it against the wall. A piebald setter followed him, its claws clicking on the floorboards; it sat down in a corner, thumping the floor so hard with its tail that the old man said: 'Stop it, Halas! Behave yourself.' The dog stopped thumping its tail, yawned and lay down.

'Well, Trofim, what news?' asked Sevryuk. 'He's our forester,' he told me.

'What news?' Trofim sighed as he sat down to table. 'All of the same sort. They've burned down the manor at Lyady. And at Staraya Guta, they've clubbed Pan Kaputsinsky to death, God rest his soul. Not that he wasn't an old scoundrel, but still . . . Nothing but murder and arson all around. You're the only one they seem to spare. It's very strange. I can't think why he leaves you alone, that Andrey Gon. Perhaps he's heard you get on well with the peasants. Or perhaps your turn is still to come.'

'He's always like that,' laughed Marina, Sevryuk's wife. 'Every time he comes he's astonished to find us alive.'

'Live long and be happy, I've nothing against it,' said Trofim. 'Have you heard about the blind man's guide?'

'No. What about him?' Marina asked quickly.

'They're having the funeral tomorrow at Pogonny.'

'We'll go,' said Marina. 'We'll certainly go.'

'For that God will forgive you your sins. You might take me with you. It's too far for me to walk now.' He looked round at the windows and lowered his voice: 'Anyone around?'

'No strangers,' said Sevryuk. 'What is it?'

'I'll tell you,' Trofim said mysteriously. 'The Masters are holding a meeting at Leiser's inn on the Braginka.'

'Who?' asked Marina's brother.

'The Masters. You know. The Old Men of Mogilev.'

'Wait a minute,' Sevryuk interrupted. 'I'll tell them. They don't know what you are talking about.'

It was then I heard for the first time the strange tale of the Old Men of Mogilev. It made me feel as if I were living in the past century, if not in the Middle Ages.

For a very long time, ever since the days of the Polish occupation, there had been a colony of beggars at Mogilev on the Dnieper, many of them blind. They were known as the Old Men of Mogilev, and they had elders among them who were known as the Masters.

The Masters trained the young members of the community in the complicated rules of their profession; they taught them the right way to chant and to beg, and they instructed them in the laws of their common life.

The beggars scattered all over the Polessye, Belorussia and the Ukraine, but once a year the Masters gathered at some secret place —an isolated inn on the marshes, or an abandoned forester's hut— and held a meeting to decide on the admission of new members and on whatever other business they had.

In times of trouble and popular disturbance, the beggars were a serious menace to the authorities. They kept the peasants' anger alive by fanning it with their ballads about the wicked rule of the Polish landowners and the wretchedness of the village folk. What I heard of the Old Men of Mogilev gave me a new conception of the countryside in which I found myself. It seemed that in this region of swamps and stunted woods, of mist and wilderness, the fires of resentment smouldered like their sunsets, without ever going out. From then on, I no longer thought that the rags of beggars smelt of bread and of the dust of the road—they smelled to me of gunpowder and arson, and when I looked more closely at the blind vagabonds, I realised that the special tribe to which they belonged was not merely that of the unfortunates but of gifted men of ruthless will.

'Why are the Masters having a meeting on the Braginka?' asked Sevryuk.

'Who knows. They meet every year,' Trofim said unwillingly. 'Have the guards been snooping round?'

'Not here,' said Sevryuk. 'We heard they were at Komarin yesterday.'

'Oh well.' Trofim rose to his feet. 'I thank you. I'll go up and have a rest in the hayloft.'

Trofim went—but not to the hayloft; he went off to the forest and only reappeared in the morning.

Marina told me about the boy who had been a blind man's guide.

Two days earlier, a blind man had come with his guide to the house of a neighbouring landowner, Lyubomirsky. They were driven away from the doors and when they got to the gate the Ingush watchman (landowners in those days often employed Ingushes as guards) let a wolfhound off its chain and sent it after them. The blind man stood dead still and the dog only sniffed at him and growled, but the boy panicked and ran. The dog chased and killed him.

The peasants had picked up the body of the boy and taken it to Pogonny, where the funeral was to be held tomorrow.

I liked the Sevryuks. Marina was a splendid horsewoman and a dead shot. She was small but very strong; she spoke in a sing-song voice and walked with a light, swift step. Her judgments were harsh, like a man's, and she had a taste for long historical novels such as Danilevsky's *Fugitives in Belorussia*.

Sevryuk had the look of a sick man, with an emaciated face and a mocking expression. He avoided his fellow landowners, preferred the company of the peasants and kept himself busy on his small estate.

As for Marina's brother, the student, he was out shooting all day. In his spare time he filled cartridges, cast smallshot and cleaned his Belgian double-barrelled gun.

Next day we went to the village of Pogonny. We crossed the deep, cold river Braginka by ferry; the wind was buffeting the willows on the bank.

Beyond the river the dirt track ran between the pinewoods and the swamps.

The marsh stretched as far as the horizon, vanishing in the hazy light; it was yellow with islands of flowers, shining with puddles like windows, and rustling with grey sedge. Never had I seen such limitless marshes. At a distance from the road, among the luxuriant green of patches of quagmire, a slanting cross marked the place where a man, who had been out shooting, was drowned.

We heard the funeral bell long before we drove into the deserted village with its tumble-down huts roofed with rotting thatch. Hens fluttered, squawking, from under the horses' hooves.

The whole village was gathered at the church. Through the open doors we could see the candles, their light falling on the garlands of paper flowers round the ikons.

We went in; the crowd silently parted in front of us. The dead boy lay in a narrow coffin, his fair hair carefully combed, his blood-less hands crossed on his breast and holding a tall thin wax candle; the candle bent in the heat and wax dripped on the yellow fingers. A priest in a black cope and with shaggy hair was praying and swinging a censer.

I watched the face of the boy: it looked as if he were trying to remember something.

Sevryuk touched my arm. Following the direction of his glance, I saw a row of beggars drawn up on one side of the coffin. They were all old men in brown tunics and leaning on thick staves shiny with age. They stood with raised heads, looking up at the painting of the Lord of Hosts above the altar. It was curiously like them; it had the same lean dark face and stern sunken eyes.

'The Masters,' Sevryuk whispered to me.

They stood quite still, neither crossing themselves nor bowing. There was an empty space around them. Behind them I could see two boys, blind men's guides with canvas sacks over their shoulders. One of them was quietly crying and wiping his nose on the sleeve of his tunic, the other stood with downcast eyes and a mocking expression.

Women sighed; men's voices were sometimes raised in the porch. The priest looked up and prayed in a louder voice and the hubbub ceased.

Afterwards the beggars moved up to the coffin, lifted it on to their shoulders and carried it out. Two blind men followed them with their guides.

The coffin was lowered into the ground. Water had already seeped into the grave. The priest said a last prayer, took off his vestment, rolled it up, and limped from the cemetery. Two elderly peasants spat on their hands and were picking up their spades, when a blind beggar with a hawk's face walked to the side of the grave and said in a loud voice:

'Wait, everybody.'

There was a deep silence. The blind man felt for the edge of the grave with his stick, bowed over the coffin, straightened himself and, staring ahead with his white eyes, broke into chant:

Beneath a hollow willow-tree, beside a shallow stream,
The Lord rested on His weary way,
And the people from all the places around
Came and offered Him whatever they had.

The crowd moved closer to the blind singer.

Women gave Him honey and homespun, girls offered Him their
    necklaces,
Old men and old women brought Him their ikons and their bread
And a small girl put a bunch of periwinkles at His feet
And ran and hid behind the barn. And the Lord smiled
And said: 'Who will give Me his heart?
Is there anyone who will not begrudge Me his heart?'

A woman in a white shawl whimpered softly. The blind man paused, turned to her and went on:

Then a young lad brought Him his heart,
Fluttering like a dove, and put it in His hands.
And the Lord saw that it was pierced and black with clotted blood.
It was tarnished and as black as the earth
From the everlasting tears it had shed and the wounds it had borne,
For the boy had wandered about the earth
Leading the blind, and had never known happiness.
The beggar stretched his hands in front of him.
And the Lord rose and lifted that heart in His hands.
He rose in His infinite power and He cursed the unrighteousness of men,
And black clouds gathered over the earth
And thunder crashed over the forests
And the voice of the Lord rang out:
The blind man smiled joyfully.
This heart is the richest gift I have received from the race of men.
I will keep it beside Me on my Heavenly throne
So that all good people may honour it.
He paused again, reflected, and continued in a powerful muffled
chant:
This bruised heart is richer than diamonds,
More splendid than flowers, brighter than stars
Because an innocent lad made of it
A humble gift to Almighty God.

Women were wiping their eyes with the edges of their dark
shawls. 'Give alms,' the blind man said, 'for the repose of the soul
of the youth Vassily, innocent and slain.'

He held out his cap and copper coins poured into it, while the
soil was being shovelled into the grave.

We went back to the carriage, Marina walking ahead, and drove
home in silence. Only Trofim said: 'Isn't it strange—for thousands
of years there have been people living on the earth, and they still
haven't learned to be good.'

After the funeral there was a feeling in the air as if danger had drawn
closer to the Sevryuks. The heavy doors were bolted in the evenings,
and in the middle of the night Sevryuk and Marina's brother got up
and, taking loaded guns with them, made a tour of inspection
outside.

Once they saw a camp fire burning in the woods; next morning

The Inn on the Braginka

Trofim reported that a stranger had spent the night there. 'Must be one of Gon's men,' he said. 'They're all over the place, prowling like wolves.'

Later that day a young man in black army trousers with faded red piping came to the house; he was barefooted and had his boots slung over his shoulder. His face was peeling with sunburn. His eyes were sullen and observant.

He asked for a drink of water. Marina brought him a jug of milk and a loaf of bread. He drank thirstily and said:

'You're brave people. Aren't you afraid to live in a place like this?'

'No one is going to harm us,' said Marina.

The boy grinned. 'How do you know?'

'Because we don't do any harm to anyone.'

'That's for others to judge,' the boy said enigmatically as he went off.

As a result Marina parted unhappily from Sevryuk when the next day he went to the nearest small town to buy provisions and gunpowder. He took me along with him. We were to return the same night.

I enjoyed the drive through the deserted countryside. The road ran between the marshes, over sandy hillocks overgrown with stunted pinewoods. A steady trickle of sand came from the wheels. It was a sultry day and we could see the heat shimmering over the marsh.

In the little Jewish town, goats were wandering about on the roofs, nibbling the moss. We passed the synagogue with its sign of David nailed over the door.

In the square, the ground was littered with straw and drowsy horses stood about, unsaddled. A detachment of Dragoons had halted in the town for its midday rest. The men were lying on the ground, their faces flushed and their tunics unbuttoned, lazily singing:

> *Soldiers, brave soldiers*
> *Where are your wives?*
> *Our loaded cannon,*
> *These are our wives.*

The officer sat on the verandah of the inn, drinking muddy looking *kvas* made of fermented wheat.

We went into the shops. They were known as 'vaults'. It was cool and dark inside. Pigeons pecked corn on the scales. The Jewish shopkeepers wore shiny black caps on their heads; they complained that there was little point in doing business because all the profit went on bribing the police Inspector. They also told us that two days earlier Gon had made a raid on a neighbouring estate and driven away four good horses from the stables. In one shop we were given tea; it smelled faintly of kerosene and was served with pink lenten sugar.

We started for home later than we had intended. Sevryuk whipped up the horses, but the sandy road had tired them out and they couldn't go faster than a walk. Clouds of flies swarmed over their rumps and they were ceaselessly swishing their long tails to whisk them off.

A storm was coming up from the south. The marsh darkened. A blustering wind rose, shaking the trees and bringing a smell of moisture. There were flashes of lightning and a faint, as though underground, rumbling in the distance.

'We'll have to turn off and stop at the inn on the Braginka,' said Sevryuk. 'We'll have to stay overnight. It's a pity we wasted so much time.'

We turned into a forest road, but we could hardly see it. The wheels kept catching on the roots of trees.

Night was falling very quickly, but now the forest thinned out, a fresh damp breeze blew in our faces and we saw the black silhouette of the inn rising in front of us.

It stood under the willows on the edge of the Braginka. Behind it the ground, falling away to the river, was thickly overgrown with nettles and hemlock. From this scented undergrowth came the anxious squawking of chickens sheltering from the storm.

The innkeeper Leiser came out on the porch. He was a stout elderly Jew in knee boots, trousers as wide as a gypsy's and a red sash round his waist.

'Oh, what an honoured guest!' he shut his eyes in an ecstatic smile. 'It would be easier to find a jewel in the forest than to tempt such a visitor into my humble inn. Please be so kind as to step straight into the front room.'

In spite of his honeyed words, he was darting wary glances at us from under his crinkled eyelids.

The Inn on the Braginka

'Don't worry,' said Sevryuk. 'I know you've got the Masters staying. It's none of our business. Anyone can spend a night at an inn.'

'What am I to do?' Leiser sighed. 'With nothing but bog and forest all around, what choice have I got? To tell you the truth, Pan Sevryuk, I'm sometimes frightened of them myself.'

We went in. The floorboards, scrubbed with sand, creaked under our feet. The house had subsided and everything in the room was a little askew. A bloated, grey-haired woman was sitting up in bed, supported by pillows.

'My mother,' Leiser explained. 'She's got dropsy. Dvoira!' he shouted, 'bring the samovar!'

A sad little face peered out from behind a curtain and Leiser's wife greeted us.

The windows were closed against the storm; flies were beating against the glass. On the wall hung a fly-blown portrait of General Kuropatkin. Leiser brought hay for our bedding, spread it on the floor and covered it with sacking.

The minute we sat down to tea, there was a clap of thunder so loud that the china on the table jumped. The darkness outside the window streamed with a grey torrent of rain continually torn by bleary flashes of lightning.

The noise of the downpour drowned the hissing of the samovar as we sat drinking tea and eating biscuits. It was a long time since tea had tasted so good to me. I loved the inn, isolated at the back-of-beyond, the sound of the rain and the thunder echoing through the woods. The voices of the Masters could just be heard through the partition wall.

Exhausted by the hot day and the long drive in the bumping cart, I fell asleep on the hay as soon as we had finished tea. I woke up in the middle of the night, drenched in sweat and stifling in the airless room with its smell of kerosene. The night-light flickered. The old woman moaned in her sleep.

'I've got to get out,' said Sevryuk, sitting up on the floor beside me. 'I'll get a heart attack in this fug. Let's go and sleep in the cart.'

We tiptoed out, found the cart in the shed and, shaking up the hay, lay down on it, covering ourselves with the sacking.

The storm had passed. The stars shone moistly over the woods.

Raindrops were dripping from the roof of the shed and there was a smell of wet grass.

A door creaked and someone came out of the inn.

'Keep quiet,' Sevryuk whispered. 'I expect it's the Masters.'

Someone sat down on a log in front of the shed and struck a flint. There was a smell of cheap tobacco.

'The moment it goes up,' said a squeaky voice, 'we'll be off, or they'll be on to us.'

'That's certain,' croaked another voice. 'The Archangels are on the prowl. We shouldn't have stayed at Leiser's as long as we did.'

'I can't see anything yet,' came a third voice, sounding young and worried. 'D'you think it's too wet after the rain?'

'It won't be too wet for Gon's men,' said the squeaky voice.

'They'll do what they said,' came the croak. 'Our wrong will be avenged. We'll see God's retribution. While we still have eyes to see.'

'Are they all ready, Petro?' asked the one with the squeak.

'Yes,' replied the young voice.

'Then tell them to come out. And keep Leiser out of it. He's been paid, the rest is not his business. Are the travellers asleep?'

'They're asleep all right. Why wouldn't they be?'

There was silence again, but when I stirred Sevryuk touched my arm. More people were coming out of the inn.

'I'll be going with Kuzma to Ovruch.' The new voice was familiar. 'I might find a guide there. The people are starving.' It was the blind beggar who had sung after the funeral in the grave-yard in Pogonny.

The voice broke off again. I listened to the silence, my heart thumping; it seemed to go on forever. Then someone said softly:

'There it is.'

The men stirred. The one with the croak said: 'Well, brothers, we'll say a prayer and be off.'

'Our Father who art in Heaven,' came a muffled chant. 'Hallowed be Thy name, Thy Kingdom come . . .'

The men rose and went away.

'What was that all about?' I asked.

'I don't know. I'll go and have a cigarette outside.'

He walked out of the shed. A moment later I heard his surprised voice out of the darkness.

'That's odd. Come and look.'

I went out. Beyond the willows on the farther bank of the river, the sky was a smoky pink. Jets of sparks shot up, so near that they seemed to come from the bushes around us. The river dimly reflected the fire-glow.

'What d'you think is burning?' asked Sevryuk.

'Lyubomirsky's house,' said Leiser just behind us. We hadn't heard him come.

'Pan Sevryuk,' he said in an imploring voice. 'I beg you to have pity on yourselves and on a poor innkeeper. Let me harness your horses, and go off with God. It's not good for you to be here.'

'Why?'

'The Dragoons may come at any moment, or the forest guards. —I've not seen or heard anything.'

'Neither have we.'

'I beg you, Pan Sevryuk, in the name of your own Orthodox God. Go away! I don't want your money, a quiet life is worth more to me. You can see what things are like.'

'All right, all right,' Sevryuk agreed. 'Go and harness the horses. What's happened to your nerve?'

The horses were soon harnessed and we left. Sevryuk dropped the reins and let them go at their own pace. The road followed the bank of the river. Wet branches kept slapping us in the face.

'So they've set fire to Lyubomirsky's house,' Sevryuk said softly.

'Who?'

'Who knows! You and I haven't seen or heard a thing. Right?'

'Right.'

A low whistle came from the farther bank of the river. We stopped. It came again. We were screened by the trees and the thick undergrowth.

'Innkeeper,' a man's voice called softly. 'Come and ferry me across.'

No one answered. As we listened to the silence, there was a splash—the man had evidently thrown himself in and was swimming across. Soon we saw him through the bushes, lit by the faint glow of the fire. He was struggling against the current in the middle of the stream. He scrambled ashore not far from us and we heard the water pouring off him. 'Just you wait, Leiser,' he said as he walked away into the woods. 'You'll pay for this crossing.'

When the sound of his footsteps died away, we drove on slowly.

'Did you see who it was?' Sevryuk asked in a barely audible voice.

'No.'

'I think it was the boy who came to the house. The one in army trousers who had a drink of milk. I think I recognised his voice. That makes it all quite clear. The Masters must have complained to Gon and he sent this boy, who is one of his men, to set fire to Lyubomirsky's house. Leiser must have ferried him over the river. But remember, we don't know anything.'

He cautiously lit a cigarette, screening the flame of the match with a fold of his raincoat.

The glow of the fire swayed with the wind. The cart creaked; the river muttered in the flooded undergrowth. Later on, a cold mist rose from the marsh. We arrived at dawn, wet and chilled to the bone.

There followed several disturbed, restless days. I thoroughly enjoyed them. I liked the feeling of danger, the whispered conversations, the rumours, Trofim's reports of Gon having been seen now here, now there.

I loved the cold Braginka, the forest infested by bandits, the mysterious hoof marks on the road, appearing overnight. Indeed, I almost wished Andrey Gon would come and raid the estate—so long as he didn't kill anyone or burn down the house.

But it was the Dragoons who came. One evening at dusk, they dismounted outside the gate; an officer in dusty riding boots walked up to the verandah where we were having tea. He apologised for disturbing us and asked:

'Are you Gospodin Sevryuk?'

'Yes.'

He turned to one of his men. 'Bring him along, Marchenko.'

Two soldiers came forward, leading a barefooted young man. His hands were tied behind his back. He wore black army trousers with faded red piping.

He stood at the foot of the verandah, his eyes fixed on Marina's face as though trying to give her a message.

'Do you know this man?' asked the officer.

We made no reply.

'Take a good look at him.'

'No,' said Marina, her face white. 'I've never seen him.'

The boy shuddered and hung his head.

'And you?' the officer asked Sevryuk.

'No, I don't know him either.'

'I see.' He turned to the boy. 'So it was all a lot of lies you told us—about being a local boy and having worked on the Sevryuk estate! You've cooked your goose all right.'

'Do what you like,' said the boy. 'The might is yours, but not the right.'

Marina sprang up and went into the house.

'That's enough from you,' said the officer. 'Take him away.'

The Dragoons left. Marina cried for a long time.

'And he was trying so hard to tell me,' she sobbed. 'How could I be such a fool! I ought to have said I knew him, that he had worked for us.'

'How could you possibly guess,' Trofim tried to comfort her. 'He ought to have given you a sign. All the same, he did a good job of the Lyubomirskys' house. Paid them out for the boy they murdered.'

Soon after this I went back to Kiev.

I remembered the Polessye as a sad and rather enigmatic place. There it was, flowering with its flags and its buttercups, rustling with its alders and its birches, but never, it seemed to me, destined to hear its church bells ring for a great popular rejoicing. So I thought then. Fortunately I was proved wrong.

31
My Grandmother's Garden

My maternal grandfather had died several years earlier. After his death, my grandmother Vikentia Ivanovna had stayed on in Cherkassy with her daughter Euphrosine. But Aunt Euphrosine died the summer I went to the Sevryuks, and Grandmother came to live with one of her other daughters, Vera, who was married to a rich businessman in Kiev. They had a big house in the suburb of Lukyanovna, and they put Grandmother in a cottage in the garden.

After having been her own mistress for so long, Grandmother felt like a poor relation in Aunt Vera's grand household. Her only comfort was that she didn't have to live in the house itself and could do her own cooking in the cottage—to this extent at least, she felt independent and not in her daughter's debt.

Grandmother was lonely and she talked me into giving up my room in Wild Alley and moving in with her. The cottage had four small rooms. My grandmother lived in one, an old 'cellist called Gattenberg in another and I was given the third. The fourth room, though called the sun porch, was cold and had nothing in it but flower pots.

When I came back from Polessye, Kiev was empty; it was midsummer and everyone was away in the country. Even Borya had gone to Ekaterinoslav to get practical experience in a temporary engineering job. The only people at Lukyanovka were my grandmother and Gattenberg.

Grandmother had aged, become bent and lost her strictness, but she had remained faithful to her habits. Every morning she got up at dawn and flung the windows wide open. Then she made coffee on a spirit lamp.

My Grandmother's Garden

After coffee she went to sit in her wicker armchair in the garden and read her favourite books—endless novels by Krashevsky and stories by Korolenko and Elise Ozhenko. There I often found her—a white-haired old lady in a black dress, with her thin arms resting on the arms of her chair—fast asleep over her book.

Butterflies came and settled on her sleeves and her widow's cap. Ripe plums fell on the grass with a soft thud. The warm wind chased shadows of leaves across the paths.

A hot sun shone down on Grandmother from high overhead—the clean hard sun of the Kiev summer—and it occurred to me that it was here, in the warmth and freshness of this garden, that Grandmother would some day fall asleep for the last time.

We were great friends; I was fonder of my grandmother than of any of my other relations. After bringing up five daughters and two sons she was now alone in her old age. We were both lonely and this helped to bring us together.

I found that we had a lot in common in spite of the difference between our ages. She liked books, poetry, the sky, the trees and her own thoughts. And she never bullied me—except when I had a cold.

Her only weakness in my eyes was that, at the slightest sniffle, she insisted on treating me with her own well-tried remedy which she called 'the spiritus'. A vicious mixture of wine, wood-alcohol, ammonia, turpentine and any other spirits she could get hold of, it was a blood red liquid as corrosive as nitric acid. This she rubbed into my chest and back, and its pungent smell spread through the cottage. When this happened Gattenberg at once lit a fat cigar which added its bluish mist to the medicinal vapour.

It was usually while Gattenberg was playing his 'cello that Grandmother fell asleep in the garden.

He was a handsome old man with a curly white beard and piercing grey eyes. He often played a composition of his own, entitled 'The Death of Hamlet'. The 'cello sobbed, and the chords, as though reverberating beneath castle vaults, rose to their solemn climax:

> *Let four captains*
> *Bear Hamlet like a soldier to the stage,*
> *For he was likely, had he been put on,*

> *To have proved most royally: and for his passage,*
> *The soldiers' music, and the rites of war*
> *Speak loudly for him . . .*

Listening to the music, I imagined the great hall at Elsinore, the slender Gothic shafts of sunlight, the trumpets, the huge banners over Hamlet's body—tall and light, they dipped and rustled. The stream had long since borne Ophelia's bouquet to the sea; the waves, far from the shore, buffeted the rosemary and the rue, the last gauge of her unhappy love. Of this too the music spoke.

Grandmother woke up and said, 'Goodness! Couldn't you play something cheerful?' and to please her, Gattenberg played her favourite Pastorale from *The Queen of Spades*: 'Sweet friend, O shepherd mine . . .'

Music wearied my grandmother. She got a rest from it in the evening when Gattenberg took himself off to play in the orchestra at the Merchants' Park.

I often went to these concerts. The band played on a floodlit stand which was painted white and shaped like a shell. The audience sat in the dark under the open sky. There was a strong sweet smell of stocks and tobacco flowers; the beds were watered just before the concert. The women's dresses glimmered in the dark. The trees rustled. Sometimes there were flashes of summer lightning.

But the evenings I preferred were those when the sky was overcast and hardly anyone came to listen to the music. It seemed to me then that the band was playing only for me and for an unknown girl in a hat with a drooping brim who was always there.

She came to nearly every concert. Sometimes I knew that she was looking at me. I watched her furtively, but I only once met her eyes. It seemed to me that they flashed an amused, conniving glance.

My dull summer filled with dreams of the unknown girl and ceased to bore me. It was a summer echoing with loud rains. The rain came down from a great height and busied itself among the leaves in the garden. The glass drops as they flew from the clouds seemed to strike the keys of a musical instrument, each sounding a different note and filling my room with their tremolos. It seemed to me a miracle that ordinary rain—the kind that drips off a roof into a green tub—could make such music.

My Grandmother's Garden

'It's raining blind again,' said my grandmother. 'Oh well, it's good for the harvest.'

Somewhere beyond the light haze of the 'blind rains' and the flashing of the rainbows, the unknown girl lived—just round the corner from us. I was grateful to her for appearing in my world and immediately transforming it.

Even the yellow brick pavements with small puddles in their hollows became as curious and fascinating as something out of a Hans Andersen fairytale. Grass sprouted between the bricks; ants struggled in the puddles. Once I was inside my region of make-believe, everything, even the pavements, astonished me.

I still cannot define this state of mind. I never noticed what started it. There was no exultation in it. On the contrary, it was tranquil and restful. And it always vanished at the slightest worry.

I had a need to find expression for it, so that summer with its 'blind rains' I began to write.

I kept my writing a secret from my grandmother. When she asked me why I sat scribbling for hours in my room, I said I was making notes of my holiday reading in preparation for school.

On days when there was no concert in the Merchants' Park, I went off to the Dnieper, or to the outskirts of the town where there was a neglected park called 'Fly-away-Sorrow'. It belonged to Krulzhenko, a well-known Kiev patron of the arts.

For a few cigarettes, the keeper let me in. The park was deserted and had gone wild. The ponds were choked with duckweed; the jackdaws made their racket in the trees; the wooden benches sagged. The only human being I ever came across was an old painter who sat sketching under a large umbrella. I only saw him from a distance; he gave me such black looks that I never dared to come any nearer.

I used to make my way to an empty house tucked away at the far end of the park and sit reading on the steps of the verandah.

Sparrows scratched on the floor behind my back. Often I interrupted my reading to look into the distance of the park. Smoky shafts of sunlight fell between the trees. I was waiting. I felt certain that here, in this park, I would meet the stranger.

But she never came and I went home, taking the most round-about way—by bus across the Podol and on foot along the Kreshchatik.

I stopped on the way to call at Idzikovsky's library. In summer it was empty. A pale young clerk with a damp drooping moustache changed my books. In the condition I was in, I could read nothing but poetry. For my grandmother I borrowed novels by Spielhagen or by Boleslav Prus.

I arrived home tired and happy, my face burning from the sun and the wind. My grandmother was waiting for me. Supper was ready on a small round table with a white cloth. I told her about Fly-away-Sorrow. She nodded understandingly. Sometimes she said that the day had been long and dull. But she never scolded me for coming home late. 'Youth has its own laws,' she used to say. 'It's not my business to interfere with them.'

Later, in my room, I undressed and lay on my narrow camp bed, looking at the lamplight on the crooked branches of the apple-tree outside the window. Drifting into a first light sleep, I was conscious of the darkness and the limitless quiet of the night. I liked night time, though it frightened me to think of Orion and Virgo, Aquarius and Sagittarius passing overhead in the stillness high above Lukyanovka and our cottage.

I wrote a story about that summer. I put everything into it—the 'cellist, the girl in the Merchants' Park, Fly-away-Sorrow, the nights, and a dreamy, slightly ludicrous boy.

I tormented it for weeks, until the words lost their sharpness and turned to cottonwool and even I found the purple passages a little tiresome. There were moments when I despaired.

At that time a periodical used to come out in Kiev, curiously entitled *The Knight* and edited by a well-known Kiev literary and artistic figure, Evgeny Kuzmin. After many hesitations I took my story to Kuzmin.

The editorial office was in his flat. A small, polite schoolboy opened the door and took me to Kuzmin's study. A spotted bulldog sat on the rug, dribbling and fixing me with its inflamed eyes.

It was stuffy. There was a smell of scented candles. The black walls were decorated with white masks of Greek gods and goddesses. Every piece of furniture was piled high with books in cracked leather bindings.

I waited, listening to the crackling of the bindings. Kuzmin came in. He was very tall and thin, with white fingers which shone with antique silver rings.

My Grandmother's Garden

He spoke to me with his head bowed in an attitude of respect. I mumbled and blushed, wondering how soon I could get out. I knew I was a fool and my story was rubbish.

He flicked the pages with his limp fingers and sidelined one passage with a very sharp nail.

'I regard my periodical as a forum for young writers,' he told me. 'I would be happy to welcome a new contributor. I will read your story and send you a postcard.'

'If it's not too much bother, would you send your answer in a sealed envelope?'

He smiled understandingly. I left.

I shot out of the house. The pavements were being sprinkled with water out of hosepipes. The water gurgled and the spray blew in my face. It made me feel a little better.

Anxious to escape from the very district, I jumped on a moving tram. The passengers watched me with amusement. I jumped off and walked.

Dust was rising from the Corn Market. Round clouds, all identical in shape and size, were sailing in a row above Lvov Street, which was as dull as usual. There was a sharp smell of horse manure. A scraggy grey horse went by, pulling a coal cart; a man with a coal-black face was walking alongside, shouting 'Coal!'

I remembered my story lying on the desk in Kuzmin's airless room and overflowing with purple passages and vague and noble thoughts about life. I burned with shame and swore never to write another.

'It's all wrong, it's all wrong,' I muttered to myself. 'It isn't what I meant at all. Or perhaps it isn't wrong but just bad?'

I no longer knew anything, I was in a complete muddle.

I walked in the direction of Podol. Cobblers with cold faces were hammering away at the soles of old shoes. The hammers struck trickles of dust from the leather. Boys with slings were shooting sparrows. Women were hanging up coloured clothes in their back yards.

It was a windy day. The wind sent dust and litter flying in the air above Podol. High on its hill, Rastrelli's Cathedral of St. Andrew shone above the city with its red pillars and silver domes.

I went into a tavern and drank some sour red wine, but this didn't make me feel better.

I got home late and with a bad headache. My grandmother rubbed me with 'spiritus' and put me to bed.

I was sure that I had made an irreparable mistake. Not only had I written an appallingly bad story but I had thereby cut myself off from writing for the rest of my life. There was no one of whom I could ask what to do now. I longed with my whole being to become a writer and I knew with complete certainty that my efforts were doomed. How was it possible?

Gattenberg was playing softly in his room. This time it was not 'The Death of Hamlet' but the 'Masque of the Red Death', a composition he was working on and of which he had played us several fragments.

My grandmother couldn't get over his predilection for gloomy themes. 'When it isn't death it's pestilence!' she complained. 'I can't understand it. I always think music ought to cheer people up.'

Gattenberg had come to his favourite passage:

> *They wept beside the streams*
> *That now run peacefully*
> *Through the wild paradise*
> *Of your native land.*

'That's better,' I muttered. Suddenly I knew what I had to do—work, persevere, live for writing. Clearly the way was hard and long, but for some reason this knowledge gave me peace.

Two days later I received a postcard from Kuzmin. He had disregarded my request for a sealed envelope. He wrote that he intended to publish my story in the next number of his magazine.

Needless to say, Grandmother had seen and read the postcard. It had actually made her cry.

'If only your father were alive!' she sighed. 'He used to laugh at me, but he was a good man.' She made the sign of the cross over me and kissed me. 'Well, work hard. God is very good to send me this joy in my old age.'

She was more excited about the publication of my story than I was myself. When the next number of *The Knight* came out, she baked a 'mazurka' and cooked a special lunch in honour of the occasion.

She even put on her black silk dress—the one that in my childhood I only saw her wear for Easter, and she pinned a bunch of artificial heliotropes on her breast. But the dress no longer made her look young as it used to in those days. Only her eyes laughed as she looked at me.

The wasps buzzed in the jam pot as we ate, and Gattenberg—as though guessing what the occasion was—played Vinyavsky's 'Mazurka' and beat time to it with his foot.

32
Latin

'You! A boy in the eighth form!' Suboch looked at me round-eyed, his moustache bristling.

What had given us the idea of making a 'psychological experiment' on Suboch was that there were six stout metal hooks sticking out of our classroom wall. Pictures had once hung on them; they had long since been removed but the hooks had stayed.

Suboch moved about the school like a whirlwind. Every morning he arrived in our classroom with his coat tails flying and his pince-nez flashing, he slammed the door and sent the mark book whizzing through the air to land on his desk with a thud. The class jumped up with a clatter of desk lids and made the same noise as it sat down. The glass jingled in the windows; the sparrows shot out of the poplars outside and made for the other end of the garden.

This happened daily. Coming to a stop, Suboch drew a tiny note book from his pocket, held it up an inch from his myopic eyes and froze in a menacing stillness: he was hunting for the name of his latest victim.

One morning, six of the smallest and lightest of us, including myself, were hung by our belts from the metal hooks (the hooks prodded our backs, hurting abominably). Then, just as Suboch was bursting in, all the others leapt on their desks and stood on their heads with their legs in the air.

Suboch—in mid-career and unable to stop—flung his mark book as usual at his desk. The instant it landed, the class reversed its position, stood upright and sat down; the six of us undid our belts, dropped to the floor and also took our seats.

There was perfect silence and order in the room. Our faces were expressionless.

When Suboch started to rant, we denied everything. With quiet assurance we maintained that no one had ever stood on his head or hung from a hook. We even hinted obliquely that Suboch was suffering from delusions.

He called up the six of us and inspected our clothes, but there were no traces of plaster on us; neither were there any on the floor. Suboch was shaken. He worried a lot about his health.

Calling in the supervisor, he asked him if he had heard anything strange at the beginning of the lesson.

'No,' said Platon Fyodorovich.

'No unusual noise?'

'The class always makes rather a lot of noise getting up and sitting down,' the supervisor said diplomatically, with a puzzled look at Suboch.

'All right. Thank you. It seemed to me there was something unusual.'

'What kind of thing?' the supervisor asked gently.

'Nothing, it doesn't matter,' Suboch suddenly lost his temper. 'Sorry I troubled you.'

The supervisor shrugged his shoulders and went out.

'I'll be back in a minute,' said Suboch, picking up his mark book and leaving the room. He returned a few moments later with Inspector Varsonofy Nikolayevich, known as Varsopont.

Varsopont gave us a curious look, went up to the wall, climbed on a desk and tugged at one of the hooks. It came out quite easily in his hand.

'Well, well,' said Varsopont, putting it back.

We were all watching him.

'Well, well,' he said again. 'It's certainly very strange.'

'Well,' he repeated and, shaking his head, left the room. Suboch sat down and stared, motionless, at his mark book. Then he leapt to his feet and dashed out. The door slammed. The sparrows shot out of the poplars. A draught rustled the pages of our books.

No one came until the end of the study period and we sat as quiet as mice. The success of our experiment had alarmed us; we wondered if Suboch might really go out of his mind.

The sequel was less tragic. Rumours of the incident flew round the school and the youngest boys, green with envy, tried the 'experiment' on one of their own masters. It is well known, how-

ever, that a work of genius can never be reproduced. The attempt
failed disastrously.

Suboch heard about it, flew into a rage and accused us in terms
worthy of Cicero's address to Catalina: 'How long, O Catalina,
shall our patience continue to be abused?'

What took us by surprise was that he was much less annoyed by
the deception practised on himself than wounded by our lack of
respect for Latin.

'Latin, the tongue of Ovid and of Horace!' he thundered. 'The
tongue of Cicero, Titus Livius and Marcus Aurelius! The tongue
venerated by Pushkin and Dante, Goethe and Shakespeare! And
they did more than venerate it, let me tell you—they knew it a lot
better than you do. Every word of Latin could be cast in pure gold
—there is not an atom of dross in it! And you dare to jeer at it!
You dare to turn your Latin class into a circus! Your cheap little
minds are stuffed with nothing but rubbish. Football! Snooker!
The cinema! That's all you can think about! You ought to be
ashamed of yourselves!'

We were! Indeed we felt crushed. But we were also offended.
Most of us knew a great deal of Latin.

An armistice was concluded, and in the end Suboch owed to it
the greatest triumph of his life.

We were very fond of Suboch and, to make up for the pain we
had caused him, we worked furiously on his subject. Thus finally
the day came when he could not, in justice, give anything less than
top marks to any boy he called to the board.

'A most fortunate occurrence,' he muttered, grinning into his
moustache.

We repeated our performance the next time, hard as he tried to
trip us up and drove us through our 'unseens'. Suboch beamed.
But there was a shade of worry mixed with his joy. The event was
completely unprecedented. It was too much like a miracle.

When the miracle happened for the third time, he looked frankly
upset. Our brilliance had become the talk of the school and was
giving scandal. Ugly rumours were going round. It was said
that Suboch was giving us better marks than we deserved in order
to build up his own reputation as a successful teacher.

'Do you think perhaps I'd better give some of you a little less
than top marks today?' he asked us in an uncertain voice.

Latin

We looked at him, hurt and silent. It seemed almost as if he would now be happy if one of us were to deserve a nought. Was he perhaps even regretting his inspired speech?

But we would have no truck with it. We could not unlearn our Latin and we were none of us prepared to fail our tests just to put a stop to the gossip.

In the end Suboch, driven desperate by the suspicions of his colleagues, arranged a public demonstration. He invited the Vice-Chairman of the district school board, the Director of the school, Inspector Varsopont and Father Olendsky, who was an eminent Latin scholar, to be present at one of our lessons. He harried us unmercifully and with all his cunning but we fought back staunchly and acquitted ourselves with spectacular success.

The Director rubbed his hands, Varsopont ruffled his hair, the Vice-Chairman smiled condescendingly, and Father Olendsky said: 'Just look at those young devils!'

After that our standard went down a little. We could not have stood the strain much longer. But by then the reputation of Suboch as the best teacher on record was established and unshakable.

33
The Humanities

Russian literature was taught us by Shulgin, an elegant old man with a glistening white beard and bright blue eyes—but who could be put in an ungovernable rage by a senseless remark. On such occasions he tore text books to shreds, or else clasped his hands, shook them in our faces and implored us:

'Get out! Yes, you. Please get out! Out!'

These fits were followed by complete exhaustion. He was ill, of course; we realised it, and so did the other teachers and the supervisors. If an attack continued for too long, Platon Fyodorovich tiptoed in, put his arms round Shulgin's shoulders and took him to the teachers' common room where he revived him with essence of valerian.

When he was in his right mind, Shulgin was almost too gentle. Literature, as taught by him, was a realm of unclouded peace. His system of marking our work was haphazard, and a small boy in a junior form had only to come and cry on his shoulder for him to change his marks to better ones than he deserved.

One day we were writing an essay for Shulgin on the worn out theme of the female characters in Turgenev's novels, when a cheeky and affected boy called Gudin said: 'The green parrots are now on the boulevard.'

It was the kind of remark calculated to set Shulgin off. He fell on Gudin, shook him so that his teeth rattled and tore at his jacket until the buttons flew off.

Matushevich grabbed Shulgin's arms while another boy went for the supervisor.

Shulgin sat down, clutched his head and burst into sobs. Several of us couldn't bear it and hid our heads under the lids of our desks.

Platon Fyodorovich hurried in with Varsopont and they led Shulgin from the room.

A dead silence followed their departure. Matushevich walked up to Gudin and said:

'You bastard! Get out or we'll kill you.'

Gudin stared idiotically and didn't move.

'Get out!' Matushevich repeated, and Gudin walked unsteadily to the door. There he turned and tried to say something, but such icy hostility met his gaze that he hunched his shoulders and slunk out. He never came back—it would have been impossible. His parents sent him to Falkner's technical school, a refuge for idlers and hooligans.

Shulgin also disappeared for good. He was ill for a long time and his doctors forbade him to go back to teaching. We occasionally saw him in Nicholas Square, sitting on a bench, his chin propped on the pommel of his stick. We bowed, but he only gave us a look of terror.

Shulgin was replaced by Trostyansky, a tall thin man with a pale arrogant face who divided writers in two categories—decent citizens who deserved to be studied and seditious characters who wasted their talent and of whom the less said the better.

He annoyed us and in the essays we wrote for him we reversed his judgments, praising his villains and attacking his gods. He calmly and politely explained to us that we were wrong and gave us zero.

Trostyansky was replaced by Selikhanovich who taught us psychology as well as Russian literature. He looked like Byron and wore a frock coat buttoned to the neck.

Selikhanovich was gifted and sensitive. He 'washed' the image we had formed of the Russian writers. It was as though a good restorer had cleaned a painting: he washed off the accumulated mud of boredom, *clichés* and petty judgments, and to our amazement, revealed the play of colour and the depth of meaning they had concealed.

We learned a lot from Selikhanovich, and not only about recent Russian writing. He introduced us to the nineteenth century philosophers of the West, as well as to Hans Andersen and to the *Song of Igor* of which until then we merely knew the Slavonic text.

He had a remarkable talent for exposition. Once he had

explained them, the most complex philosophical theories became clear, harmonious structures which bore witness to the admirable play and freedom of the human mind. Scholars, thinkers, writers, poets, whose names had suggested nothing to us except a string of dates and of their 'services to humanity', became living people set in their historical background.

Giving us a lecture on Gogol, Selikhanovich conjured up the Rome of Gogol's time, its hills and its ruins, its painters and its carnivals, its very air and the colour of its sky. Its outstanding figures appeared before us, quickened by a magic which he made us feel to be available to all of us, since it was only the magic of a passionate and imaginative scholarship.

Being taught literature by Selikhanovich was a breathtaking journey through time and space. We visited the armouries of Tula and the Cossack outposts on the road to Daghestan; we felt the very drizzle of the 'autumn in Boldino'; we moved from the debtors' prisons of Dickensian England to the market places of Paris, and from Chopin's sick bed in the ancient monastery on the island of Majorca to the unpeopled valleys of Tasmania where the sea winds rustled through the fields of maize.

Thus we followed the lives of the men to whom we owed our knowledge, such as it was, of our country, of the world and of beauty—Pushkin, Lermontov, Tolstoy, Herzen, Ryleyev, Chekhov, Dickens, Balzac and many others—and were filled with pride in the power of the human spirit and of art.

More surprisingly, Selikhanovich also instructed us on how to be polite and even tactful. This was one of the problems he set us:

'You are in a drawing-room with several other people. All the armchairs are occupied. A lady walks in. Her eyes are red with weeping. What should a well-mannered person do?'

'Get up and offer her his chair.'

'And what will he do if he is not only polite but considerate?' We didn't know.

'Turn the chair with its back to the window, so that other people shouldn't notice she has been crying.'

What astonished me was his remark to me one day when he was talking to me of my wish to be a writer: 'I wonder if you'll have enough endurance.' I hadn't thought of it as a qualification and only realised much later how essential it was.

Another day he stopped me in the school corridor and told me:

'You must come to Balmont's[30] lecture tomorrow night. If you want to write prose you must learn about poetry.'

The lecture was on 'Poetry and Magic'. I went to it. The hall at the Merchants' Club was crowded and hot. Waiting for the lecturer was a small table covered with a green velvet tablecloth and lit by two bronze candelabra.

Balmont entered. He was dressed in a frock coat with a flowing silk tie and a modest daisy in his buttonhole. His thinning yellowish hair curled over his collar. His eyes were fixed on a point above our heads, their expression enigmatic and a little arrogant. He was no longer a young man.

He spoke in a slow, vibrating voice. At the end of every sentence he paused and listened, like a pianist with his foot on the loud pedal, listening to the vibration of a chord.

After the interval he recited his own poems. To me, they held all the singing quality of the Russian language itself. He stood with his small red beard pointing at the ceiling and the music of his poetry broke over the auditorium in waves.

He stopped; the pendants of the candelabra shook with the applause. He held up his hand for silence.

'I am going to read you "The Raven" by Edgar Allan Poe,' said Balmont. 'But first I want to tell you a story which shows that fate is occasionally very kind to poets. When Poe died and was buried in Boston, his good Quaker relations ordered a very large and heavy tombstone. They evidently wanted to make sure that the restless spirit of the poet stayed where it belonged and did not come back to disturb the peace of mind of decent hard-working Americans. But the stone split as it was being placed on the grave. And there it still lies, over Edgar's bones, with pansies growing out of the cracks. Incidentally, Pansy was the name Edgar gave to his lovely wife Virginia, who died before him.'

Balmont read the poem and its dark splendour filled the hall. No longer did the Kreshchatik twinkle with chains of bluish lights outside the windows of the Merchants' Club—only the wind howled over the snow-covered plain, and the iron notes of 'Nevermore' fell into the emptiness like the striking of a tower clock.

Could it really be never more?—His mind could not accept it. Would he never see Virginia again, never hear her light, shy knock on the heavy door? Would there never be youth and love and happiness again? 'Nevermore' croaked the raven, and the man—the unimpressive little man who was the great, rejected poet Edgar Allan Poe—shrank with loneliness in his worn armchair and looked into the cold future with the eyes of a sick child.

All my life I have been grateful to Selikhanovich for awakening in me the love of poetry. It was poetry that revealed to me the possibilities of language. It refreshed the meaning of words and restored their power. My eyes were opened to the world of poetic imagery as though a bandage had been removed from them.

If Selikhanovich opened our eyes to literature and philosophy, Klyachin introduced us to the modern history of the West. Scraggy, with a prominent Adam's apple, always unshaven, his frock coat never done up, his eyelids crinkled and his eyes unseeing, he spoke in a harsh voice and in fragments of sentences.

He flung his words like lumps of clay at the image he was creating for us of Danton or Baboeuf or Marat, or of Napoleon or of Gambetta. His voice rattled in his throat with indignation as he told us the story of the 9th Thermidor or of the treachery of Thiers. He so far forgot himself that he sometimes lit a cigarette in class, though he quickly pulled himself together and put it out.

Klyachin was an authority on the French Revolution. That he was tolerated in our school at that time, remains a mystery. He was a complete anachronism—a survival of the past as well as an omen of the future.

He sometimes seemed to us to be the last of the Montagnards— a Montagnard who had somehow escaped the guillotine and the swamps of Guyana and, surviving his generation by a century, turned up in Kiev without any diminution of his fervour or austerity.

On the rare occasion when he was too tired to talk about the Revolution itself, he told us about its Paris background—the streets, the houses, the lighting of the squares, the clothes worn by the women, the songs, and what the newspapers looked like. He often made us wish we could go back a century and see for ourselves the great events which he described to us.

34
Assassination at the Opera

The polished parquet in the Assembly Hall was like a lake mirroring the dark blue rows of schoolboy uniforms with bright buttons, and the chandeliers burning in full daylight. The low murmur in the hall broke off. A Colonel walked in with a jangle of spurs, a short man with light, prominent eyes. He stopped and gave us a searching look. The bugles sounded with brassy voices. We were standing at attention.

The Colonel—Nicholas II—was followed by the Empress who came in, bowing her head to right and left, very thin and tall in a stiff white dress and a large hat; ostrich feathers drooped over the brim. Her face was lifeless, beautiful and ill-tempered. Following her in Indian file came four small girls in equally stiff white dresses and with pale thin lips; the dresses were without a bend or a fold, as though they were made of cardboard. Following the little girls came their governess, Princess Narishkina, an enormous lady, bulging, billowing and loudly rustling in lilac silk trimmed with black lace, a gold rimmed pince-nez on her nose, a satin ribbon across her chest, and fanning herself with a small lace handkerchief.

The occasion was the school centenary, but it had been ruined in advance because two days earlier, Stolypin had been assassinated by Bagrov, an old pupil of the school.

The Emperor was hidden from us by the courtiers, officers and members of the Government who accompanied him. All we could see now were bald heads and red ribbons, white trousers with gold braid strapped to patent leather shoes, and the silver belts and wide trousers and boots of Cossack Generals.

Nedelsky, who was top of the school in elocution, greeted the Tsar with a poem of his own composition, reciting it painstakingly in a loud, wooden voice and addressing the Emperor as 'thou'. Then the retinue parted, leaving a wide passage for the Tsar, who approached us and, fingering his light brown moustache, said slowly:

'Good day, gentlemen.'

We replied as we had been instructed, our voices clear but not too loud:

'We wish Your Imperial Majesty good health.'

Being the shortest boy in the top form, I was standing at the end of my row and the Emperor stopped in front of me. He had a slight nervous twitch in his cheek. With a distracted smile which only touched his eyes, he asked my name. I told him.

'Are you a Ukrainian?'

'Yes, Your Majesty.'

His glance passed to the next boy. He stopped in front of each boy and asked him his name. After the inspection came the concert. No one sat down for it because the Emperor remained standing.

We were watching the Tsar and his suite; the contrast between them astonished us. The Tsar, unimposing and even a little clumsy-looking, seemed lost among his crowded retinue. They flashed, gleamed and clinked with gold and silver, polished boots and cartridge belts, sword belts and swords, epaulettes, pelisses, medals and spurs. Even when they stood still they emitted a faint jingling of arms and regalia.

The Emperor was frankly showing how tired he was of galas and receptions. The courtiers were yawning behind his back. The whole thing was boring and unnecessary. The programme was cut short. The school orchestra played 'Glory, glory to our Russian Tsar', a boy recited the 'Song of Oleg' and the choir sang a cantata. After listening to the concert with a stony face, the Emperor left.

It had originally been decided to promote the school, on the occasion of its centenary, from a 'gymnasium' to a 'lycée' but after the assassination of Stolypin the plan was cancelled. It was hardly fitting to grant special privileges to an institution which turned out political criminals. The school was merely renamed 'Emperor

Alexander Gymnasium', in honour of Alexander I and our new badges were engraved with the initial A and an imperial crown.

An enormous number of festivities had been arranged for the week of the Emperor's stay in Kiev—the unveiling of an ugly bronze statue of Alexander II and of even uglier plaster monuments to St Olga and Sts Cyril and Methodius, military manœuvres on the outskirts of the town, and various inaugurations, processions, pageants and command performances.

All the high-school boys in Kiev were paraded on the race course. We marched past the Emperor, raising clouds of dust; the brass bands blared; the sunset was in our eyes, blinding us. We so lost our heads that we forgot to reply to the Emperor's greeting; a full General galloped up to us and, jerking irritably at his reins, gave us a dressing down; his horse pranced, its ears flat back.

Finally there was the gala performance at the Opera to which all the boys' and girls' high-schools sent their top forms.

We were taken up the dark stairways and passages to the gallery and locked in. We were not supposed to go down to the lower tiers. Polite but cheeky policemen stood at the doors. Occasionally they winked and let a pretty schoolgirl go through.

I was sitting in the back row where I could see nothing. It was very hot. The ceiling was just over my head. Not until the interval did I manage to push my way through to the front. I leaned on the balcony railing and looked down into the hall. It was veiled in a light haze; jewels came to life in it here and there and gave off coloured sparks. The imperial box was empty; the Emperor and his family were in the sitting-room at the back of the box.

Several courtiers and cabinet ministers were standing by the railing which separated the front row of the stalls from the orchestra pit. The musicians in their black tail coats were sitting in front of their music stands but not, as they usually do, tuning their instruments. I watched the audience and listened to the confused murmur of voices.

Suddenly there was a sharp crack. The musicians jumped up. There was another crack. I didn't at once realise that they were shots. A girl next to me cried out:

'Look! He's sitting down on the floor!'

'Who?'

'Stolypin. Over there, by the orchestra rail.'

The theatre was unusually quiet. Sitting on the floor by the orchestra rail was a tall man with a ribbon across his chest. He was fumbling with his hands as though trying to find a hold by which to raise himself. There was an empty space round him.

A young man in a tail coat was walking away down the aisle. It was too far for me to see his face, but I noticed that he was walking calmly, without any appearance of haste.

Someone screamed. There was a thud; an officer jumped to the floor from one of the first tier boxes and seized the young man's arm. A crowd immediately surrounded them.

'Clear the gallery,' a police officer said behind me. We were hurried out on to the landing. A muffled hum of voices was coming from behind the doors of the auditorium, which had been closed. It died down and the band played 'God save the Tsar'.

'He's killed Stolypin,' Fitsovsky whispered to me.

'No talking,' shouted the police officer. 'You are to leave the theatre at once.'

Going down the same dark stairs and corridors, we came out into the brightly lit square. It was empty. The mounted police had dispersed the crowd in front of the doors of the theatre and were driving it farther up the side streets. The horses were backing, pawing the ground and filling the square with the drumming of hooves.

A bugle sounded; an ambulance came up at a swinging trot; orderlies jumped out of it, carrying a stretcher, and raced up the steps.

The police were hurrying us out of the square, but they were themselves so confused that we paid no attention and hung back. We saw Stolypin being carried out on the stretcher and put into the ambulance, and the ambulance dashing away down Vladimir Street with a police escort galloping alongside.

When I got home and told my grandmother and Gattenberg what had happened, Grandmother said it was wrong to shoot in a theatre because innocent people could be hurt; Gattenberg got excited, blew clouds of cigar smoke, said the scoundrel had asked for it and went off in search of further news. He returned after midnight and told us that straw had been put down in the street in front of the hospital in which Stolypin was lying, and that the Black Hundreds were calling for a pogrom against the Jews.

'That was all we needed,' my grandmother said indignantly. Gattenberg said there was no danger of a pogrom so long as the Tsar was in Kiev.

Next morning my grandmother asked me if I was going into town. I said I had to go to school.

'Why?'

'We are rehearsing the reception for the Tsar.'

'As if the Tsar had nothing better to do! Why don't you say you've got a headache and stay at home? Everybody's rushing about like a lunatic, wasting time as if God will make it up to them. Sit and read in the garden. I'll make you a *strudel*. I can't think how people can dash about the streets in this weather.'

In the end I gave in and missed the rehearsal.

The weather was indeed wonderful. The leaves on the apple trees were turning pink and crinkly. Some of them had rolled up into little tubes and were tied with cobwebs. Red and white asters were flowering beside the paths.

Yellow butterflies fluttered among the trees and came down in clusters on the stone steps of the verandah, the tin watering can left out on the lawn and any other surface warmed by the sun.

As though diminished by the autumn, the sun travelled slowly overhead, taking a long time to reach the tops of the hazel trees.

I was reading in the garden, sitting in my grandmother's wicker armchair. Sometimes music reached me, coming from the town. After a while I put down my book and watched the path. There was thick grass on either side of it and the verges were dark with velvety moss. A patch of white showed against the velvet; a wood anemone had come up for a second time from a seed which somehow had blown into our garden.

A white duck waddled up from the yard, saw me, quacked with displeasure, and waddled back. Sparrows were preening themselves on the roof and craning their necks to see if there was anything interesting going on below: they were waiting. My grandmother came out, wrapped up in a warm shawl, and threw a handful of crumbs. The sparrows flew down and began to jump about like small grey balls.

'Come and have dinner,' Grandmother called me. I went up the verandah steps. A smell of apple pie came from the room.

'There's a royal feast for you,' said Grandmother, glancing at the garden. 'What more do people want?' The garden was indeed a feast of sunshine and clean warm air.

35
Razgulyay

I was travelling to Moscow to spend Christmas with my mother. The train passed close to Bryansk, but it was snowing blind and I could only guess at the familiar little town with its snow-carpeted streets and the glassed-in verandah of Uncle Kolya's house, somewhere behind the curtain of the blizzard.

It was my first trip to Moscow. I was excited at the thought of seeing Mama, visiting the capital, and going so far north from our southern, provincial Kiev.

With every hour we were moving farther into the white plains, slowly climbing to the edge of the dove-grey sky. There, in the dark haze on the skyline, it seemed to me that the daylight merged with the polar night.

What worried me was the weather in Moscow. I had mittens and a hood but no winter overcoat. The bells at the stations clanged and echoed in the cold air; felt boots creaked on the snow. My neighbour offered me bear steak; it smelled of pine pitch.

Somewhere beyond Sukhinichi, in the middle of the night, we got stuck in snowdrifts. The wind howled in the tin ventilators. The guards kept hurrying through with lanterns, as white and shaggy with snow as woodmen, banging the doors and waking me up.

In the morning I went out into the corridor and the air bit my face like sharp crystals; snow had blown in through the cracks of the doors and drifted along the floor. The carriage door opened with difficulty. The blizzard had died down. The snow was so deep that you could drown in it. A small blue bird sat chirruping on the roof of the carriage, peering to right and left. The white sky merged with the white earth. It was so still that I could hear the water dripping from the engine.

Dyma met me at the Bryansk Station in Moscow. He was wearing the uniform of the Technological Institute and had a small, black, bristling moustache.

I was chilled through and we went to have tea in the buffet. I was surprised to see that the Moscow station was a low wooden building, like an enormous tavern.

The orange sunlight fell on the counter with its nickel-plated dishes, the blue potted palms, the steaming teapots and the muslin curtains. The windows had patterns of arrow-shaped leaves made on them by the frost; we could hear the cab drivers shouting outside.

We drank tea with broken sugar and were served with crisp pastry sprinkled with flour. Then we went outside and stood on the steps. Shaggy horses were steaming; the drivers had patched coats with metal badges glinting in the sun: pigeons fluttered about and pecked the manure on the snow.

'Where to, Your Excellencies?' yelled the drivers, smacking their lips and shaking the reins.

One of them broke through and swept up to us; he folded back the worn wolfskin rug and we got in and sat down in the narrow sleigh, our feet on a bale of straw. I looked about me in amazement. Could this possibly be Moscow?

'To Razgulyay, but go through the Kremlin,' said Dyma.

'Any way you like. It's all the same to me,' said the driver.

Immediately outside the station square we got into a melée of sleighs, bells, tall painted yokes, horses' heads breathing steam at us, policemen's faces with frozen moustaches, and the sound of church bells rocking the air.

We drove over Borodino Bridge. The windows across the river were sullenly smouldering with the sunset. Yet the round-faced clocks at the crossroads were showing only two o'clock. Everything was wonderful and bewildering.

'Well, how do you like Moscow?' Dyma asked me.

'Very much.'

'Wait till you see the rest.'

Beyond Arbat Square we turned into a narrow street. At the

end of it I saw a hill and, on it, crenellated walls and towers, the
tops of green-roofed palaces and grey cathedrals, all of it veiled in
the reddish smoke of the sunset.

'What's that?' I asked, taken by surprise.

'Don't you recognise the Kremlin?'

I gave a deep sigh. I was not prepared for this encounter. The
Kremlin rose above the noisy city like a fortress of pink stone,
gold, and stillness. Here was Russia's history! 'Who so proud as
not to bare his head before the Kremlin's holy gate . . .' We drove
through the Borovitsky Gate, past the Tsar Bell, the Tsar Cannon
and the belltower of Ivan Veliki pointing at the evening sky, and
bared our heads as we passed through the dark entrance of the
Spassky Gate. A lamp was flickering before an ikon. The chimes
struck with a calm indifference overhead as we swept out, and downhill towards the river.

'Whatever's that?' I grabbed Dyma's arm. Rising from the
hillside was a cluster of intricate onion-domes, like gaily coloured
heads of burdock.

'Don't you know St Basil's?' he grinned.

There were bonfires in Red Square, and cab drivers standing
round them, warming their hands; the smoke hung over the pavements. And here on the walls, I saw the posters of the Moscow
Arts Theatre with its seagull in the corner, and others printed in
thick black type with the words 'Emile Verhaeren'.

'What's that?' I again asked Dyma.

'Verhaeren is in Moscow for a few days.' He laughed at my
expression. 'You'll get many more surprises before you're through.'

It was dark by the time we got to Razgulyay. The sleigh stopped
before a two-storeyed house with thick walls. We climbed the steep
staircase, Dyma rang the bell, and the door was flung open by
Mama. Behind her stood Galya, craning her neck at the dark
landing.

Mama kissed me and cried. Her hair had turned completely
white.

'Goodness!' she kept saying. 'You're completely grown up!
And so like your father! My goodness, how like him you've grown!'

Galya drew me close to the lamp and carefully examined my face.
I realised from her strained expression that she couldn't see me,
although she kept repeating that I hadn't changed at all.

The furniture was poor and unfamiliar. All the same, I found a few things I remembered—Mama's jewel case, an antique bronze alarm clock and, hanging over Mama's bed, a photograph of my father as a young man.

Mama got flustered because dinner wasn't ready and went off to the kitchen. Galya, as usual, asked me silly questions—what the weather was like in Kiev, why my train was late, and whether Grandmother still took coffee for breakfast. Dyma was silent.

I felt that our lives had been so eventful in the past two years that it was hard to know where to begin. Then it occurred to me that there was no real need to talk about anything that mattered. We had grown so far apart that the gap was too wide to bridge in the ten days I was to have in Moscow.

So I said nothing about my story—either to Galya and Dyma or even to Mama.

The thought of my grandmother, and of my room in the Lukyanovka came to me with a faint nostalgia. It seemed as if my real home were there. Here, everything now struck me as a little strange—the gloomy, two-roomed flat, and Dyma's Institute, and Galya's questions. Only Mama's eyes were unchanged. But even she was fussing about trifles to which in the old days she would never have given a thought.

I was waiting for her to talk to me about my plans, but it was not until we were having dinner that she asked casually:

'What will you do when you leave school?'

'I'll go to the University.'

After dinner Mama took out of her jewel case some theatre tickets—grey slips with the imprint of the seagull. 'They're for you,' she said.

They were for *The Living Corpse* and *The Three Sisters*. Mama had queued for them all night in the frost. I hugged her, touched and overjoyed. It was nothing she said, smiling; she had enjoyed herself, standing in the crowd of students; she had rarely had such a nice time.

The Three Sisters was on that evening, so Dyma and I went out immediately after dinner. We took the tram to Theatre Square; it was very cold; the cable crackled and shot blue sparks.

The Square was filled with small spangles of snow; they hung in the air and were clearly visible under the lamps. The windows of Muir & Marie Lise threw wide shafts of light on the pavement; in one of them there was a Christmas tree festooned with gold and silver tinsel.

We turned into Kamerger Lane and entered the modest-looking theatre. The floor was covered with grey felt. People walked noiselessly. A hot wind blew from the radiators. Everything was austere and yet festive.

My cheeks were so hot and, I suppose, my eyes were so bright that our neighbours glanced at me and smiled. 'Pull yourself together or you won't see or hear a thing,' said Dyma.

I was in torment for the characters in Chekhov's play. Yet so great were the play and the performance that I was also happy and refreshed.

All the sad and unattractive things I had seen in Razgulyay now seemed to me passing and unimportant. For all the poverty and failure of our lives, I was bathed in the inextinguishable light which came to me from the mysterious country of art; no one could deprive me of my wealth; no one had the key to it except myself.

In this mood I spent the whole of my holiday. Mama kept glancing at me and repeating that I had become astonishingly like my father.

'I can't see you ever becoming a steady, positive character,' she said once. She paused and added: 'No, you'll never be a prop. Not even to yourself. Not with your flights of imagination and with your frivolous outlook on life.'

I said nothing. She put her arms round me and drew me close to her.

'It doesn't matter, darling. All I want is your happiness. Nothing else is important.'

'I'm happy as I am,' I said. 'I wish you wouldn't worry. I've managed all right for two years. I expect I'll go on managing.'

Mama had taken to wearing spectacles. Their frame was broken and held together by a piece of tape. She took them off and fiddled with the tape; then she gave me a long look.

'How cold and formal we've all become,' she sighed. 'And so secretive. It all comes of being poor. You've told me nothing about yourself. And I don't tell you anything either, I keep putting it off. We really must have a talk.'

'All right. Only don't upset yourself.'

'Galya is blind.' She made a long pause. 'Now she's getting deaf as well. Without me she wouldn't last a week. You have no idea of the amount of care she needs. I've simply got no strength now, except for her. God alone knows how much I love you—you and Dyma and Borya, but I can't tear myself in pieces.'

I said I understood it all perfectly, and that I would soon be in a position to help her and Galya—just as soon as I was through with school. I no longer intended, as I had done in the past, to go back to live with her. But I felt sorry and affectionate and unwilling that she should torment herself on my account. I reassured her as best I could and, feeling more cheerful myself, went off to the Tretyakovsky Gallery.

I felt a stranger in my own family. There was too great a contrast between the sparkling city with its snow and sky, its church bells, its theatres, its museums, and the pinched and dreary life we led in our two cold rooms in Razgulyay.

It amazed me to see Dyma looking perfectly satisfied with his life—pleased with his Institute, and with his chosen profession which to me was utterly alien—as well as to notice that there was never anything to read in his room except a few textbooks and mimeographed lecture-notes.

As for Galya, her blindness restricted her to a continuous, cautious preoccupation with insignificant tasks. She was always having to grope for things; she did everything by touch. Her life had stopped when she began to go blind. Now she lived in her memories; they were small and monotonous, and they were getting fewer and fewer—she was beginning to forget things.

Sometimes she just sat in silence with her hands folded in her lap. Occasionally Mama snatched an hour in the evening to read to her, usually from Goncharov or Turgenev. When she stopped, Galya questioned her in detail about what she had just heard, trying however vaguely to recover the thread of the plot. Mama patiently replied.

There was hardly anyone at the Tretyakovsky Gallery. It seemed as if the winter had silently shifted the Gallery to the suburbs, where not a sound of the city was to be heard. Only the ancient crones—guardians of the masterpieces—drowsed in their chairs.

I stood looking at Nesterov's 'Vision of St Bartholomew'; with its thin birch trees as pale as candles and its confident young grass, reaching to the sky, it struck me by its undemanding beauty.

Sitting on the divan in front of the picture and aiming her lorgnette at it was a stout, middle-aged lady in black. A girl with auburn plaits sat next to her.

I moved aside, not to block their view, when the lady turned to me and said:

'Doesn't it remind you of the hills at the back of the park at Ryovna, Kostik?'

I looked at her, startled. She smiled. 'All you young people are so unobservant! Don't you remember the Karelins—Sasha and Lyuba and myself? We met at Ryovna. It's true it was ages ago.'

I blushed and said how do you do. Now I recognised her— Maria Timofeyevna, the mother of the little girls—but it took me some time to recognise Lyuba without her black hair ribbons and looking quite grown-up.

'Come and sit down,' said Maria Timofeyevna. 'How you've grown! I suppose I shouldn't call you Kostik. Tell me what you're doing in Moscow. Do you miss Ryovna as much as I do? What a marvellous place! We really must go back there next summer.'

I told her about myself and she told me that she and Sasha were still living in Oryol, but had come to spend Christmas with Lyuba who had finished school and was now at the Moscow College of Painting and Sculpture.

'Where's Sasha now?' I asked her.

'She's staying at the hotel. She's got a sore throat.'

Lyuba was silent but occasionally gave me a sidelong glance. We left the Gallery together. I saw them back to their hotel and they insisted on my coming in with them to get warm and have some coffee.

The large two-roomed suite was dark with heavy curtains and carpets.

Sasha greeted me as an old friend and at once asked for news of Gleb Afanasyev; so far as I knew, he was still at school in Bryansk. She had a ribbon tied with a bow round her neck, like a cat.

'Come along,' she seized my hand and dragged me to the other room. 'I'll show you Lyuba's pictures.' But Lyuba seized my other hand and pulled me back.

'Nonsense,' she said, blushing. 'You'll look at them another time. We'll see you again, won't we?'

'I don't know,' I hesitated.

'You must greet the New Year with us,' cried Sasha. 'At Lyuba's—she's got a studio in the Kislovka. You simply must come and look at all her bohemians, Kostik, you can't think what they're like! There's one woman, a painter, straight out of a French novel, you'll fall in love with her at once! She always goes about in a black satin dress—frou-frou-frou—and the scent she wears! It's called "Sorrow of Tuberoses"!'

'The rubbish you talk!' said Lyuba. 'No wonder you're always getting a sore throat.'

'That's only because it's delicate—like a nightingale's,' said Sasha, making a languid face. 'The rigours of the Russian winter are too much for it!'

'Seriously though, do come to my New Year's Eve party,' said Lyuba.

'I'm afraid I have to be at home. We always greet the New Year at home.'

'So you shall,' Maria Timofeyevna said firmly. 'Greet the New Year at home and come to Lyuba's afterwards. They'll be there all night if I know anything of them.' I promised to come.

When coffee was brought, Sasha dropped four lumps of sugar into my cup—it was quite undrinkable—and Maria Timofeyevna lost her temper with her. Lyuba sat in silence, with downcast eyes.

'Look at that Sleeping Beauty!' said Sasha. 'Isn't she beautiful, Kostik? Just look at her. Not like me—I'm the Ugly Duckling.'

'Stop it now. That's enough.' Lyuba pushed her cup away and stood up. I looked at her. Her blue eyes flashed angrily. She really was very beautiful.

At home, Mama was delighted when I told her I had seen the Karelins and they had asked me for New Year's Eve.

'Of course you must go. You'll enjoy it. You haven't had much fun in Moscow. They're nice people and very cultured.' Culture was Mama's yardstick—if she liked people, she said they were cultured.

It was still two days before the New Year. They were wonderful days, white with hoar-frost and mist. I skated on the rink at the Zoo; the ice was much harder and blacker than in Kiev; the attendants swept it with enormous brooms. I raced a bearded man in a small black sheepskin hat and always won. He reminded me of the artist at the house near Smela where I had once been with Aunt Nadya.

Mama kept meaning to take me to Aunt Nadya's grave at the Vagankovo cemetery, but we never managed to go.

I went to see *The Living Corpse* at the Moscow Arts Theatre and liked it even better than *The Three Sisters*. I enjoyed the scenes of Moscow, the trial, the gypsy songs.

Improbably, in the December frost of Moscow, a very different holiday came to my mind. I remembered Alushta, Lena, my parting from her. All these years I kept meaning to write to her, but I never did.

Thinking of her, I was struck by the number of people who had gone out of my life—Lena and Aunt Nadya, my grandfather who kept bees, and my father, and Uncle Yusia and others. How strange and how sad it was, and how much I had already experienced in my eighteen years of life! Since I had loved them and they had all taken something of my love away with them, it seemed to me I must be poorer than I had been. And yet I knew that my love of life was growing greater year by year.

Because of the many people who had left me for ever or for a long time, I felt that my meeting the Karelins again—I had completely forgotten them—had a special significance, as though it were meant.

I greeted the New Year at home. Mama baked a lot of biscuits and Dyma bought cold meat and cakes and wine. At eleven he went out. Mama said he had gone to fetch his fiancée; her name was Margarita. She assured me that Margarita was a remarkable girl who would make Dyma a wonderful wife, and I expressed nothing but joyful surprise, although privately I disliked the sound of her name and the fact that she came of a family of government officials.

I helped Mama lay the table. There was a smell of scorched hair; Galya had been waving hers with a curling iron and had burned off a long curl. She was very upset. I tried to comfort her.

I unpacked the presents I had brought from Kiev—a length of grey material for Mama, slippers for Galya, and a box of mathematical instruments for Dyma—a really beautiful box which I had wheedled out of Borya. Mama was so pleased that she even blushed.

A few minutes before midnight, Dyma arrived with a tall, pale girl. She had a long, sad face and wore an ill-fitting lilac dress with a yellow sash; a lace handkerchief was pinned to her bodice. She blushed continuously, and ate biscuits with a fork.

Galya immediately engaged her in a conversation on how children ought to be brought up. Margarita answered yes and no, glancing at Dyma, who sat with a tight smile and said nothing.

The alarm went off with a furious clatter, cutting Galya's reflections short. We drank a glass of wine each to the New Year.

Mama was clearly trying to make a good impression on Margarita, while covertly watching her every look at Dyma, as though weighing the quantity of love in each.

I talked nineteen to the dozen, trying to show I was full of the party spirit, but keeping my eye on the clock.

After drinking more wine, Mama cheered up and began to tell Margarita about our Easters in Cherkassy and our life of ease and happiness in Kiev long ago. She looked as if she didn't quite believe what she was saying and kept asking me for confirmation, which I gave each time.

At half past one I excused myself and went. Mama came with me to the front door and asked me conspiratorially what I thought of Margarita. I said she was delightful, and Dyma was very lucky. I realised that the truth would only have hurt her to no purpose. 'Please God,' Mama whispered. 'I think she likes Galya.'

Outside, in Basmannaya Street, I stopped and drew a deep breath of the cold air. I went to the Kislovka by cab, the driver quarrelling with his horses all the way.

The door was opened by Sasha who had a new ribbon tied with a large bow round her neck. The hall filled with a flight of twittering girls; they were followed by a handsome old man in a student's uniform, but there was no sign of Lyuba.

The girls giggled as they unwound my scarf and pulled off my coat, while the old man sang in a young voice 'Three goddesses upon a hill began an argument at dusk' from *La Belle Hélène*.

'His eyes, his eyes!' the girls shouted, and Sasha covered my eyes with her hands. My breath was taken away by the smell of hair and scent and the touch of Sasha's small hard fingers pressed on my eyelids.

I was seized by the arms and led. A hot breath on my face told me that the door of the inner room had opened. There was a sudden silence and a woman's imperious voice said:

'Swear.'

'What?'

'That tonight you will think of nothing but happiness.'

'I swear.'

'Now swear allegiance.'

'To whom?'

'To the one whom we have chosen to be our queen.'

'Swear!' Sasha whispered, her breath tickling my ear.

'I swear.'

'As a sign of obedience, you will kiss the hand of the Queen,' said the same voice, shaking with laughter. 'Sasha, take your big paws away.'

Sasha took away her hands and I saw the room, brilliantly lit and crowded with pictures. A haggard young man was lying in the pose of Vrubel's Demon on top of the piano, his arms twisted above his head and his eyes staring at me tragically. Another young man, with a snub nose, struck the keys. The crowd parted and I saw Lyuba.

She was sitting in an armchair on a round table. The folds of her light, white, clinging silk dress drooped to her feet. Her bare arms hung down, and she held a black ostrich-feather fan in her right hand. She was looking at me, trying not to smile.

I went up and kissed her hand. The old man dressed as a student gave me a glass of ice cold champagne; I swallowed it at a gulp.

Lyuba rose to her feet. I helped her off the table. She caught up her long skirt and bent over me.

'We haven't frightened you with our nonsense? Why have they given you an iced drink? You must have something warm. I think there's some mulled wine left.'

I was dragged to a table and offered food, but the intention was at once forgotten and I was laughingly pushed, together with the table, back against the wall, to clear the floor for dancing.

The snub-nosed youth struck up a waltz. The Demon jumped

off the piano and whirled away with Lyuba. She was leaning far back in his arms, her fan half over her face, and every time she swept past me she smiled through the feathers.

The old man was dancing with the woman whom Sasha described as the heroine of a French novel and who broke into peals of sinister laughter.

Sasha dragged me from behind my table and we danced. She was so thin, I felt she might break in two.

'Mind you don't dance with Lyuba,' she said.

'Why?'

'She's stuck up.'

After the dancing, the Demon finished off the wine in the bottles and got drunk.

'I thirst for summer!' he roared. 'Away with icicles! Let there be rain!'

The old man sat down the piano and sang in a heart-breaking voice:

> *My distant friend*
> *Will you not come?*
> *I weep . . .*

When we stopped, we heard rain—a fresh abundant downpour, somewhere just out of sight. There was a frightened silence, then we all dashed down the passage to the bathroom. The Demon was standing in the bath tub, dressed in an old mackintosh and galoshes, a heavy shower drumming on the black umbrella over his head.

'Gold! A rain of gold from heaven!' he was shouting.

The shower was turned off and the Demon dragged out of the bath.

The general hubbub went on, in which I too was shouting, laughing and reciting poetry. I didn't come to myself until Lyuba put out the chandelier and the room filled with the bluish haze of dawn.

Everyone fell silent. The faint blue daylight mixed with the light of the table lamp; faces looked shadowless and beautiful.

'This is the best moment of an all-night party,' said the old man. 'Now we can sip wine and relax, and talk about this and that. I love the dawn. It rinses the soul.'

The Demon hadn't sobered up. 'No soul rinsing!' he shouted.

'I refuse to listen to anyone rinsing his soul. Light consists of seven colours. This I respect. The rest I spit upon.'

There was a long silence. We were half asleep. Lyuba was sitting next to me. 'My head is swimming,' she said. 'And everything looks so blue. But I don't at all want to go to sleep.'

'This is the catharsis!' the old man said portentously. 'The cleansing of the soul by tragedy.'

'I don't know about that,' said Lyuba, becoming thoughtful. Her eyes reflected the blue of the morning.

'You are tired,' I said.

'No, just happy.'

'Are you really going to Ryovna this summer?'

'Yes. Will you come?'

'Yes. If Uncle Kolya is there.'

'Only "if"?' she smiled.

Soon we got up and began to say goodbye. I was the last to go. I was seeing Sasha back to her hotel, and she was waiting for her throat to cool after a hot cup of tea.

When we came out, we found smartly dressed young men and women—we thought they were actors—playing at snow-balls in the street . . . The snow was sprinkled with confetti. The sun was rising, its shaggy flames bursting through the mist.

I felt ashamed of going back from the party to our wretched flat with its everlasting smell of kerosene. But the thought only passed through my mind. An instant later the world was again vibrating as if the snow, the sun, the sky, the touch of Lyuba's hand resting for a moment in mine as we said goodbye, and indeed the whole of life in general were all part of a quiet orchestral music.

I left Moscow two days later, by the night train. Mama came to see me off and stood on the platform, bent and muffled up in her thick shawl. Dyma was at the theatre with Margarita. Galya had spent the day worrying that I would miss my train.

'Don't be angry,' said Mama. 'I may have said you were like your father, but you are a good boy, I know you are.'

The train moved. For a long time I stood watching the lights of Moscow, wondering which of them was burning in Lyuba's room.

36

A Tale about Nothing

The thaw started in February. With it came the fog. The warm wind drove it away. Lukyanovka was full of the smell of melting snow and wood bark; the wind carried it from across the river, where the woods were darkening with the approach of spring.

The roofs dripped, the icicles tinkled, and only at night—and not always then—did the wind sweep away the clouds, so that the puddles froze and the stars came out. You could only see them in the suburbs. In town, there was so much light from windows and lamps that no one ever suspected their presence.

On raw February evenings my grandmother's cottage was particularly warm and cosy. The lights were on and the shutters closed; the wind blustered in the empty garden outside.

I was writing another story, this time about Polessye and the Old Men of Mogilev. The longer I tinkered with it the staler it became. But gutted and limp though it sounded in the end, I took it to the periodical *The Flames*.

The address was in Fundukleyev Street; the office was a small room facing the yard. A jolly looking, tubby little man was getting ready for tea and slicing salami on a pile of galleys when I came in. In no way surprised by the appearance of a schoolboy with a manuscript, he took it from me, glanced at the ending, said he liked it and told me to wait for the editor.

'Is that your real name?' he asked, pointing at my signature.

'Yes.'

'That's a mistake. The periodical is Left Wing. You are still at school, you might get into trouble. Better think of a pseudonym.'

I meekly crossed out my name and put 'Balagin' instead.

'That'll do,' he approved.

A Tale about Nothing

A gaunt, sallow man, with a tangled beard and sunken, piercing eyes, walked in from the street. Coughing and cursing, he took a long time unwinding his long scarf and taking off his snow boots.

'The editor.' The tubby man stopped peeling his salami and pointed at the newcomer with his penknife.

The editor went to his desk without glancing at me, sat down, stretched out his hand and said in an alarmingly hollow voice: 'Hand over.' I put the manuscript in his hand.

'You know that rejected manuscripts are not returned?'

'Yes.'

'Good,' he grunted. 'Come back in an hour and I'll give you my answer.'

The fat man winked and grinned.

I went away discouraged, wandered up and down the Kreshchatik and dropped in at the library where I met Fitsovsky; he had just borrowed a volume of Ibsen and attacked me for not reading more of him; *Ghosts*, he said, was the greatest masterpiece ever written. We left the bookshop together and, as the hour was not yet up, went into a dark courtyard to smoke. Smoking was forbidden and we didn't want to be caught by a teacher or a proctor.

Fitsovsky came with me to the door of the office and, being curious, offered to wait, but I begged him to go—I couldn't bear the thought of facing him if I came out with my story rejected.

I went in. The editor looked at me searchingly and said nothing. I too remained silent but felt waves of heat coming from my face.

'Can I have my manuscript back?' I asked at last.

'What?' He laughed and collapsed into a fit of coughing. 'Certainly, by all means, take it and put it in the fire. Only as it happens, I want to publish it. Believe it or not, I like it.'

'Sorry, I didn't realise,' I muttered.

'Don't be so impetuous. You'll need a lot of patience if you're going to be a writer.—Come back for your fee on Wednesday,' he added icily. 'And whatever you write next, kindly bring it along.'

I dashed out and saw Fitsovsky standing by the gate. He had waited after all.

'Well?' he asked nervously.

'They've taken it!'

'Come on,' he said, 'let's celebrate. We'll go to my room. I've got some muscatel and some pickled apples.'

Between us we drank the bottle of muscatel. By the time I went home, the trams had stopped. The streets were empty. The lights were out. If I had met a beggar I would certainly have taken off my coat and given it to him. Instead, I met a white dog shivering beside a fence. I stroked it and it immediately attached itself to me. I talked to it all the way home, and it jumped up and snapped at my coat sleeve to show that it understood.

'Listen,' I said, stopping. The dog pricked up its ears. Something rustled behind the garden fences, as if last year's leaves were being stirred.

'That's spring,' I explained. 'And then it will be summer. And then I'll go to the country. And perhaps I'll see the most perfect woman in the world.'

The dog jumped, snapped, and we continued on our way.

There was not a light in any of the windows. The whole city was asleep. How could they, I wondered; they ought all to be out in the street, watching the dark, scudding clouds and listening to the thaw—the snow softly crunching, the water slowly dripping from the melting, hollow snowdrifts. It was wrong to be asleep on such a night.

I don't remember how I finally got home. Grandmother was asleep. The dog politely followed me to my room. Supper was waiting for me on the table. I gave the dog some bread and meat and made it comfortable for the night in the corner by the stove. It fell asleep instantly. Now and then it wagged its tail without waking up.

My grandmother saw it in the morning, but she wasn't annoyed with me. She took pity on the dog, called it Cadeau, fed it, and the dog stayed with her for good.

Spring was getting closer and closer, and so were our final examinations. We had to revise everything we had ever learned at school. The spring made it even harder.

At the end of the Easter holidays Uncle Kolya came over for a few days from Bryansk, to see my grandmother. He shared my room. Aunt Vera was annoyed because he didn't stay at the big house, but he laughed it off. We lay on our beds in the evenings, laughing and talking. If my grandmother heard us, she got up, dressed, and came and sat with us late into the night.

One evening I went with Uncle Kolya to one of Aunt Vera's

command supper parties. I detested them. Aunt Vera gathered round her what my grandmother described as a collection of *monstres et créatures*. One I particularly disliked was a fashionable oculist called Dumitrashko, a squeaky little man with a curly golden beard and golden locks tumbling down over the collar of his frock coat. He arrived rubbing his hands and immediately started to poison the air by venting his rage against all intellectuals: Aunt Vera's husband, a pimply, swarthy tycoon, egged him on. Another habitué was a retired general, Pyotukh, who came with his three daughters, all old maids, and talked of nothing but the price of logs, in which he traded in a small way. Aunt Vera tried to make small talk but with poor success. 'Mind you,' she began (her every other sentence began with 'mind you'), 'Madame Bashinskaya never wears anything except lilac,' or 'Mind you, the apples in this pie are from our own garden,' but the conversation never took fire. To help her to entertain her guests, she made her daughter Nadya sing and play the piano. Unnerved by the drilling stares of the General's daughters, the wretched girl sang shakily a romance fashionable at the time, called 'The Swan' ('The drowsy creek, the silent waters smooth as glass . . .') and made a mess of the accompaniment. Her German music teacher watched her anxiously. She wore her hair in a tall hayrick and had a nose so thin that the bright lamplight shone through it. She was always a silent witness at these parties.

After supper we went back to my grandmother. Uncle Kolya sat down with a sigh of relief and said, 'How nasty that was!'

To take away the nasty taste and think of something else, he invited Gattenberg to Grandmother's room and arranged a concert. Gattenberg played his 'cello and Uncle Kolya sang Polish folk songs for Grandmother:

> O Vistula, so blue,
> You flow to foreign lands,
> Your way is long . . .

My grandmother listened, her hands folded in her lap. Her head was shaking and her eyes clouded with tears. Poland was so very far away! She knew that she would never see the Vistula, or the Niemen, or Warsaw again. She was already finding it difficult to get about and had even given up going to Church.

Before he left, Uncle Kolya told me that he was going back to

Ryovna that summer and made me promise to come—not that I needed any pressing!

From that moment on, everything looked different. I even began to think I would pass my exam. It was a long time to wait, but the expectation of happy days is sometimes the best part of them—though I as yet had no idea of this curious aspect of human life.

37
The End of School

Our school leaving examinations began at the end of May and went on for a month. The rest of the school was by then on holiday. Ours were the only footsteps to echo through the cool, spacious building, resting after the hurly-burly of the winter.

The windows of the Assembly Hall, where the exams were held, stood wide open. Dandelion seeds blew round the room in the sunshine, winking like small white lights.

Dress uniform was obligatory. The stiff, silver braided collars scratched our necks. We undid them in the garden where we sat under the chestnut trees waiting for our turn.

We were frightened of the examinations, and sad to be leaving school. We were used to it, it was what we knew. The future was vague and alarming, chiefly because we were bound to scatter and lose touch. It was the end of our cheerful, closely knit family life.

Before the start of the exams, a meeting was held in the garden, to which everyone came except the Jews who knew nothing about it.

There it was decided that the best of the Russian and Polish scholars should deliberately get less than top marks in some subjects in order to forfeit their chance of a gold medal. We were determined that all the gold medals should go to the Jews who were not admitted to the University without one.

We swore to keep our decision secret, and to our credit, we never spoke of it to anyone outside, either then or at the University. If I break my promise now, it is because hardly any of my school friends are still alive. Except for a handful, they were all killed in the great wars which have taken place in my lifetime.

There was also another meeting. This was to decide which of us should help which schoolgirl to write her essay. For some reason the top form of the Marinskaya Girls' High School sat for its written examination in Russian with us.

Stanishevsky, who had conducted the negotiations, brought a list of six girls who needed help. I was allotted one called Bogushevich, whom I had never seen in my life.

We sat at separate desks, the boys on the left and the girls on the right of a central aisle. Supervisors walked up and down the aisle, watching to see that we didn't pass notes or bits of blotting paper or any other suspicious objects.

We knew that the six girls sat, each at the end of her row, closest to the aisle. The name Bogushevich suggested a plump Ukrainian; there was a fat one with thick plaits who I thought must be her.

The Director walked in; we stood up, he ripped open the stout envelope in which the set theme for the essay was sent over from the District Department of Education, and wrote slowly on the blackboard: 'True education includes moral as well as intellectual training.'

An anxious mutter went round the room. The subject was full of pitfalls. There was no time to lose; I got down to writing a synopsis for Bogushevich at once.

We were allowed to smoke during our final examination on condition that we asked permission one at a time and went to the smoking room at the end of the passage. The proctor on duty in the smoking room was the now decrepit Kazimir—the one who had taken me to my prep form on my first day at school.

On my way down the corridor, I rolled up the crib and fitted it into the hollow mouthpiece of my cigarette. I smoked the cigarette and left the stub in a pre-arranged place on the windowsill. Kazimir was peacefully chewing a sandwich and saw nothing.

The rest was up to Littauer who followed me to the smoking room, picked up my stub, substituted his own, extracted the crib on his way back and dropped it on Bogushevich's desk as he walked down the aisle. Littauer was followed by Stanishevsky, Régamé and two others. My job was easier than theirs, which required sleight-of-hand.

I watched Littauer but never saw him drop the note. Only the feverish way in which a girl started to write told me that the operation had been successful. But it was not the fat girl with thick braids; all I could see of this one was her thin back with the white straps of her pinafore crossed over it and the reddish curls at the nape of her neck.

We had four hours to write the essay and most of us finished earlier. Only the girls were still sweating at their desks. We went into the garden. There were so many birds in the trees that they seemed to have gathered from all over Kiev.

Littauer and Stanishevsky had a clash. Littauer said the conspiracy had been planned in an idiotic way. Stanishevsky, proud of its success and expecting to be congratulated, was furious.

'What was idiotic?'

'There was not the slightest need for each of us to know the name of the girl he was supposed to help. Six girls—six cribs. Any girl could have used any one of the cribs. It only made an extra complication when it came to dropping the notes.'

'Good Lord! Have you no imagination? Are you a complete cretin? Don't you understand that I did it deliberately?'

'What on earth for?'

'Because it made it more interesting, that's why, you idiot! How do you know that a burning passion won't spring up between the rescuer and the rescued? I suppose that hasn't occurred to you!'

'No, I must say, it hasn't.'

'Well, you're an ass,' Stanishevsky cut the argument short. 'Let's go to François'.'

François' was a café where after every exam we squandered our savings on an orgy of five or six ices each.

The subject which terrified me most was trigonometry, but I scraped through. The exam dragged on into the evening. Afterwards we waited to hear the results. Overjoyed because no one had failed, we rushed into the street, making a tremendous din. Stanishevsky flung his textbook into the air; the leaves came fluttering down from the sky and scattering all over the pavement. Pleased with the sight, we all threw our textbooks to the sky and in another moment the whole street was white and rustling. A policeman blew his whistle at our backs.

We turned into Fundukleyev Street and gradually scattered to our homes until only five of us were left: Stanishevsky, Fitsovsky,

Shmukler, Khorzhevsky and myself. We went to the Galitsky Market where there were a lot of beer halls and restaurants. The exams were virtually over—only Latin was left and we none of us were afraid of Latin—so we decided to get drunk.

We walked down the street, joking and giggling; people stopped to stare at us. We went into a beer hall. The floor boards stank of beer. There were cubicles along the walls, lined with pink wallpaper and described as '*cabinets particuliers*'. We took one, and ordered vodka and Boeuf Stroganoff.

The proprietor tactfully drew the curtain, but we made so much noise that people kept looking in. We offered them all drinks, and they all drank to our 'successful finish'.

Late in the evening, the proprietor came in and muttered, with a warning glance at the curtain: 'There's a snooper.'

'What kind of a snooper?'

'A policeman in plain clothes. You'd better get out quietly. Go through the back door. There's a passage from the yard into Kudryavskaya Street.'

We didn't take it very seriously; all the same we left through the back door, across the dark, smelly yard with its dust bins and its woodshed, ducked under the clothes lines and came out. No one had followed us.

The pavement was dimly lit. Waiting for us was a round-shouldered man in a bowler hat.

'Good evening, Gentlemen,' he wheezed menacingly, raising his hat. 'Have you had a good time?'

We said nothing and went on. The man followed us.

'Thought you'd get away through the back? Aren't you a bit young?'

Stanishevsky stopped. The man also stopped and put his hand in his pocket.

'I don't know what you want,' said Stanishevsky, 'but you can leave us alone and go to hell.'

'So that you can slink into another tavern!' the man burst out. 'High-school boys, boys from the Emperor Alexander Gymnasium going to beer halls! Did you know you can get a wolf ticket for that?'

'Come on,' said Stanishevsky. 'We don't have to listen to that fool.' We walked on.

'Fool, am I?' said the detective, keeping a yard behind us. 'It's you who are fools. I was at high school myself once.'

'You look like it,' said Stanishevsky.

'You don't believe me,' he shouted hysterically. 'Well, it's true. I went to high school and I got expelled with a wolf ticket for getting drunk. And you imagine I'll let you get away with it! I'll see you're expelled with wolf tickets if it's the last thing I do. You can say goodbye to the University here and now, and you needn't worry any more about exams—they won't help you. I heard you in the beer hall. Did you speak against the Government? You did. Did you joke about the Emperor's family? You did. It's as easy as winking. And don't you try any tricks on me. I'm reporting you to the security police and that's that.'

We turned off into the tangle of narrow streets which led to the wasteland. We thought that he would be afraid to follow us to such a place, but he stuck to us like a leech.

'Can't we deal with him—five of us?' Stanishevsky whispered. We stopped. The man pulled out his revolver and showed it to us with a snigger.

We took him on an endless walk through back alleys, avoiding the crossroads where there were policemen. Fitsovsky suggested that we should disappear one by one; the detective was bound to follow those who stayed together until only one was left—that one would be caught but not the rest. But we refused to consider throwing one of us to the wolves.

We jeered at him mercilessly. We each made up a version of his biography and discussed it in loud voices, adding more and more monstrously insulting details. He was panting with rage and obviously getting tired, but he limped after us with lunatic obstinacy.

By the time the sky was getting lighter in the east, it was clearly necessary to take action. We made a plan and took a long way round to Stanishevsky's house. It had an eight foot wall facing the street, smooth except for a projecting ledge near the bottom. At a given signal, we sprang on the ledge and swung ourselves across, thankful for the gymnastics we had done at school.

Finding a heap of broken bricks at the foot of the wall, we sent them flying at the detective who had remained outside. He yelled, jumped back on to the road and fired his revolver. The bullet zoomed unpleasantly overhead.

We dashed across the yard, into an inner courtyard and up the stairs to Stanishevsky's flat on the third floor. Within seconds we were undressed and lying on sofas and divans, listening to the noises outside. Stanishevsky's father, a respectable lawyer, strode up and down the flat in his dressing gown, his hair bristling. He shared our fighting mood but implored us to keep away from the windows.

First we heard shouting in the street, and someone furiously shaking the gate and cursing the porter, then the voices of the detective, the porter and several policemen arguing in the yard. Fortunately the inner courtyard had a back way out and the porter assured them that we must have escaped that way. After a few minutes they left.

We slept like the dead until midday, when Stanishevsky's sisters went to reconnoitre, reported that there was nothing suspicious to be seen, and we all went home.

We had escaped a serious danger by the skin of our teeth. The detective had certainly meant to get us, and a wolf ticket was a fate equivalent to civic death.

The day came at last when we stood facing the Director across the green baize covered table in the Assembly Hall, and he congratulated us one by one and handed us our certificates.

The traditional ball in our honour was given the following night. The schoolgirls who had sat with us for the examination in Russian had been invited. The school building blazed with lights, the garden was decorated with coloured lanterns, the band was playing.

Before the dancing began Suboch made a speech:

'As fourth formers I could only just tolerate you, in the fifth form I began to teach you though the odds on turning you into human beings were small; I made friends with you in the sixth, became attached to you in the seventh and proud of you in the eighth. I am an unhappy father, I have too many children—forty of them and they change every few years. So I have forty times as many cares and troubles as fall to the lot of ordinary parents. As a result I may not have paid as much attention to each of you as I wished. Now you are going and I am sorry. I tried to turn you into decent people. You on your side gave me an aim in life. You kept me young. I hereby solemnly forgive you all your idiocies, including even your fights with Section One—I forgive you everything, it doesn't take much generosity on my part. But I ask you to be generous on yours. Heine said there are more fools in the world than human beings. Clearly he exaggerated, still he meant something. He meant that every day we meet people whose existence brings neither joy nor profit either to themselves or to those around them. Be afraid of being useless! Whoever you are, remember not to let a single day go by without writing at least a line. Work hard. For what is talent? Only work in triplicate and in quadruplicate. Love your work, and may you always be sorry to put it down. I wish you happiness. And don't think unkindly of the teachers who have grown grey in their wars with you.'

We rushed at him and he kissed us every one.

'And now, a few words of Latin,' he said. He waved his arms and broke into '*Gaudeamus igitur juvenes dum sumus.*' We joined in the chorus of our first student song.

The ball opened. Stanishevsky was master of ceremonies. Stanishevsky ordered the rescuers to dance with the rescued and introduced me to the thin girl with radiant eyes who was Olga Bogushevich. Her eyes cast down, she thanked me for my help and turned pale with embarrassment. I assured her it had been no trouble. We danced. I fetched her an ice from the buffet. After the ball we saw the schoolgirls home. Olga Bogushevich lived in Lipki. I walked with her through the dark night under the warm canopy of the chestnut trees. Her white dress was even more festive than the June night.

After that I went to Fitsovsky's. We had pooled our money to buy food and wine and invited Suboch, Selikhanovich and Johanson. Johanson sang songs by Schubert. Suboch accompanied him brilliantly by clinking bottles.

We made a lot of noise and came away when the sun was up but the streets still held their long cold shadows. We hugged and kissed in farewell and went our different ways, feeling intensely sad and intensely happy.

38
Summer Night

There it all was, just as I remembered it—the leaves of the hazel trees outside the window, the raindrops shining on them, the sun on the drenched park, the sound of the water on the mill race. I was back at Ryovna, but the Karelins' house stood empty and boarded up. Only a stray black dog lived on the verandah; when anyone came by, it yelped and hid in the bushes outside until the danger was past.

Sasha had had diphtheria and no one knew for certain whether the Karelins were coming later or not at all.

It was a summer of uncertain weather and violent storms. Uncle Kolya said it was because of the sunspots.

The rains came first, then the drought. Quiet days were suddenly torn by hot winds which brought a dry haze. The river darkened. The pines muttered and swayed. Dust chased travellers on the roads, whirling away to the ends of the earth.

'It's a hard summer,' said the peasants.

The leaves crinkled on the lime-trees. The river dropped day by day. In the mornings there was less and less dew, and when the sun came up you could hear the dry seeds popping in the grass. The hot fields were littered with white tufts of burdock.

'There's sure to be a terrible storm after such a heat wave,' people said.

The storm came at last. Gleb Afanasyev and I watched it slowly approaching all through the morning. The heat was stifling. We went to the river and lay in the lukewarm water.

The sky seemed to be full of smoke and through the smoke you could see great black bulges of petrified cottonwool—these were the storm clouds showing through the dust.

Summer Night

Everything was dead still. The frogs and the birds had fallen silent and the fish had stopped splashing. Even the leaves in the trees were motionless as though terrified. Mordan had crawled under the verandah and lay whining softly and refusing to come out. Only people continued to make a noise, walking about and calling to each other, but they too felt uneasy.

At dusk the haze dissolved and a single cloud as dark as night filled half the sky. It was shivered by lightning but there was no sound of thunder. A blurred moon rose in the east and advanced alone upon the cloud, with not a single star at its back. At every flash of lightning it turned pale.

Finally the earth drew a deep, refreshing sigh. The thunder rolled over the woods and away across the waving cornfields to the south. While its mutter was still dying down, a second peal followed it in the same direction, shaking the ground.

'The Prophet Elijah driving his carriage in heaven,' said Gleb.

The edges of the cloud curved downwards. There were yellow eddies in it, and black caverns where the lightning exploded and flickered from cave to cave.

The village church bell tolled the signal to put out all fires—two quick strokes followed by a pause, repeated again and again. We damped the stoves, closed the doors, windows and shutters, and sat down on the verandah to wait.

Somewhere far away beyond the park there arose a roar as vast as the earth. Aunt Maroossya couldn't stand it and went inside. The roar came upon us like a tidal wave. It was the wind.

Everything was whistling and howling. The lime-trees creaked. A yellow darkness raced low over the earth. A glass pane cracked and tinkled. An unbelievably white light flared and there was a bang as if the house had been driven up to its roof into the ground. A ball of yellow fire ran smoking and crackling along the tree-tops and burst with a dry crash like an artillery shell.

'I wish it would rain,' Aunt Maroossya kept saying. 'If only it would rain.'

The rain fell. Grey torrents streamed through the dishevelled park. The downpour reverberated, gathering strength. To its reassuring sound, we went to bed and were soon fast asleep.

I woke up in the middle of the night to hear dogs barking and horses snorting, then footsteps, laughter and the clatter of dishes.

Gleb was awake, too. The rain had stopped but the lightning still flashed continuously.

'My prophetic soul tells me that someone has arrived,' said Gleb. 'But who? Listen.' We lay listening, then Gleb jumped up and began to fling on his clothes in the dark. 'Come on, it's them. I hear the divine strains of Sasha's voice.'

I got up and began to dress. 'Yes, Kostik's here, he's been here a long time,' I heard Aunt Maroossya saying. 'So is Gleb. We must wake them up.'

'Let them sleep,' said Maria Timofeyevna. 'They can talk tomorrow. How we ever got here, I still don't know. For two hours we were held up by the storm at Ryabchevka!'

'Come along,' said Gleb.

'You go first.'

'Oh, so you're nervous.'

'Why should I be nervous?'

'Well then, let's go together.'

The ground floor was lit up. Aunt Maroossya was pouring out tea. There was a pile of wet suitcases by the door.

Sasha ran to meet us and hugged us. We kissed Maria Timofeyevna's hand. She pinched my cheek and said: 'How sunburned you've got.'

Lyuba was kneeling on the floor with her back to us, digging inside a suitcase.

'Lyuba,' said Maria Timofeyevna. 'Don't you see Kostik and Gleb are here?'

'I'm coming, I can't find the lemons.' She got up slowly.

'Well, don't bother, we can do without.'

Lyuba turned round, smoothed her hair, and held out her hand to me. She gave me a quick glance and looked away.

'Come and sit down,' said Aunt Maroossya. 'Your tea will get cold.'

We could hear Uncle Kolya outside on the verandah. He was splashing water on somebody's hands and the other man was washing, snorting and protesting: 'Please don't bother, it's too kind of you, thank you so much.'

'Who is that?' I asked Sasha.

She took me by the shoulder and muttered in my ear:

'Lenya Mikhelson. A college friend of Lyuba's. He's a painter. An infant prodigy.'

'Who did you say?'

'You'll see for yourself. I hate him.'

'Stop whispering, Sasha,' said her mother.

Lyuba gave her sister an annoyed look and cast down her eyes.

Uncle Kolya brought in a tall young man in spectacles, with a long face and big teeth, who gave us an open, good-natured smile and shook hands. His short-sightedness made him clumsy, but it was clear that, as Mama would have said, he came of a good family. He had manners and assurance, but he was equally clearly city-bred.

'What a charming rural scene,' he said, after accepting tea from Aunt Maroossya, thanking her and sitting down.

Gleb snorted. Sasha said: 'Have some jam, it's strawberry.' Aunt Maroossya gave Gleb a worried look and Uncle Kolya frowned at him, but immediately smiled.

After tea we carried the Karelins' luggage to their cottage. The park was whispering and shaking off the rain. The cocks in the village were crowing in various keys. Dawn was breaking over the tree tops.

The Karelins got on with their unpacking. The sun touched the verandah railing with gold and disclosed the amazingly clean, fresh landscape. Lenya Mikhelson stood on the sandy path in front of the cottage, drawing on it with his stick.

'What a morning! Let's go and bathe,' said Gleb, after we had taken the last of the luggage across. We had also tried to help with the unpacking but Maria Timofeyevna had thrown us out.

We got our towels and went to the river, passing Lenya's drawing on our way. It was a face very like Lyuba's, with a round sun shining down on it, and written beneath it were the words 'Oh, sun-spun radiance!'

'Sloppy decadent!' Gleb fumed. He walked on, swinging his towel. After a while he said without looking at me:

'Chuck it, Kostik. Honestly! You'll only spoil your holiday. Stop thinking about it. Come on, I'll race you.'

He ran and I ran after him. Frogs jumped out of our way in the wet grass. The white sun rose higher and higher. The clean sky shone brighter and brighter.

By the time we got to the river, I almost thought that I had shed my sorrow. I was hot and out of breath, my heart was pounding and I told myself it was absurd to break my heart over a conceited girl on a morning like this and with a long hot summer day in front of me.

Uncle Kolya joined us by the river. We dived and swam, and disturbed the water so much that we could see the water lilies bobbing on the ripples as far away as the dam. I almost forgot to grieve over Lyuba's treachery. All I wanted was to show her that I didn't mind in the least—my life was much too full of interesting things for me to be upset about a holiday romance with its vague sighs and half-hinted confessions.

'Well, isn't it true, after all?' I asked myself. 'What's so special about my infatuation with Lyuba—is it more important than this sunshine' (the sun was reaching through the trees to the dark water below) 'or this remarkable smell of uncut hay, or even this small green beetle scurrying up the plank to the bath house?'

I consoled myself without much difficulty, presumably because my surroundings were so pleasant.

Gleb climbed on the roof of the bath house, stretched his arms to the sun, chanted in a nasal voice, 'Oh, sun-spun radiance', and jumped into the river with a yell.

'Come out, you hooligans,' called Uncle Kolya. 'After tea we'll go exploring.'

'Where?'

'Up the river, past Chalk Hill.'

I got out and walked along the dry planks on which my wet footprints vanished before my eyes. My bathing towel smelled of the sea. The sun was warm on my chest and my damp head, and all I wanted was to laugh, and talk, and race Gleb all the way back to the house. This I did; Mordan and Chetvertak raced after us, yapping, leaping and trying to snatch our towels out of our hands.

We tore past the Karelins' cottage with a frantic noise of laughing and barking, and burst into our house, nearly giving Aunt Maroossya a fit.

After tea we explored the bank of the river with Uncle Kolya; Gleb and I traced it on an imaginary map and invented names for every bend, backwater and creek. We waded through grass and bushes. Our shirts were yellow with flower pollen. 'I don't believe in being melancholy,' said Gleb with an air of deep thought.

So the summer went by.

The heat wave was soon over, and storm after storm broke over the park, piling the clouds on top of the trees. The clouds caught in the branches and left damp tatters clinging to them as they tore themselves free and raced off in blind terror.

The park rocked and moaned. The leaves of the water lilies stood straight up. The rain beat on the roof, and our top floor was as noisy as the inside of a drum.

Everyone cursed the weather except Uncle Kolya, Gleb and I. We put on our raincoats and went to the dam to check our fishing lines, and to fill our lungs to bursting with the raw wind. The wind tore leaves off the trees and sealed them to our faces. Our raincoats turned as stiff as wood. We shouted to each other.

We got into the very thick of the storm, and choking, turned our backs to it.

'Marvellous!' Uncle Kolya yelled. 'Absolutely marvellous! Mind you don't get blown away!'

'A charming rural scene,' shouted Gleb.

We went on a tour of inspection. The old willows thrummed as they caught the wind, all their branches taut and their leaves turned black and grey. Hollow trees cracked and splintered. Jackdaws rode the wind, dishevelled and shrieking inaudibly—we could see their open beaks but could hear no sound.

There was one place behind the tall dam which was always sheltered. To reach it, we had to climb down through dense weeds; the nettles lashed our faces but didn't sting us. It was there that Uncle Kolya kept his rods hidden under a log. We took them out with shaking hands. What would Aunt Maroossya say if she knew what we were up to? Even she didn't think us lunatic enough to go fishing in a storm.

We cast our lines. The wind howled a yard above our heads, but below it was still.

'I don't suppose for a moment they'll bite,' said Gleb. 'They aren't as crazy as we are.'

He said it to reassure the fish, pretending not to care but in reality desperately longing for a catch. By a miracle, the float sank.

Uncle Kolya gave a shout. We tugged at the strong, tinny looking fish. The wind had become a hurricane. Flurries of rain scudded over the water. But we were past noticing.

'Are you cold?' shouted Uncle Kolya.

'No. Wonderful!'

'Want to go on?'

'Of course!'

The storm lasted five days and died in the night. No one saw it happen.

I woke up in the morning to the twitter of birds. The park stood deep in mist. The sun was struggling through it. The mist was light blue—evidently the sky above it was clear.

Uncle Kolya had lit the samovar and was letting it smoke outside the verandah. The smoke rose straight up. A faint smell of burnt fir-cones drifted into the room.

I lay in bed, looking at the top of the lime-tree in front of the window. Something wonderful was happening to it. A shaft of sun had broken through the leaves and lit hundreds of small green and gold lights. It was a sight no painter could have put on canvas —certainly not Lenya Mikhelson.

In his pictures there were orange skies, blue trees, faces as green as water melons, and all of it was as much an invention as my love for Lyuba now appeared to have been. I was quite cured of it. What perhaps had contributed most to my recovery was the five-day storm.

I watched the sun piercing the tree deeper and deeper. It fell on a single yellow leaf, then on a tomtit, then on a raindrop, quivering and ready to fall.

'Kostik! Gleb! Do you hear?'

'What?'

'The cranes.'

We listened. A sound came from the blue haze as though water were splashing in the sky.

39
A Dose of Poison

The village chemist was called Lazar Borisovich. He sometimes called on Uncle Kolya.

He struck me as a very unusual chemist. Dressed in a worn out student's uniform, with a crooked pair of pince-nez on a black cord wobbling on his thick nose, he was short, squat, whiskered up to the eyes, and known for his sharp tongue.

We knew that he came from Vitebsk, had studied at the University of Kharkov but not taken his degree, and now lived over the shop with his hunch-backed sister. We guessed that he was somehow connected with the revolutionary movement.

His pockets were stuffed with pamphlets by Plekhanov; passages in them were underlined in thick red or blue pencil, and their margins were scribbled over with notes and exclamation marks. On Sundays he took them to some quiet corner of the park, spread his jacket on the grass and lay reading, his legs crossed and one thick boot swinging in the air.

One day I went to the chemist's to get some powders for Aunt Maroossya. She was starting a migraine.

The shop was the front room of an old peasant cottage, very clean, with floor mats, a geranium, porcelain jars on the shelves, and a strong smell of medicinal herbs. Lazar Borisovich gathered and dried or distilled them himself.

Never have I known such a creaky place as that house. Every floorboard had its own squeak, and so had the chairs, the wooden sofa, the shelves and the counter on which Lazar Borisovich wrote his prescriptions. Every movement you made set up so many squeaks, in so many keys, that it seemed as if there were several invisible fiddlers in the shop, scraping their bows on very dry, taut strings.

Lazar Borisovich had a very fine ear for all these sounds and could tell exactly where each came from.

'Manya, can't you hear?' he shouted to his sister. 'Vaska's in the kitchen, he's after the fish.'

Vaska was the chemist's old, baldish, black tom cat.

'Please don't sit on that sofa,' the chemist sometimes begged a customer, 'it starts such a concert that it's enough to drive you out of your mind.'

Sometimes, as he ground his powders in his mortar, he told us that, thank goodness, the shop was less noisy now that the weather was more damp.

Suddenly the mortar let out a screech, the customer jumped, and Lazar Borisovich said triumphantly:

'So you also suffer from nerves!'

Setting my teeth on edge as he prepared Aunt Maroossya's medicine, he told me:

'As you may know, Socrates was poisoned with hemlock. Well, there's hemlock growing as thick as a jungle on the marsh, down by the mill. I'm warning you. It's got white umbrella-shaped flowers. The poison is in the roots. Look out for it if you go that way. Though actually, in small doses the poison is useful. Personally I believe that everyone ought to have a small dose of poison added to his food now and again, to clear his brain.'

'You believe in homeopathy?'

'As a psychological remedy—yes,' the chemist said with conviction. 'You don't understand what I mean? All right, let me try an experiment on you.'

I agreed out of curiosity.

'Well now, I know that some allowance has to be made for young people. Especially for young people just out of school and on the point of going to the university. Your mind must be like a merry-go-round. All the same, it's about time for you to start doing some hard thinking.'

'What about?'

'As if you didn't know!' Lazar Borisovich lost his temper. 'Here you are, starting out in life. Right? Well, what are you going to be, may I ask? What are you going to do with yourself? Or do you think you can just go on having a good time, treating every-thing as a joke and shrugging your way out of every serious problem? Life isn't all a holiday, young man! Don't you believe it. One thing I can tell you—we are on the eve of great events. I know your uncle laughs at me, but that doesn't prove he's right. So that's why I'm curious—what kind of a person do you intend to be?'

'I want to be . . .'

'Stop!' shouted Lazar Borisovich. 'I know what you'll tell me. You want to be a doctor, or an engineer, or a scientist or this or that. That doesn't interest me in the least. That isn't the thing that matters.'

'What is then?'

'Jus-tice!' he shouted. 'You've got to be on the side of the people. You've got to stand up for them. You can be anything —a dentist if you like—so long as you struggle for the people to have a good life. See what I mean?'

'But why are you saying this to me?'

'Oh, for no special reason. I'm just talking in general. You're a nice enough lad, but you don't do much thinking. I've been noticing it for a long time. So now, do me a favour and get down to it.'

'I'm going to be a writer,' I said, blushing.

'A writer?' Lazar Borisovich adjusted his pince-nez and gave me a look of shocked amazement. 'A lot of people want to be writers. I wouldn't mind being a Leo Tolstoy myself.'

'But I've already started to write . . . I've had some things published.'

'In that case,' Lazar Borisovich said briskly, 'be so kind as to wait a minute. I'll just weigh out these powders then I'll see you home, we've got to clear this up.'

He was obviously excited; he dropped his pince-nez twice as he was making up the packet.

We went out and walked across the fields. The sun was setting in the woods beyond the river. Lazar Borisovich picked a sage leaf, rubbed it, smelt it and said.

'This is a big thing you want to do, and it needs great knowledge of life. Right? At present you've got very little of it, if any. Do you realise how much a writer needs to know? It's frightening to think of! He's got to understand everything. He's got to work like an ox and not think about fame. One thing I'll tell you. You've got to go everywhere and see everything. Go to fairs, factories, night-shelters, peasants' huts. And to theatres, and to hospitals, and to mines, and to prisons—everywhere. So that in the end life is distilled in you like valerian in alcohol. So that you get a genuine essence. Then you can offer it to people as a miracle cure. In specified doses of course. Yes, indeed.'

He talked about what it means to be a writer until we came to the park. There he said goodbye.

'You're wrong if you think I don't take things seriously,' I told him.

'Oh, but I don't!' He seized my hand. 'I'm very happy! Can't you see? But admit there's something in what I said—and that you'll do a bit more thinking after my little dose of poison—eh?'

He kept hold of my hand and peered into my eyes. Then he sighed and walked away. I watched him across the field—a short shaggy little man, plucking at the sage. In the middle of the field he took a penknife out of his pocket, squatted on his heels and dug up a root.

The experiment worked. I realised that I knew next to nothing and had given very little thought to many things that mattered. I took the comic little man's advice and soon went out into the world, into that school of life which no amount of books or theories can replace. It was hard work. But being young made it easier—I didn't ask myself if I had the strength to go through with it, I was sure I had it.

That evening we all went for a walk up Chalk Hill. It was a steep hill overgrown with young pine trees; from its top the ground fell sharply away to the river. We sat on the edge of the cliff and looked out into the huge, warm autumn night. The sound of the water by the dam came from below. Birds were stirring in the branches, settling down for the night. Summer lightning flashed over the wood. When it did, you could see clouds like puffs of smoke.

'What are you thinking about, Kostik?' Gleb asked.

'Just things in general.'

I was thinking that I would never believe anyone who told me that life—with all it contained of love, and of longing for truth and for happiness; with its summer lightning and its distant sound of water in the night—that it could be without reason or meaning. I would strive to assert its meaning always and everywhere for as long as I lived.

Notes

1   *Niva:* illustrated weekly published in Petersburg, 1870-1917. Among its contributors were Chekhov and Tolstoy.

2   *Kantonisti:* sons of soldiers who, under an early 19th century law, were destined for the Army from birth and brought up in special primary schools in preparation for their military training. Knights of St. George: holders of the George Cross, a Tsarist decoration.

3   Taras G. Shevchenko (1814-1861): probably the greatest Ukrainian poet. *Kobzar* (1840) was his first collection of poems, one of which is entitled 'Katerina.'

4   Adam Mickiewicz (1798-1855), Polish poet and patriot, leader of Romantic school in Polish literature. After a term in a Russian prison, he lived in Russia for five years.

5   *Makhorka:* cheap tobacco.

6   Hetman: originally a Polish military title, retained by the Cossacks.

7   *Zaporozhye:* The Dnieper region where the main part of the Cossack army was settled between the 15th and the 18th century.

8   'Bloodletting of Uman ': massacre of Jews and Poles by Ukrainian Cossacks in 1768.

9   The *Gymnasium* (translated throughout the book as High School) was an eight year secondary school. Most *gymnasiums* were State schools, though some were private. The Matriculation certificate gained at the end of the course qualified the student to enter the University.

10   Alexander I. Herzen (1812-1870): Russian liberal thinker and writer who emigrated to the West in 1847; many of his works were banned by the Tsarist censors. Henryk Sienkiewicz (1846-1916): well-known Polish novelist, author of *Quo Vadis*, winner of Nobel Prize for literature in 1905.

11   *Russian Word:* daily newspaper with a very large circulation, published in Moscow, 1894-1917. *The Thought of Kiev:* the most important pre-1917 provincial paper; Left-wing, closed down by Petliura in 1918.

12   V. V. Vereshchagin (1842-1904): realistic painter well known for his battle scenes. Mikhail A. Vrubel (1856-1910): Symbolist painter, muralist, book illustrator and theatrical designer. One of his most famous pictures is ' The Demon ', inspired by Lermontov's poem.

Notes

13 Science School ('real'noye uchilishche') was a secondary school with a scientific, technical and mathematical slant, as against the classics and humanities slant of the *gymnasium*.

14 Anton G. Rubinstein (1829-1894): famous Russian pianist, composer of fifteen operas, including *The Demon* (based on Lermontov's poem), and founder of the St. Petersburg Conservatoire.

15 Contract Fair: so called because the contracts made at it each spring regulated the sugar production for the whole of Russia; it was moved from Dubno to Kiev in 1797.

16 M. Y. Lermontov (1840-1841): famous Romantic poet and writer, much influenced by the Caucasus where he served twice on military missions; it was the setting of his 'Demon', probably the most popular poem in 19th century Russia. Shamil (1798-1871): leader of a Caucasian revolt against the Tsarist Government; regarded as a hero by the early revolutionaries but classed as a reactionary during the chauvinist period under Stalin.

17 The oldest and most important monastery in pre-revolutionary Russia.

18 N. N. Miklukho-Maklaï (1847-1887): explorer, best known for his travels in the New Guinea where he became an expert on the Papuans.

19 Bartolomeo Rastrelli (1700-1771): architect of Italian origin who designed many buildings in Russia, including the Winter Palace in Petersburg and the St Andrew's Church in Kiev.

20 The populists (*narodniki*) were 19th century Russian revolutionaries who based their programme on the peasants and opposed Marxism.

21 Fet: pen name of Athanasy Shenshin (1820-1892), a lyrical poet who influenced the Symbolists and a wealthy landowner with an estate in the Kursk province.

22 '*Chernosotenets*', i.e. member of the Black Hundreds, reactionary gangs, often financed by Tsarist officials, who organised violence against Jews and liberals.

23 Lieutenant Peter P. Schmidt (1867-1906): executed for leading the mutiny on the cruiser *Ochakov* in the Black Sea.

24 Admiral Pavel S. Nakhimov commanded a squadron which destroyed the Turkish fleet in the Black Sea in 1854 and was later killed in the defence of Sebastopol. The writer Count Leo Tolstoy (1828-1910) served with the garrison in Sebastopol in 1854; his *Sebastopol Stories* appeared while the city was still under siege.

25 The play by Alexandre Dumas is based on the life of the English

Notes

Shakespearean actor Edmund Kean (1787-1833) whose heavy drinking led to his mental breakdown.

26 M. F. Bulgakov (1891-1940): Soviet playwright and novelist, born in Kiev, best known for his play *The Day of the Turbins*.
Gogol's *Dead Souls* performed by the Moscow Arts Theatre.

27 Valentin A. Serov (1865-1911): realistic painter, pupil of Repin, best known for his portraits but who also painted scenes of country life and dramatic compositions, and drew caricatures for the revolutionary press in 1905. Isaak I. Levitan (1860-1900): landscape painter influenced by the Brabazon school; close friend of Chekhov. Alexander N. Skryabin (1872-1915): famous Russian pianist and composer. Vera Kommissarzhevskaya (1872-1915): great dramatic actress who founded her own theatre in Petersburg in 1904; sister of famous producer, pupil of Stanislavsky, Fyodor Kommissarshevsky.

28 G. V. Plekhanov (1827-1918): founder of Russian philosophical Marxism, one-time friend of Lenin but opponent of Bolshevik revolution. N. G. Chernyshevsky (1828-1889): radical whose novel *What is to be Done* was an inspiration to generations of Russian revolutionaries. Prince Peter Kropotkin (1852-1921): leading theorist of anarchism. S. M. Kravchinsky (1852-1895), better known by his pen name Stepnyak, was also in the revolutionary movement, supported terrorism and was forced to emigrate in 1880.

29 N. N. é (1831-1894): painter, studied in Italy, much influenced by religious ideas of Tolstoy whose portrait he painted in 1884.

30 Konstantin D. Balmont (1867-1943): son of landowner of Scottish origin, Symbolist poet, translator of Poe, Shelley, Whitman and Calderon; emigrated in 1918 and died in Paris.